Other books by Jan P. Norbye:

Sports Car Suspension (1965)
The New Fiat Guide (1969)
The Wankel Engine (1971)
Chassis Tuning (1973)
The Gas Turbine Engine (1974)
Streamlining and Car Aerodynamics (1977)

Other titles in the Marques of America series
published by Motorbooks International:

Chrysler: The Postwar Years
Hudson: The Postwar Years

Marques of
America

Buick:
The Postwar Years

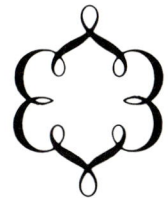

Motorbooks International
Publishers & Wholesalers Inc
Osceola, Wisconsin 54020, USA

Jan P. Norbye   Jim Dunne

©1978 by Jan P. Norbye and Jim Dunne
ISBN: 0-87938-044-6
Library of Congress Number: 77-25850

Printed and bound in the United States of America
Book and jacket design by William F. Kosfeld

Library of Congress Cataloging in Publication Data

Norbye, Jan P
  Buick.

  (Marques of America ; 3)
  Includes index.
  1. Buick automobile. I. Dunne, Jim, 1931-
joint author. II. Title. III. Series.
TL215.B84N67   629.22'22   77-25850
ISBN 0-87938-044-6

Preface

WITHOUT BUICK, GENERAL MOTORS would not be what it is. Without Buick, there would not have been a General Motors at the time it was formed. Without Buick, there might *never* have been a General Motors, and without Buick, General Motors might have failed. We must also realize that without General Motors, Buick might have failed, not once, but at various times in its history. And yet, we are free to suspect that Buick's troubles may have stemmed from corporate decisions as to the role Buick was to play in the overall scheme of GM's affairs.

Over the years Buick has been used as a training ground for top officials of General Motors. Harlow H. Curtice, who was GM president from 1953 to 1958 was a Buick man. Charles A. Chayne, who was GM vice president of engineering from 1951 to 1963 was a Buick man. And the men who started the companies that built the Nash and Chrysler cars were trained at Buick.

Judged against its American rivals, Buick cars have always been technologically advanced. Although Buick did produce side-valve engines for some years, it has always had a valve-in-head engine in production. Buick's pioneering of the automatic transmission is legion. And yet there has never been anything experimental about the Buick car. Buick engineering could be described as stolid as well as solid, and a strong concern for quality has dominated the minds of the men responsible for the design and construction of Buick automobiles. This concern was given overt expression in a slogan used in Buick's publicity material and advertisements for many years: "When better automobiles are built, Buick will build them."

Not that mistakes were never made. Some technical innovations were prematurely released for production. Some engineering matters were neglected, to be corrected tardily and at incalculable cost. In years when the sales department put pressure on the manufacturing side to increase production volume and exploit peaks in consumer demand, quality control was allowed to slip.

The history of Buick since 1945 has been eventful. It has been a series of ups and downs, some due to Buick's own initiatives. This question of initiative bears a moment's reflection. As a member of the organization that dominates the entire automobile industry, Buick is bound by corporate plans and budgets to an increasing extent. The division's autonomy has steadily eroded over the years. The initiatives Buick is free to take do not include the launching of an all-new car, for instance. At the product end, the division can select new combinations of off-the-shelf parts, and play with the model lineup, introduce new model names, and vary the product mix (which is the model-by-model proportion in the total output) in accordance with market needs. Buick, in common with all other GM car divisions, is undergoing a slow but relentless transformation from a manufacturing organization to a sales and service branch.

We will examine this process in considerable detail over the years since 1945. And in order to develop a complete understanding of how it affects the Buick cars as well as the management of Buick Motor Division, we need to look back at Buick's traditions. We will admire Buick in its days of grandeur, and share in Buick's suffering in its moments of misery. We will pay tribute to the men who made Buick; and honor Buick for the incomparable experience it gave to men who went on to great careers in other companies as well as within General Motors.

Jan P. Norbye
Jim Dunne

Table of Contents

CHAPTER 1

Buick—Backbone of General Motors

ONCE, BUICK CAME CLOSE to becoming the nation's number one producer of automobiles. That was in 1910, when Buick built 30,525 cars, coming within 1,500 units of matching Ford's output of 32,053 cars. Once, Buick would probably have gone out of business if it had not had the strength of the General Motors Corporation behind it. That was in 1933, when model-year production fell to 46,924 cars, less than one-fifth of capacity, and Buick plunged to sixth position in new-car registrations, behind Chevrolet, Ford, Plymouth, Dodge and Pontiac. What had gone wrong? The industry as a whole found itself in the depths of the economic depression following the Wall Street collapse on October 29, 1929, and the car market shrank from 3.8 million in 1929 to 1.1 million in 1932. But in 1933 other makes advanced and the market expanded to 1.5 million cars, while Buick's fortunes continued to decline. Buick's output had been dropping year by year since 1927, when a quarter of a million cars were produced. In 1930, Buick built 181,743 cars. The following year, Buick produced only 138,965 cars. And in 1932, only 56,790 Buicks were made.

Mismanagement? Hardly. Buick's president in those years was Edward T. Strong, who had taken over that office in 1926 and immediately raised Buick's sales and profits to record heights. He could not explain, however, why Buick sales began to slip while the industry was enjoying a booming trade during 1928 and 1929. Probably the customers stayed away from Buick because the cars did not look new. The Buick appearance hardly evolved from 1925 to 1929, and it was in these critical years that both the industry and the public became conscious of automobile design as an art form. Over at Chevrolet, sales manager Richard H. Grant spent $10 million on advertising the car simply as a thing of beauty. The 1927 La Salle was a roaring success, and this was attributed primarily to its styling, and secondarily to its being a Cadillac product.

The 1929 Buick was to get the benefit of a new design from the recently established GM Art & Color Section, but was a resounding flop. It became known as the 'pregnant' Buick. The body had a prominent bulge below the belt line, starting at the cowl and running the entire length of both sides, linking up around the rear body panel. For 1930, Buick reverted to fairly straight body lines. Strong had correctly analyzed the situation so far as to conclude that the product was the key to solving his problems, and it was not his fault that the Art & Color Section misjudged the consumers' readiness to accept controversial design features. In the auto industry's prosperous days of 1928-29, Strong also felt the Buick should be upgraded, and wanted to offer a new eight-cylinder engine instead of the old six. He directed his chief engineer, Ferdinand A. ('Dutch') Bower, to design a straight-eight and get it into production as soon as possible. For the 1931 models, the new straight-eight replaced the six across the board. Buick's

This 1905 Buick Model C had two cylinders.

A Buick Model 10 Single Rumble (1908-1910) with a 92-inch wheelbase, 18 hp and four cylinders, cast in pairs. The single seat in the rear was popularly called the 'mother-in-law seat.'

David Dunbar Buick was an inventor who cycled helplessly between fortune and famine throughout his life. He was a successful manufacturer of bathtubs and plumbing supplies before turning his attention to engines and cars.

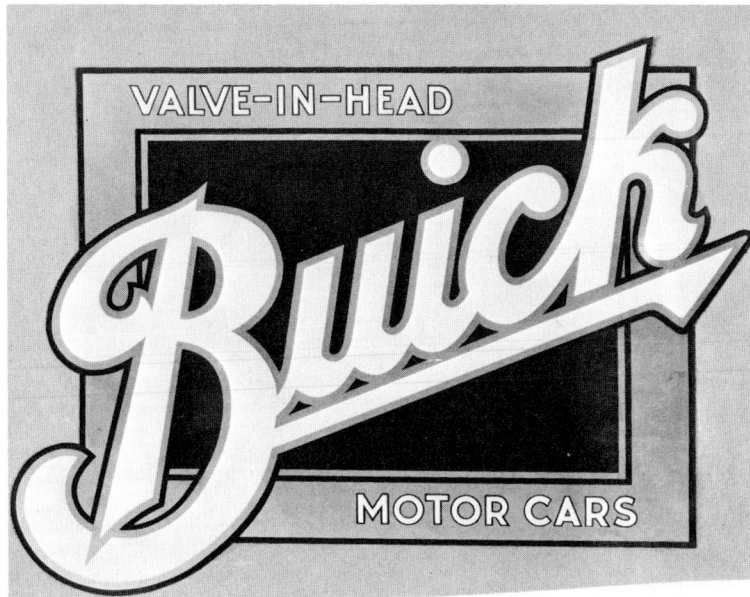

The script of the Buick emblem was begun in 1908; later the rectangular background was added.

price levels were held, but the new upgraded Buicks seemed frivolous in the depressed economic climate of 1931, and their sales curve dropped sharply.

Strong's solution had been at least partially correct, but the market conditions had been turned upside down, and what would have been right for 1929 was wrong for 1931. Strong worked himself nearly to the point of collapse in his efforts to make Buick profitable again, and resigned in April of 1932. He was replaced by a reputable trouble-shooter, Irving J. Reuter, who was general manager of Oldsmobile and Oakland, and accepted the added burden of running Buick as well.

Reuter pooled the sales management for all three divisions, but it did not pay off for Buick. Pontiac and Olds dealers baulked at having to handle the Buick, though Buick dealers got a shot in the arm by selling Pontiac and Oldsmobile cars. Still, Buick lost twenty-five percent of its dealers in this period. It became apparent that Reuter did not have the answer for Buick, and his health was threatened by this tremendous work load. In the fall of

1933, GM transferred Reuter to Germany, where he took charge of Opel for a year, and then went into retirement in North Carolina.

Who could save Buick? GM President Alfred P. Sloan and Executive Vice President William S. Knudsen thought the best-qualified executive talent inside the GM ranks was a man named Harlow H. ('Red') Curtice, who was then working as president of AC Spark Plug Division. (The AC headquarters were in Flint, Michigan, just a couple of blocks from the Buick offices.) He was nicknamed Red because of the color of his hair—a nickname that stayed long after he started graying and going bald.

Curtice was a native midwesterner, born in Petrieville, Michigan in 1893, the son of a fruit merchant. While still in school, he was helping his father with the bookkeeping, and also worked as a clerk in a wool mill. He capped his formal education with a business course at the Ferris Institute in Grand Rapids, Michigan, and in 1914 found a job as a bookkeeper with AC Spark Plug Company. He was made comptroller of the company about a year later, when he was twenty-one. During World War I he served in the U.S. Army, and then returned to AC Spark Plug. By 1923 he was assistant general manager, and four years later he became vice president, succeeding to the presidency of AC in 1929.

Curtice took over as general manager of Buick on October 23, 1933, about two months after the 1934 models went into production. They had dramatic new styling, and featured 'knee-action' independent front wheel suspension (a Cadillac development) at the usual low prices. But that was not enough for Curtice. He announced the Buick Special. The name did not indicate a high-priced, exclusive extra-special model, but was to be understood in the usual retailer/restaurant sense, implying a special price reduction. It was a merchandising creation—not an engineering innovation. The car was hurriedly prepared, using a Buick engine and front suspension, but was built on the Pontiac frame and wheelbase with several body panels from the lowly Chevrolet. Production costs were reduced so that the car would be profitable even at its low list price of $855. And it did the job it was supposed to do in the market place.

Buick's production volume soared to 71,009 cars in the 1934 model year, still far below capacity but the first increase in seven years. The dealer organization was restored, and the joint marketing program with Pontiac and Oldsmobile was given up. The Special was officially known as Series 40. Since 1931 the Buick models had been identified by two-digit numbers, the first numeral indicating the series and the second numeral the body style. The model range included Series 50, Series 60, Series 80 and Series 90. Curtice wanted to get rid of the dull numbering system and use colorful names to add sales appeal to Buick cars. He introduced the Century name in 1935. The first Buick Century was developed from the former Series 60 and outfitted with a 120-hp engine that was claimed to give it a top speed of 100 mph. That magic number was the reason for the model name Century. It combined the division's lightest vehicle with the most powerful engine, and was definitely a high-performance car. The Century was geared for high-speed cruising and not for acceleration, so that it also ran quietly at high speed, and gave surprisingly good gasoline mileage. But the 1935-model Buicks were hard to tell apart from the 1934 models, and sales slipped again. Model-year output in 1935 was only 53,249 cars. Curtice wanted a dramatic change in the exterior appearance of the Buick, and called on the head of the Art & Color Section (later to be renamed GM Styling), Harley J. Earl. The two were good friends.

Automotive historian Mike Lamm reported in an article ("The Buick Boom"—*Motor Trend*, June 1969) that the following conversation took place between Curtice and Harley Earl at the beginning of 1934: "What car do you drive, Harley?" Curtice asked. "Cadillac" was the laconic answer. "Then," continued Curtice, "how about designing me a Buick you'd drive yourself?" Earl said he would try. The result was a car that went into production as the 1936 Buick. It was startlingly new in appearance, with a bold new grille, two-piece V-type windshield, long fender skirts and a built-in trunk. The 1936 models also had important engineering changes. The straight-eight engine received aluminum pistons, and hydraulic brakes were adopted.

Curtice renamed Series 80 the Roadmaster, and Series 90 became the Limited. Series 50 was suspended. Now the Curtice formula began to pay off. Buick built 168,596 cars in the 1936 model year, but was still seventh in the sales race for the calendar year, with a market share of 4.72 percent, behind Chevrolet, Ford, Plymouth, Dodge, Oldsmobile and Pontiac. In 1937, Buick model-year production soared to 220,346 cars and took sixth place by pushing Oldsmobile back to seventh. The following year, there was a general setback in the market, but with an output of 168,689 cars, Buick secured an 8.8-percent share of the market, all but equaling its 1927 market penetration of 8.86 percent. Their market share was not to drop below eight percent again, before car production was interrupted by World War II. Buick had made a complete recovery.

The Buick car was born in 1903—a year that also saw the birth of three other makes destined for prominence in America's auto industry: Cadillac, Ford and Maxwell. Buick built only sixteen cars that first year, a dwarf compared to Oldsmobile's 3,750 and Cadillac's 2,286. The name Buick was chosen for the product because it was the name of the company's founder and president, David Dunbar Buick (1855-1929). He was born in Scotland and his parents moved to Detroit when he was two years old. As a boy, Buick delivered newspapers and later worked in a brass foundry. He

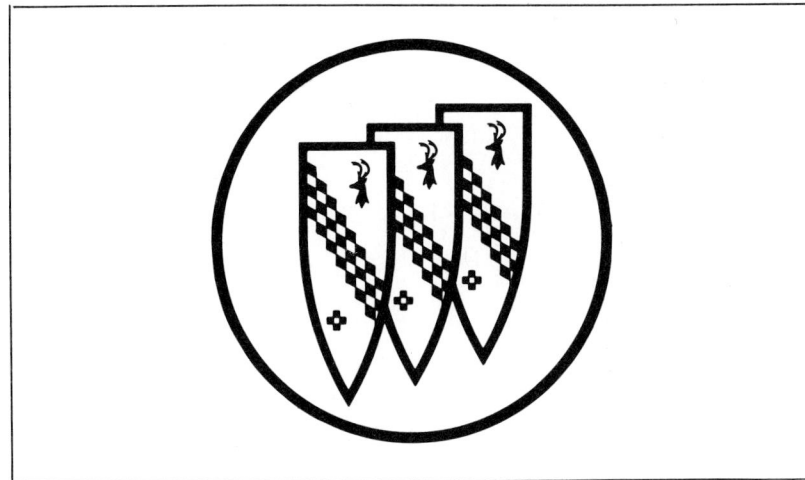

The Buick crest was inaugurated in 1937, representing the coat of arms of the Scottish Buik family (later the spelling was changed to Buick). The crest design incorporates a checkered diagonal, a buck's head and a pierced cross. The tri-shield emblem was adopted in 1959.

took out a patent for a lawn sprinkler and went into the plumbing supply business. Buick made his fortune on a process of applying enamel to the surface of cast iron bathtubs, sold the plumbing business, and started a new venture to build gas engines of his own design. In 1901 he hired a French-born engineer, Eugene C. Richards, who had studied engineering in Philadelphia, and had experience from the Olds Motor Works, to develop a marine engine. Richards created the Buick flat-twin valve-in-head engine, which he patented in his own name.

With marine engine production under way, Buick's interest turned to automobiles, and he engaged another engineer, who had built a car in Detroit, to take charge of the project. He was Walter L. Marr, who was to be Buick's chief engineer until 1917. Native of Michigan, Marr had gone to Cincinnati as a young man, where he ran a bicycle shop and took part in bicycle races. He also worked on a perpetual-motion machine, but as he matured, he wanted to design and build cars. This desire brought him to the center of the auto industry, Detroit. To get car production started, Buick

Harley J. Earl headed GM Styling and was responsible for many generations of Buick bodies, beginning with the 'pregnant' Buick of 1929. He is personally identified with the 1936 models and the 1942-48 Buick bodies.

The 1936 model was dramatically different in exterior appearance. It had a bold new grille, two-piece windshield, long fender skirts and built-in trunk.

secured financial backing from Benjamin Briscoe (1868-1945), one of America's largest manufacturers of radiators and sheet metal parts for the auto industry.

Buick started production, like many other famous auto makers (from Ford on the low-priced end of the scale to Duesenberg in the prestige and luxury field), with a model named after the first letter in the alphabet. Buick's Model A was a simple and straightforward design, with a front-mounted engine and rear-axle drive. Two seats were placed near the center of the straight ladder-type frame. The power plant was based on Richards' two-cylinder marine engine, with overhead valves, claimed to develop 21 hp. The drive was taken via a cone clutch, two-speed planetary transmission and single chain drive to the rear axle.

Buick car production stumbled when Briscoe suddenly sold his Buick stock to James H. Whiting (1842-1919), president of the Flint Wagon Works, in 1904. Briscoe had decided to back the Maxwell instead. After Whiting had settled Buick's debts in Detroit, he moved the car shops to Flint, with David D. Buick, Walter L. Marr and other key personnel. But Whiting, busy with his other duties, neglected the management of Buick; and David D. Buick was an inventor, not a business leader. To Whiting's disappointment, Buick produced only thirty-seven cars in 1904, and Whiting began to look for someone to take the whole business off his hands.

He found a buyer in the person of William C. Durant (1866-1946), president of the Durant-Dort Carriage Company in Flint. Though born in Boston, Durant grew up in Flint. He left school at the age of sixteen to work in his grandfather's lumber yard. Before he was twenty-one, he had a reputation as a business wizard, credited with the reorganization of a gas company and a water works. Small in stature, he had all the energy of an atom bomb. His bent for adventure was boundless, and his flair for money-making opportunities uncanny. Durant's fascinating story has been told in an excellent book by Lawrence R. Gustin, *Billy Durant, Creator of General Motors*. After his purchase of Buick, Durant's organizational ability and salesmanship began to tell almost immediately, and Buick production rose to 750 cars in 1905. As an example of his business methods, consider his use of the Durant-Dort carriage dealers as outlets for the Buick car. It was a ready-made distribution setup, whose basic product was in a decline. The following year Buick joined the industry leaders with an output of 2,295 cars, behind Ford, Cadillac, Maxwell and Rambler.

Under Durant's management, Buick's capitalization went up from $75,000 to $1.5 million in less than four years. In 1908 Buick made a serious attack on Ford's lead in production, and built 8,820 cars against Ford's 10,202. As business grew, Durant began to think in terms of an automobile 'trust.' This idea led him to organize the General Motors Company, incorporated on September 16, 1908. On that date, General Motors was just a paper tiger. Its assets were the Buick Motor Company and that was all. Buick was not just the nucleus of General Motors; Buick *was* General Motors. But Durant moved quickly. Olds Motor Works was added in November 1908, and Cadillac in July 1909. Oakland was also absorbed in 1909. In fact, Durant did not stop buying up companies. He thought about consolidation, but time ran out on him before he could integrate the various companies and rationalize their product lines. The day of reckoning came in September 1910, when Durant lost control of General Motors to a group of investment bankers in New York.

At Buick, it was business as usual. Durant had taken little part in its day-to-day affairs since he formed GM. The man who held the title of president of Buick from 1908 to 1910 was William M. Eaton, but he was replaced by Charles W. Nash (1864-1948) whom Durant had brought into Buick from the Durant-Dort Carriage Company. Nash worked as manufacturing manager of Buick, with a work force of 12,000 men, and in 1910 was named general manager. In 1912, Nash was elected president of General Motors.

One of the things Nash had arranged at Buick was to hire away the general manager of the American Locomotive Company's Pittsburgh plant and make him works superintendent in Flint. His name was Walter P. Chrysler (1876-1940). And it was Chrysler who replaced Nash as president of Buick, a post he was to hold for seven years.

Under Walter L. Marr's technical direction, the Buick car had developed considerably over the years. He designed Buick's first four-cylinder engine, which was a side-valve unit of the T-head type (crossflow cylinder head) that was built from 1906 to 1909. Its cylinders were cast singly, and it was

Harlow H. 'Red' Curtice put Buick back on its feet in the mid-thirties and assured Buick's prominence and autonomy within General Motors after 1945. He became president of GM in 1953 and retired in 1958.

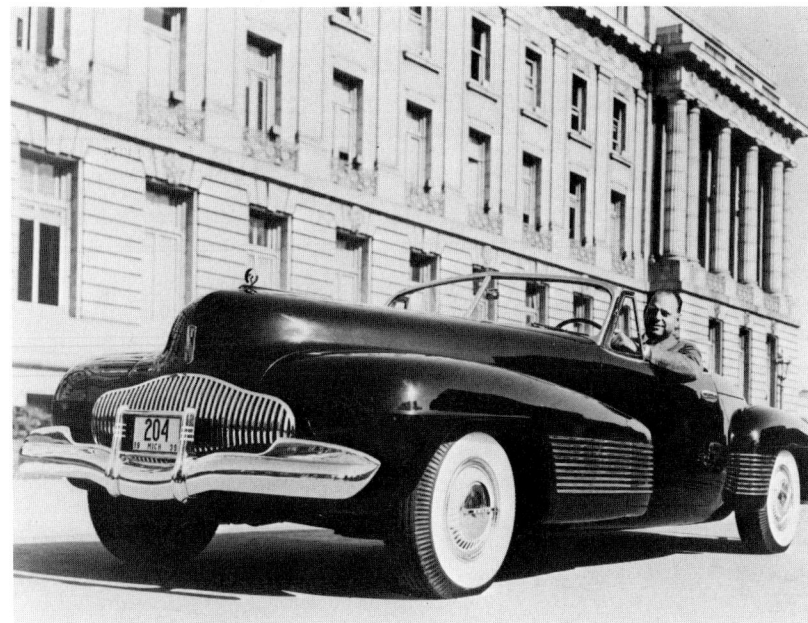

Buick's Y-Job was created in 1939 and Harley Earl used it as his personal car for a long time. Most of its styling features were adopted for the 1942 models, and its influence stretched into the 1950's.

Front end of Y-job foreshadowed Buick grilles up to 1958. Here the car is shown in its original form, with concealed head lamps. Open head lamps were fitted later. Harley Earl is at the wheel.

used in the Model D, a high-priced model at $2,500. Marr's assistant, Enos A. De Waters, was the designer of the first low-priced four-cylinder Buick, the Model 10 of 1908. It had a vertical in-line engine, with the same valve-in-head design that had proved so valuable on the flat-twin engines. De Waters was mainly responsible for Buick's changing from chain drive to shaft drive in 1907, using a torque tube design that was to be a lasting Buick feature.

De Waters had a Bachelor of Science degree from Kalamazoo College, where he graduated in 1899. He was born in that city on July 22, 1874. In 1901 he got an engineering degree, crowning two years' studies at the University of Chicago, and then he worked for two years as a test engineer with the Thomas Motor Car Company in Buffalo, New York. After that experi-

ence, he got a job with Cadillac in Detroit as a layout draftsman in 1903, and the following year he moved to Buick in Flint. He started as a general foreman of the drawing office, later De Waters became a layout man, assistant engineer, and chief engineer.

Buick advertisements claimed that in 1912, the company was manufacturing the entire car itself, except for lamps, carburetors, coils and magnetos. The first six-cylinder Buick appeared as a 1914 model. The block was cast in pairs, and the engine delivered 48 hp from its 331.2-cubic-inch displacement. The car was called B-55 and had a 130-inch wheelbase. Buick's entire line of cars that year had Kettering's Delco electric starter.

David Buick had left the company in 1908. He moved to California and invested in gas and oil field exploration, and lost all. He sold his Buick stock to get money to survive. He invented a carburetor and got Durant to finance him in manufacturing it, which brought him back to Michigan. But later he went to Florida to cash in on real estate development, only to lose his investment again. He returned to Detroit in 1927 and for the last two years of his life worked as a clerk in a small industrial trade school.

Other personnel changes were to leave greater marks on the Buick organization. Durant, financed by the du Pont family, regained control of General Motors in 1916, which brought Nash to resign. Chrysler stayed on as president of Buick till January 1920, when he left in protest against Durant's mercurial decision-making, and was replaced by Harry Bassett. Ten years after starting to build the Chrysler car, Chrysler told his own story in a series of articles for the *Saturday Evening Post,* which were later reissued in book form under the title *The Life of an American Workman.*

Bassett had started his career as an office boy with the Remington Arms Company, but left to join Weston-Mott Company, axle manufacturers. He was appointed assistant superintendent within a year, and after six years with the company, Bassett became general manager. When Buick took over Weston-Mott in 1916, Bassett was made assistant general manager of Buick, ranking next to Walter P. Chrysler. Under Bassett's management, Buick production kept pace with the other industry leaders, and ran third (behind Ford and Willys-Overland) in 1919, 1921, 1923 and 1924.

In the meantime, Durant had lost control of GM's finances. He sacrificed his personal fortune to support GM stock prices, but to no avail. The du Pont family agreed to take over his debts in return for his resignation from GM—and his GM stock holdings. The corporation now entered the Sloan era of management by committee. Durant, like Henry Ford, had exercised centralized, autocratic control over all aspects of the operation. Sloan, while retaining final authority, separated responsibilities for decision-making to committees made up of a small number of executives, such as the General Purchasing Committee, General Technical Committee, Operations Committee, General Sales Committee, Financial Committee and Executive Committee. This proved to accelerate the technical evolution of the Buick product while at the same time boosting output. The one-millionth Buick was a 1923 six-cylinder convertible. That year it was decided to drop the four-cylinder models completely. The lowest-priced four-cylinder Buick cost about $650 more than a Ford Model T or a Chevrolet Model 490, and the Buick engine was no smoother or quieter than those of the low-priced cars. From 1924 through 1930 all Buicks were sixes. During 1928, Buick produced its two-millionth car. Keeping pace in chassis engineering, Buick introduced four-wheel-brakes on its 1924 models, using drums with external-contracting bands, and a mechanical linkage with rods and levers to both front and rear brakes. Internal-expanding drum brakes were adopted for the 1930 models, and hydraulic brakes were introduced on the 1936 models.

In the General Motors organization of the thirties, Buick ranked next to Cadillac, above Chevrolet, Pontiac and Oldsmobile. This ranking referred to price level, not to the division's commercial importance. Chevrolet outranked them all in that respect. Price level ranking, however, also meant prestige, and that was a marketable commodity. The scheme of assigning a price bracket to each car division, with a certain margin for price overlap, was devised by Alfred P. Sloan (1875-1966), who became president of General Motors on May 10, 1923.

Sloan was a graduate electrical engineer, with a degree from the Massachusetts Institute of Technology. A native of New Haven, Connecticut, he settled in Newark, New Jersey, at the age of twenty, having landed a job as a draftsman with the Hyatt Roller Bearing Company there. As he rose through the ranks at Hyatt, he used his savings to acquire a heavy financial interest in the company. In 1916 he sold the company to General Motors and became vice president of a GM subsidiary controlling a group of parts manufacturing companies. In 1920 he became a member of the Executive Committee of General Motors and began to map the corporation's future.

At that time, six out of the corporation's eight makes of cars were losing money. The only profitable ones were Cadillac and Buick. "It was Buick that made any kind of General Motors car line worth talking about," Sloan was to write in 1963 in his autobiographical work, *My Years with General Motors.* To his boss, Pierre S. du Pont (the du Pont family owned thirty-six percent of GM stock), Sloan stated as early as 1921: "It is far better that the rest of General Motors be scrapped than any chances taken with Buick's earning power."

Buick was so important in Sloan's mind that he assigned two market segments to the Flint division. The four-cylinder Buick was to compete in the $900 to $1,200 price range, and the six-cylinder Buick in the $1,200 to $1,700 price range. The low end of Buick's market would overlap with Oakland's (later Pontiac), and the upper end would overlap with Oldsmobile's. Chevrolet was restricted to the low-priced market and Cadillac to the luxury-car market. The other makes—Sheridan and Scripps-Booth—were phased out. In the decade that followed, price overlap between the divisions increased from a small margin to head-on internecine conflict, and in no case more so than between Buick and Oldsmobile—by the mid-thirties, their relative standing was reversed.

Buick's model designations over the years need a little explanation. The letter system instituted with the original Model A in 1903 lasted through the Model S in 1908, but only the C, D, F, G, K and S reached production. The F lasted through 1910, so there was a two-year overlap with a new numbering system, starting in 1908 with a $900 Model 10 and a $2,500 Model 5. The numbers were issued chronologically, in a coded sequence, but refer to the date the design was started rather than to the date production began. Thus, there was a Model 7 in 1909 and Models 16 and 17 in 1910, followed by Model 14 in 1911. The Model 14 was Buick's last two-cylinder car.

Harley Earl with the Y-Job. Scale of this compact-looking roadster is shown by Earl's six-feet four-inch frame. Heavy chrome decor on fender sides became a postwar celebration of the end of shortages and the return to 'the good life.'

Beginning in 1911, Buick went to higher-number designations, but they now meant something else. They were an indication of horsepower, but usually not the exact horsepower. Model 30 and Model 31 of 1913, for instance, shared the same 32 hp engine, which had also been used in the previous year's Models 28 and 29. Model 40 of 1913 *was* rated at 40 hp. After three years, this had caused a lot of confusion, especially as to year of manufacture, and it was time for another change. The numerals were retained in 1914, but they were again given new meaning. The first digit indicated engine type, so that numbers beginning with 2 or 3 denoted 4-cylinder cars and 4 and 5 indicated 6-cylinder cars. The second digit indicated body style in code: 5 and 9 meant open touring cars, 4 meant a roadster, 1 meant a brougham, 0 meant a coach (two-door) or a sedan (four-door), 6 meant a coupe and 8 a victoria coupe. To identify the cars by year, a letter code was used, so that B-55 meant a 1914 six-cylinder touring car. For 1915, all models switched to the prefix code C. The letter D was used for both 1916 and 1917, and E for 1918. For some reason, the alphabetical sequence then broke up, and H was used for 1919 and K for 1920. Then the letter code was abandoned and replaced by a two-digit prefix, giving the year (21 for 1921, and so on). As a result, cars became identified by four numbers, hyphenated in the middle, such as 22-45, which was a 1922 six-cylinder open touring car. These designations were not just internal codes, but were used in advertising and sales literature as well. Buick had no model names yet, but that was to change in 1925. Buick built two separate car lines that year, Standard Six and Master Six. The numeral code was

still retained, but receded into the background. Model 26 was a Standard Six coupe, and Model 48 a Master Six victoria coupe. It's easy to see how this system evolved into the Series 40, Series 50 and Series 60 which replaced the Standard and Master labels in 1930.

As mentioned, we have seen how Harlow H. Curtice changed Series 40 into the Special, and Series 60 into the Century. Yet Buick retained the number code for its own use. Thus in 1937, Model 61 was a Century four-door sedan and Model 46 a Special coupe. Series 90 was renamed Limited in 1936, after the Series 80 had assumed the Roadmaster title. Series 50 became the Buick Super in 1935 but was suspended after a year, to be revived as a 1940 model. Starting in 1940, the Roadmaster was downgraded to Series 70, while the Limited was built in two sizes, Series 80 and Series 90.

By the time Buick car production was suspended in 1942, the division had reinforced its status both within General Motors and in the industry as a whole. Buick's strong showing in the late thirties pushed Cadillac to the point where it had to give up the La Salle. In spite of its higher prices, Buick sold fifty percent more cars in the 1939-1941 period than arch-rival Oldsmobile, and even led the vigorous, snob-value-bargain Pontiac in sales. Buick sales ran consistently about twice Studebaker's level, well ahead of Dodge and about three times higher than the Chrysler. Nash and Hudson were no threats to Buick's dominance in its market segment, and even Ford's bright new Mercury could not put a dent in Buick's sales success.

CHAPTER 2

The Straight-Eight Engine

To MOST PEOPLE, the Buick engine was the heart of the Buick automobile. There was something majestic about it, standing bolt upright in the chassis, and running the full length of the enormously long hood, from right behind the radiator to within the barest necessary clearance of the cowl. It was rock steady, even when idling at 450 rpm or less, reminding one of a lazy giant marine engine. At the same time it just reeked of power, the way the big steam locomotives did. Its styling—if you can talk about the styling of an engine—gave eloquent expression to the idea that this huge, tall hunk of metal was a force, an irresistible force that could conquer all in its way. Yes, you can talk about the styling of an engine. Enthusiasts of exotic cars like Alfa Romeo, Bugatti and Bentley will certainly support that view. The Buick eight could not, of course, compete with such esoteric machinery in terms of technical sophistication.

The styling of the Buick engine rather tended to play down its brute force. The gentle radius on the rocker cover edges and corners were sort of a dissimulation—a disguise of its true character. But then the large manifolds and the vacuum-cleaner-size air filter would give it away, showing off the engine's vast breathing needs. On the ignition side, what impressed one most was the multiplicity of things, such as eight spark plugs, neatly lined up, with short wires to the distributor. One would also be impressed by the open spaces on the cylinder block. Smaller engines often become dominated by the clutter of accessories. Not the Buick eight. Between the fuel

pump at the front and the starter motor at the rear end, there was just the distributor, towering on its shaft, extending at an angle from the block. The water pump assembly occupied the space between the cylinder head and the cooling fan. Behind the fan belt pulley on the crankshaft was a prominent casing for the timing gears and chain. The fan belt also turned the pulley on the generator, which was mounted on the left side of the block. Below manifold level, the block was uncluttered, visible to anyone who opened the hood, proudly baring its surface as a work of art, an iron sculpture.

All who had the experience of driving a Buick, knew that the engine was much more than a piece of statuary. It was functional. All its parts were designed for function rather than beauty. This added to its beauty in the eye of the beholder, if he was a car enthusiast who knew his auto mechanics. To the uninitiated, the obvious functionality of the thing must have added to its mystery, and to their sense of aesthetics. The Buick eight was as dynamic in appearance as American auto engines could be, since the disappearance of the Stutz and the Duesenberg.

For the 1946 models, Buick built its straight-eight in two sizes, 248 and 320 cubic inches. The basic engine was unchanged from 1936, and the first eight-cylinder Buick dated from 1930 (1931 model). An extensive redesign for the 1936 models had been made for tooling reasons, not because the first-edition straight-eight had any bugs in it. But the industry had made

Continuing from a long stroke, the Buick straight-eight also had long connecting rods and long pushrods. Camshaft was chain-driven from the front, and the cylinder head supported the rocker-arm shaft assembly.

great strides in engine manufacturing techniques since the eight-cylinder engine machining line was rigged up, and completely new tooling was installed in 1935. This, of course, necessitated redesign of all the major components, to take advantage of new machining processes and new methods of materials handling. At the same time, the engine was modernized to incorporate the fruits of recent development work carried out at Buick. These changes will be described in greater detail later on. The point we wish to make here is merely the engine's ancestry.

So, here was Buick in 1945/46 with a ten-year-old engine. Yet it was a more advanced design than anything Chrysler, Hudson or Packard was building at the time. It was also a more modern engine than the straight-eight-cylinder units then produced by Pontiac and Oldsmobile. And even the Cadillac V-8 was pretty obsolete by then. Consequently, Buick could happily plan to continue making the same engine for a number of years to come.

Buick's straight-eight was a monobloc unit with a detachable cylinder head. The crankshaft was a 2-4-2 type, which means it was arranged like a four-cylinder engine in the middle, with a two-cylinder engine on each end. The firing order was 1-6-2-5-8-3-7-4. Buick chose the 2-4-2 arrangement because it gave a smoother engine than the alternative layout, which is known as a 4-4 type, and represents two four-cylinder engines placed end to end. Both gave evenly spaced firing impulses, but the sequence of torque impulses with the 2-4-2 crankshaft made for a smoother running engine. The crankshaft was a one-piece steel forging of tremendous strength, running in five main bearings. There was a main bearing at each end, and one between each pair of cylinders. Crankpin journals were of two-inch diameter, and had a width of 1.22 inches. The shaft was counterweighted and carried a torsional vibration damper at the front end. This damper consisted of a laminated steel flywheel supported on steel leaf springs.

Cylinder block and head were both iron castings. The crankcase was integral with the block, which extended to a level well below the crankshaft center line in the interest of maximum strength and rigidity. At the bottom, a pressed-steel oil pan was fitted, containing a gear-type oil pump and a fixed-position oil filter. The camshaft had a bevel gear that turned an inclined shaft, extending down to drive the oil pump and upwards to drive the ignition distributor. The smaller 248-cubic-inch version had a 3.093-inch bore and 4.125-inch stroke, giving a stroke/bore ratio of 1.333:1. Stroke/bore ratio, when seen in relation to the number of cylinders and total piston displacement, is an indication of the engine's performance potential. In general, a high stroke/bore ratio indicates a slow-running high-torque engine, while a low stroke/bore ratio usually means the engine is designed for high crankshaft speeds and tends to be poor in low-range torque. The larger

320-cubic-inch version of the Buick straight-eight had a bore of 3.437 inches and a stroke of 4.312 inches, which gave a stroke/bore ratio of 1.254:1. Both versions were designed to reach peak torque (i.e. the strongest pull) well below 2000 rpm, and to run out of revs before reaching 4000 rpm.

Buick held the bore between three and 3½ inches in order to obtain a compact combustion chamber, which is a requisite for efficient burning of the air-fuel mixture. The engine with the larger bore, however, had more space available for valve heads, and with larger valves, it could obtain more mixture in a given time. Stroke was kept within the four- to 4½-inch range. A longer stroke would have led to problems in the bottom end, for longer stroke means greater crank throw. With greater crank throw, the crankcase must be widened to make room, and that tends to add weight. Greater crank throw also means that the crankshaft must be beefed up to maintain its rigidity. Unbalanced forces are higher with a longer crank throw, and simultaneously, space considerations make it more difficult to counterweight the crankshaft for balance. In addition, side thrust on the pistons is stronger when the crank throw is lengthened, which means higher friction and greater wear. Bearing friction and bearing loads are higher the longer the crank throw. In order to minimize the side thrust on the piston, Buick used very long connecting rods: 7.625 inches center-to-center on the 248-cubic-inch engine, and 8.25 inches center-to-center on the 320-cubic-inch engine.

Buick could not shorten the stroke (and the crank throw) without losing some of its low-end torque. And it was the strong low-end torque that gave the Buick its marvelous tractability and flexibility. It could be driven in top gear down to a walking pace without losing its smoothness, and it would accelerate smoothly in top gear whenever one stepped on the gas. It could start from standstill in second gear—the same second gear that was good for at least 60 mph.

The cylinder head was of the reverse-flow type (as opposed to crossflow), with both intake and exhaust manifolds on the same side—the left side. The valves were positioned vertically in the head, with ports arranged symmetrically along the engine's axis. Though intake ports were larger than exhaust ports, both were small in relation to the cylinder bore, and the gas flow path through the manifold and cylinder head was a tortuous one, describing a vague S-shape.

Spark plugs were inserted from the right, at an angle of about thirty degrees (from horizontal), into one 'corner' of the wide and shallow combustion chamber. There was a recess in the cylinder head, produced as part of the casting and not machined, and roughly symmetrical in shape. The pistons, on the other hand, had an offset dome on the side away from the spark plugs, to concentrate the combustion in the area nearest the plugs. This 'turbulator' top, as Buick called it, was cam-ground. But the dome left a 120-degree quench area. Quench area is a zone where small amounts of gas are cooled by large metal surfaces, creating an environment in which combustion cannot be sustained. This is harmful to the engine's efficiency, but auto engineers were used to accepting quench areas in return for piston shapes and cylinder head designs that minimized abnormal combustion—self-ignition, ping, knock and rumble. Buick engineers were no exception.

The camshaft was chain-driven from the crankshaft, and was located in the upper-right-hand corner of the crankcase—a long way from the valves. That necessitated the use of extremely long pushrods, which had to be substantial in diameter and weight to do their job. The pushrods tipped one end of a rocker arm, whose other end in turn opened the valve.

Mechanical valve lifters rode against the cams, and the valves were closed by single coil springs. The rocker arms were mounted in full-width bearings on a rocker arm shaft, with a ratio of about 1 to 1.35. The rocker arm ratio shows the length of the arm that opens the valve, expressed as a percentage of the arm that receives the impetus from the camshaft. By using the high ratio, Buick obtained valve lift some thirty-five percent higher than the actual cam height. This was done in order to restrict the axial motion in the pushrod. The valve gear had a great deal of slack in it, and, of course, some deflection in the long pushrods was inevitable. Despite all of Buick's experience with this type of valve gear, it was not until after the straight-eight had gone into production that the engineers started to tackle the problem. The fundamental problem lay in the fact that the actual opening and closing of the valves was at considerable variance with the specified valve timing designed into the cam profiles. Since the slack and deflection could not be avoided without going to overhead camshaft construction, Buick took another approach. The overhead camshaft idea was rejected not only because of the additional cost involved, but also because overhead camshaft drive systems tended to be noisy and to need frequent adjustment. So, having accepted the drawbacks of its pushrod-and-rocker-arm design, Buick set about to reduce its effect by developing cam profiles that took valve gear deflection and slack into account. By 1936 the new cam profile went into production.

For the 1937 models, the valves were streamlined. The neck, between the stem and the head, was fleshed out, forming a large conical section designed to avoid a sudden enlargement in cross-sectional area, because that would entail an energy loss. The next big change came when hydraulic valve lifters were introduced on the 1950-model Super, along with the new 263-cubic-inch straight-eight. This engine was a bored-out version of the 248-cubic-inch power unit. The bore was increased from 3.09 to 3.187 in-ches, while the stroke remained at 4.125 inches. The crankcase height was reduced by ⅝ inch, and the connecting rods were shortened by ¼ inch. Piston skirts were shortened by 9⁄16 inch, but remained full-skirted, each with a transverse slot, carrying two compression rings and two oil control rings, as before. The 263-cubic-inch engine was the first eight-cylinder Buick to have a uniform diameter for all main bearing journals. In previous designs, five different diameters were used. By going to uniform main bearing diameter of 2.562 inches, only four instead of ten different types of bearing shells were needed for a replacement set. Other changes on the 263-cubic-inch engine were a slower-speed fan and a low-restriction type of oil filter element.

The main difference, however, was the use of hydraulic valve lifters. They reduced valve lash to zero, which eliminated tappet clearance noise. No valve clearance adjustments were needed. Valve bounce, which can occur in solid-lifter engines when inertia loads on the valve gear exceed valve spring strength, was eliminated because the hydraulic lifters effectively prevented over-revving. This resulted in longer valve life, too. Zero lash operation meant more precise control of valve timing, which had been the basic drawback of the original engine. In 1951 the 263-cubic-inch engine replaced the 248-cubic-inch version in the Special series, and at the same time the 320-cubic-inch Roadmaster engine received hydraulic valve lifters, too.

While the straight-eight engine was heavy, it was not out of line with other in-line engines of its period. The Chevrolet six, for instance, weighed 635 pounds. The 320-cubic-inch straight-eight Buick engine weighed nearly 800 pounds—794.11, to be exact, including starter, motor and generator, but without oil and water. The block and crankcase was the heaviest single part, at nearly 250 pounds (248.67). The crankshaft weighed 114.21 pounds, while the cylinder head scaled 93.34 pounds. The camshaft and drive, with lifters and valve springs, accounted for 48.54 pounds. The manifolds, taken together, with their heat controls, weighed 46.4 pounds. A piston for the 320-cubic-inch engine weighed eighteen ounces and its connecting rod 35.6 ounces. In the 248-cubic-inch engine, piston weight was 13.5 ounces and connecting rod weight 28.5 ounces. The smaller engine also had a lighter block (212 pounds) and crankshaft (85.5 pounds). Its total weight was 672.2 pounds, which works out to 2.71 pounds per cubic inch, as compared with 2.48 pounds per cubic inch in the larger Buick engine and 2.76 pounds per cubic inch in the 230-cubic-inch Chevrolet 'stovebolt six.'

While other engineers were involved with the detail design, it is generally recognized that it was Dutch Bower who conceived and laid out the Buick straight-eight. He was a dynamic worker, a two-fisted shirtsleeve en-

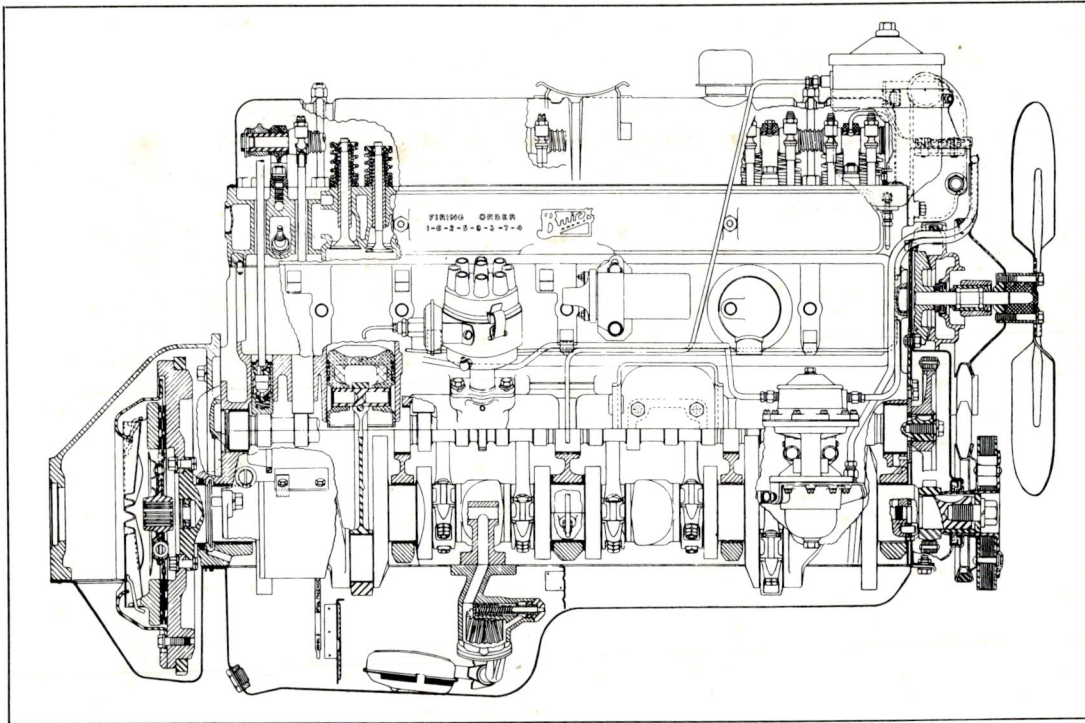

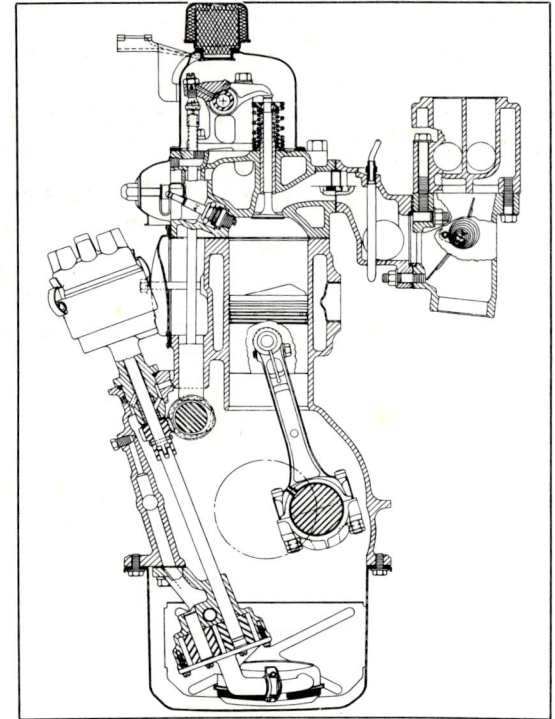

Final barrier to continued development of the straight-eight engine was flexibility in the crankshaft and crankcase, despite the large-diameter main bearings (nine in all). Designed for about 3000 rpm, it ran up to 4200 at the end. The straight-eight engine had a compact, wedge-shaped combustion chamber, with an offset dome on the piston crown opposite the spark plug. Dual-coil valve springs were used. Both intake and exhaust manifolds were on the left side of the block.

gineer of the old school. He was extremely close to the product end of engineering, and old Buick men tell stories of how he would personally go down to the garage and talk to the test drivers and get the blow-by-blow accounts of technical failures of all kinds, and then run back to the drawing office and chew out the engineers he held responsible. Working impossible hours himself, he seemed to expect all Buick engineers to work a twenty-four-hour day.

Bower began his automotive career in 1908 with Oldsmobile, and served for some time with Weston-Mott Axle Company before joining Buick as assistant chief engineer in 1918. In 1927 he succeeded Enos A. De Waters as chief engineer of Buick.

When the eight-cylinder engine was introduced in the 1931 models, it was built in three sizes: 220, 272 and 344 cubic inches. The following year, the smallest one was bored out to 230 cubic inches, and for 1934 its displacement was increased to 235 cubic inches. The largest engine remained unchanged, but the middle-size engine got a new cylinder block with 278-cubic-inch displacement for 1934. Both the 278- and 344-cubic-inch engines were replaced by a completely new 320-cubic-inch unit for 1936, whereas the smallest version continued for the Special only. It was replaced by a smaller version of the 320-cubic-inch engine in 1937, with 248-cubic-inch displacement. On its 1935 engines Buick had changed from updraft to downdraft carburetors. The new 1936/37 engines received aluminum pistons; crankshafts had improved counterweighting; full pressure lubrication was used (instead of relying partly on 'splash' lubrication, from the connecting rods being dipped into the oil pan); and the crankcase ventilation system was given increased capacity. Camshafts with new cam profiles were adopted, as explained above. The 1938-model engines were advertised with the Dynaflash label, introduced to mark the adoption of domed 'turbulator' pistons, which served to give a significant boost in power output. For 1940 the engine was balanced after assembly and its mounting system was improved with controlled rocking frequency, which caused Buick's advertising agency to announce the 'new' Micropoise Dynaflash engine. The following year the piston dome was modified and the engine renamed Fireball.

Far more important, that year Buick introduced the first compound carburetion setup as standard on the 1941 Century and optional on the 1941 Special. It was a pure Buick development, and it was not shared with any other GM division. The intake manifold which was a two-level design for 180-degree phasing, carried dual two-barrel carburetors. A progressive throttle linkage was arranged to let the engine run on the front (primary) carburetor only at cruising speeds up to 75 mph. Then the rear (secondary) carburetor would go into action. On wide-open throttle, both carburetors would open immediately, for full acceleration. The phasing was achieved by installing damper valves below the rear carburetor, with offset shafts and counterweights that were balanced by manifold pressure. This dual two-barrel setup is historically significant as the ancestor of the modern four-barrel carburetor.

The first of the postwar engines had reduced power output compared with the last of the prewar units, and the subsequent progression is shown in tabulated form in appendix number six. Some comments on the reasons for the rise in horsepower after 1946 are relevant to the eventual demise of the straight-eight in favor of the V-8. When Buick began to offer automatic transmissions in 1948, the engineers were acutely aware of the power losses associated with the early Dynaflow. In order to compensate for this, Buick cars equipped with automatic transmissions were outfitted with more powerful engines. Of course there were no mysteries about raising power output. Back in 1941, the 320-cubic-inch engine had been rated at 165 hp, and that was obtained with a low compression ratio and a single two-barrel carburetor. Its potential was far higher. But Buick was not concerned about developing the engine to its ultimate—it was a matter of providing a small increase in power, no more than five percent at first. And it was important to do this with a minimum of upset in the manufacturing end of operations.

Consequently, the first increase was made by merely providing special pistons for engines destined to go into cars equipped with automatic transmissions. They raised the compression ratio from 6.9:1 to 7.2:1. The result, in the case of the 248-cubic-inch engine, was a gain of four horsepower. As cars became heavier in the fifties, more horsepower was needed to maintain the performance level. A big step was made in 1952, when Buick switched to four-barrel carburetors.

The theory of the four-barrel carburetor showed substantial advantages for a variety of driving conditions. Basically, the idea was the same as in the compound-carburetor setup on the 1941 Buick Super. The four-barrel carburetor had two primaries and two secondaries. The primaries were small and the secondaries large. In fact, the primaries in the four-barrel carburetor were smaller than the two barrels, or venturis, in a two-barrel type. The secondaries remained closed during all normal or light-load driving. The term load in this context refers strictly to throttle position, not to the number of passengers or the amount of cargo carried. As a result, the engine would operate with lower fuel consumption most of the time. But for full acceleration, the secondaries opened, and the volume of air rushing into the engine just about tripled. That meant near-instant response, with a power reserve that was never apparent until the accelerator pedal was pushed to the floorboards. Due to the strong response, the time the car ran with the secondaries open, for passing other traffic, or going from standstill to cruising speed, was short. To maintain a steady highway speed, the primaries provided all the air flow that was needed, and the secondaries were always ready to come to their assistance at a moment's notice.

Buick had two suppliers of four-barrel carburetors for the 1952 Roadmaster: Carter and Rochester. Carter was an old-established carburetor manufacturer, and a major supplier to General Motors. Rochester was a relatively new division of General Motors. The corporation had decided, back in 1937, to build a second plant for Delco Appliance Division in Rochester, New York. The factory began operations in 1938, and in 1939 was reorganized as Rochester Products Division. Its products were diverse, ranging from shock absorbers and starter motors to brake cylinders and air cleaners. In 1945 Rochester did not revert to its former production program, but was directed to begin the development of new fuel devices. New one- and two-barrel carburetors and fuel pumps followed in short order, and a little later came the four-barrel carburetor. Though made by Rochester, it was a Buick invention, due to a Buick staff engineer named Adolph Braun.

The 1952 Roadmaster engine contained several other modifications, such as new intake and exhaust manifolds with lower gas flow restriction. It had a compression ratio of 7.5:1, and power output went up to 170 hp. That was the summit of its development. It could go no further. The top end could still be developed further, with bigger valves, lower-restriction manifold, and higher compression. But the bottom end could not take it. It lacked structural rigidity, due to its great length. The crankshaft was flexible and, what's worse, the crankcase was flexible, too. Higher stress levels and higher rpm would jeopardize its reliability. The following year, Buick began producing V-8 engines, and the straight-eight was phased out during the 1953 model year. The basic tooling for manufacturing the straight-eight had remained unchanged for eighteen years—since 1935.

21

CHAPTER 3
Buick in 1945

UPPERMOST IN THE MINDS of the men at Buick as the world went into 1945 was the return to passenger car production. The last prewar Buick came off the line in Flint on February 2, 1942, and for three years the division had been busy with a variety of military projects and the production of war materiel. To convert the factories back to automobile production for the civilian market was not going to be easy. One of the odd facts about the auto industry is that when war comes, there is a total change in what it produces. Its wartime products cannot even be made with the same production equipment! Other industries carry on with no major change. Food and beverage companies do not retool their plants because the bulk of their output is purchased by the military instead of by civilians. Clothing manufacturers do not change machinery and factory methods because they switch from gentlemen's apparel to army uniforms. But the auto industry was called upon to make any kind of hardware for which the traditional suppliers could no longer meet the demand. The auto industry's expertise in mass production was exploited to increase the nation's output of defense equipment—not tenfold, not a hundredfold, but by the thousand. It was the auto industry above all that earned America the title 'Arsenal of Democracy.' While some truck factories were able to go through the war years producing military vehicles that contained a large proportion of standard parts from their peacetime products, Buick had no manufactured goods in its prewar product range that interested the military. All Buick had to offer

was its factory capacity, its engineering know-how, and its skilled work force.

A large part of Buick's manufacturing complex in Flint produced steel cartridge cases, and another section built tank destroyers. Wartime preparations had started before car production was suspended in January 1942, when the Army Ordnance Department sent a delegation to Buick asking if they could produce cartridge cases. How many? Oh, say 75,000 a month, for the duration. Buick's general manager, Harlow H. Curtice, and his production experts recognized an opportunity in this inquiry. It offered possible wartime uses for Buick's stamping plant, with its hydraulic presses. Buick agreed to bid on the contract, but solving the production problems—which the munitions industry could not tell Buick how to solve, since they did not then produce cartridge cases on such a vast scale—took over a year. But when the contract was awarded, Buick was ready to produce 75-mm cartridge cases at the rate of 400 an hour. After that Buick got another contract to manufacture 20-mm shell casings—another interesting tooling problem, to which Buick soon found an efficient solution. In all, Buick shipped some 2.5 million 75-mm cartridge cases and about ten million 20-mm shell casings.

By midyear 1942, other groups of Buick engineers were working on projects to produce parts for diesel engines, anti-aircraft guns and automatic transmissions for tanks. Other defense contracts were to follow. William S.

Buick Roadmaster convertible (Model 76C) of 1946 was a tremendous value at $2,651. Not all buyers were able to obtain whitewall tires, which were listed as standard equipment, due to postwar material shortages.

Knudsen, GM president since 1937, had been appointed director-general of President Roosevelt's Office of Production Management (OPM) in 1940 and began to prepare the nation's industries for war. One of Knudsen's problems was to find a manufacturing company with the skill, tools and machinery to make the fourteen-cylinder Pratt & Whitney double-row '1830' radial aircraft engine in large quantities. This was the power unit for the four-engined B-24 Liberator bomber. Each engine weighed 1,450 pounds and delivered upwards of 1,200 horsepower.

His choice fell on Buick, and Curtice accepted the responsibility. At first, they were talking about 500 engines a month, with deliveries to begin in March 1942. But when Buick had completed its plans for the new plant, the government doubled the order. At that point, Curtice knew that Flint's population could no longer provide enough workers for the project. Therefore Curtice abandoned all thought of building the new plant in Flint and instead chose Melrose Park, a suburb of Chicago. The manufacturing and assembly methods used in this plant were new to the aircraft industry, for they were the fruit of many years of experience with the mass production of automobile engines. While the plant was under construction, the order was

23

doubled again. It was too late to make big changes, and it took a long time before the new target was met. But Buick did it eventually.

During the first months of production, each engine required 3,062 man-hours of labor. But the whole manufacturing and assembly organization was gradually streamlined, and by April 1943, the labor cost was only 766 man-hours. Buick was then building about 2,000 complete engines a month at Melrose Park.

The Pratt & Whitney engine had aluminum cylinder heads, and Buick contracted to manufacture them. This marks Buick's introduction to aluminum parts other than pistons, which casts an interesting light on Buick's later experience with aluminum engines. It was decided to set up an aluminum foundry in Flint. The government financed it and Buick leased it. The aluminum foundry was drawn up in detail, and redrawn nine times, each new plan a little better than the preceding one. Between the ninth and tenth sets of plans, the order came to increase production volume from 25,000 cylinder heads a month to 75,000. While the plant was under construction, the target was raised to 125,000 a month. Cylinder head production in the new foundry began five months from the date the ground was broken.

While the aluminum foundry was being built, the U.S. Army asked Buick to design a new kind of war machine—a tank destroyer. The specifications called for a lightweight full track-laying vehicle, with a low silhouette, lightly armored but highly mobile, carrying a 37-mm cannon in a 360-degree turret. "The first stages of the design for the M-18 was handled by one of the groups which later became the vehicle development group at the GM Engineering Staff," according to Buick chief engineer, Charles A. Chayne. The final product was designed at Buick. This was something new for Buick's engineers, but at least it was a motor vehicle of sorts. The original specifications stipulated a diesel engine, but the Army agreed to use gasoline engines in order to speed deliveries. The Buick engine was too small for the task—even a pair of them would not have had the power to propel this machine at the targeted cruising speed of 50 mph. Instead, the Continental C-4 was selected.

When the basic design had been approved, Buick was asked to build two prototypes for testing. Exhaustive tests at the Aberdeen proving grounds in Maryland led to modifications in the armament, but no major alterations in Buick's initial design. The cannon caliber was increased to 76 mm, and provision for machine gun mounting was added. It had been developed under the army number T-70, but the production version was known as the M-18. The Buick workers who assembled it gave it the name Hellcat. Buick was given an order for 1,000 Hellcats and production got under way in 1943; a total of 2,507 were built. This summary of war production will make it clear what shape the Buick factories were in when government orders dried up.

Hellcat production lasted till V-E Day, and the munitions plants were running till shortly before V-J Day. Still, Buick built its first 1946-model car in October 1945. One thing that saved a lot of time was the fact that the engine line had been kept intact. The machinery had been removed and put in mothballs, but it was not dismantled or converted to other uses. And when the signal was given, the machinery was installed where it had been in 1941. Fisher Body had preserved the dies for the prewar models, and was ready to resume supplies to Buick and the other GM divisions in good time. Frames came from outside suppliers who were able to fill large orders quickly. Tires were in short supply, but the situation improved almost weekly, and no Buick left the factory unshod, but many customers who ordered whitewalls had to accept blackwalls.

The 1946 Buick model range was simplified, compared with the 1941/42 lineup. The new range included only the Special (Series 40), Super (Series 50) and Roadmaster (Series 70). The bodies were practically unchanged from 1942. If the engine was basically the same as in 1936, the frame was even older, having originated in 1933. Earlier Buick frames were strictly ladder-type, with two long side-members and a number of cross-members. In 1933 cross-bracing of the center section was introduced and the number of cross-members reduced. The 1946-model frame had two long side-members, which were horizontally straight except for the kickup over the rear axle. In plan view they were also straight except for the narrow section between the front wheels. There was a cross-member at the extreme front, one over the rear axle, and one at the extreme rear. The center section was filled by a deep cross-bracing with a cage in the center of the X to let the torque tube pass through it. The 1946 Roadmaster frame had a girder depth of 6.2 inches, with a maximum box width of 2.25 inches and a thickness of 0.156 inches. The Super frame was basically the same, but with slightly less girder depth, at 6.126 inches. A shortened version of the Super frame was used for the Special.

Rear axles on the 1946 models were part of a torque tube drive system, similar in principle to the torque tube designs used by Buick since 1907. The term torque tube is largely descriptive, for some of its functions are connected with torque reactions. But its principal duty is to take up the driving thrust. All parts of the Buick drive train were enclosed. The only visibly rotating parts were the wheels. The shafts, couplings, and gears that transmitted the rotation turned inside tubes and casings. To start at the rear end, the wheels were turned by shafts revolving inside an axle casing. It was a semi-floating axle with hypoid gears. The term float does not refer to the axle housing or its suspension, but to the type of hub bearing used between the axle shaft and the casing. Semi-floating means that the shaft is carried directly in roller bearings in the axle housing. Road wheels being attached to the tapered end of the shaft by a nut and washer, completely overhung in relation to the bearing. Semi-floating axles were common on passenger cars, while trucks and other heavy-duty vehicles usually had full-floating axles. Here, the wheels are carried entirely on two sets of bearings housed in an extension of the axle casing. The housing then carries the load. The shaft has no other duty than to transmit rotation to the wheel. Some cars used a three-quarter-floating axle, which means that a single ball bearing with high load capacity is mounted with its inner race in the axle casing and its outer race located in the wheel hub. The load is therefore split between the casing and the shaft, which carries a flange that is bolted to the wheel hub. Buick used the simplest and lowest-cost type of construction.

Hypoid gearing had been used by Buick since 1938. What it means is that the pinion does not engage the ring gear at center height, but at a point lower down on the ring gear. This involves complex gear-tooth shapes: Hypoid gearing reduces gear noise and provides better stress distribution on the gears. It also allows the propeller shaft to be lowered in the chassis (which in turn permits a lower floor inside the car). The torque tube was integral with the rear axle housing which contained the pinion, ring gear and differential. It was a straight tube enclosing the propeller shaft, running the full length from the gearbox extension to the rear axle housing. At its front end, it was pivoted at two points, one on each side, in a frame cross-member. It had freedom to move up and down, but not sideways. The torque-absorption aspects of the design are easy to explain once one knows about Newton's law, which says every action has an equal and opposite reaction. When the axle shafts turn one way, to drive the car forward, the axle casing tends to turn the other way, and must be restrained. In other words, the axle housing tends to lift at the nose. With a long torque tube, this reaction is prevented, and because of the leverage in the tube, the forces upon it are quite low.

Now, for the question of driving thrust. The term thrust indicates a linear force, while torque is a twisting couple. The driving thrust stems from the tires' contact with the roadway—their 'foot-prints.' As the wheels turn, their motion must be transferred to the car. On the Buick, it's the torque tube that does that. The thrust from the wheels is carried via the axle into the torque tube and its anchorage points on the frame. These anchorage points must be rugged, because of the high forces transmitted to them, and at the same time be so constructed that they permit up-and-down movements in the torque tube. The torque-tube anchorage points constitute a front pivot point for the torque tube; each has a vertical crescent-shaped

slot to provide a passage for the propeller shaft. The anchorage bracket is secured to a frame cross-member. The car moves because the torque tube pushes against the frame. On cars without a torque tube, it is the rear suspension that must handle both the torque reaction and the driving thrust.

Buick manufactured its own axles and gearboxes. All 1946-47 models had a three-speed synchromesh transmission, which meant there was synchromesh on second and third gears, but not on first or reverse. Synchromesh was a patented GM device, adopted by Buick in 1931, which speeded up or slowed down one gear prior to engagement, so that the gears revolved at the same speed. Third gear was direct drive. Second gear had a 1.53:1 ratio and first gear a 2.39:1 ratio. All gears were helical-cut and in constant mesh, and the shift levers were located on the side of the gearbox and connected to a column-shift linkage. Buick had gone to column shift as standard for the 1939 models, having used a central floor shift from 1914 through 1938.

The 1946-48 clutch was a single dry-plate design with a facing area of 100.6 square inches for the Special and Super; 106.8 square inches for the Roadmaster. Final drive ratios differed from model to model. Special and Super had a 4.454:1 ratio as standard, which meant forty-nine teeth on the ring gear and eleven teeth on the pinion. The standard Roadmaster final drive ratio was 4.1:1 but a 'longer' 3.643:1 ratio was optional. The standard unit had forty-one teeth on the ring gear and ten on the pinion, while the optional unit had fifty-one teeth on the ring gear and fourteen on the pinion.

Buick's 1946 models had all-coil suspension. The rear springs were mounted above the axle casing, with their top ends abutting in spring housings on a frame cross-member. The axle was located laterally by a track rod, which was attached to the left frame side member at one end and at the other end to a bracket extending backwards from the axle casing, near the halfway point between the final drive bulge and the right wheel hub. The independent front wheel suspension on the 1946 Buick used two A-arms for each wheel, a long arm at the bottom and a short one on top. The outer ends held the upper and lower ends of the kingpin. The inner (broad) ends were anchored on pivot shafts. The coil spring stood on the lower A-arm, with its top end abutting against a cavity in the frame. The upper A-arm had nothing to do with the springing but served only to locate the wheel and direct its camber changes during spring deflection. Front wheel alignment was fairly typical of industry-wide practice at the time, with a caster range from ½ to 1½ degrees positive and a camber range from ⅞ degrees positive to ⅝ degrees negative. Toe-in specifications gave a tolerance from 1/16 inch to ⅛ inch. Kingpin inclination (in the lateral plane) was 4.25 degrees at ⅜-degree positive chamber. Shock absorbers

Buick Super station wagon (Model 59) from 1947 combined wood-paneled body structure with sweeping fender lines, paving the way for the all-metal wagon. The wagon came with three-speed column shift only, and non-assisted steering.

in 1946 were still vane-type hydraulics, double-acting. At front they were mounted so that the lever swung with the upper A-arm, and at the rear the unit was carried inside the frame side members, with the levers reaching back to brackets on the rear axle casing.

A steering system which Buick advertised as Permi-Firm was standard on all 1946 models. All models had a steering ratio of 24:1. This was not the steering gear ratio but the overall ratio, which meant that it took twenty-four degrees of steering wheel movement to obtain a one-degree change in steering angle of the road wheels. The steering gear was manufactured to Buick specifications by Saginaw Steering Gear Division. It was a recirculating-ball worm and nut system with a 19.8:1 ratio, and was

geared to need 4½ turns from full left lock to full right lock. The turning radius for the Roadmaster was 21.35 feet for both left and right turns. The brake system was hydraulic on all four wheels, with cast iron drums of twelve-inch diameter. Each brake assembly had one primary and one secondary shoe, with a total lining length per wheel of just over twenty-three inches. Linings were 2.25 inches wide and ³⁄₁₆ inches thick. The parking brake was mechanical, with cable control, applied by a pedal mounted to the left of the clutch and higher up. The parking brake was released via a rod with a small handle that ran along the kick panel on the driver's side; a simple pull released the brake. Oil-bath air cleaners were adopted for all series, with a long 'silencer' intake duct. Carburetors were either Carter or Stromberg. The exhaust pipe ran alongside the left frame side member, with the muffler right in the middle. The muffler was a cylindrical design about forty inches long. Fuel tank capacity was nineteen gallons on all models.

Such was the engineering on the first postwar Buick, as directed by the man who had been Buick's chief engineer since 1936—Charles A. Chayne. Chayne came from Harrisburg, Pennsylvania, where he was born on February 6, 1898. He graduated from the Massachusetts Institute of Technology with a bachelor's degree in science in 1919, and found his first job that same year with the National Advisory Committee for Aeronautics—the forerunner of the National Aeronautics and Space Agency (NASA). After working for about a year in the NACA laboratories, he went back to M.I.T. as an instructor in mechanical engineering and stayed there for six years. As the years went by he became more and more interested in working inside the auto industry, and he also longed to return to the hills and rivers of Pennsylvania where he had grown up. Both desires were fulfilled in 1927 when he found an opening for an experimental engineer at Lycoming Motors in Williamsport. Lycoming was then building four-, six- and eight-cylinder engines for such famous makes as Auburn, Elcar, Gardner and Roamer, and was getting ready to make the Duesenberg Model J engine. But Chayne stayed only nine months with Lycoming before he joined Marmon in Indianapolis as an engine designer. Here he worked under Thomas J. Litle, Jr., and George H. Freers on such projects as the Roosevelt Junior-8 car and improvements for the senior Marmons. He had become well known among his colleagues in other companies, and one day he was invited to go to work for General Motors. This led to contact with Buick executives, and he joined Buick as head of the engine design section in January 1930. The Buick eight design was frozen before his arrival, but he started the development program that led directly to the revised engine range in 1936-37.

By 1933 Chayne had been promoted to assistant chief engineer of Buick and began to set his personal mark on the entire car. Chayne's laboratory work at Buick resulted in eight patents, covering such diverse inventions as steering linkages, spring suspensions, transmission control, valve gear temperature regulators and chassis frames. Another talent of Chayne's was hiring competent engineers to assist him. He was given free rein in this area when Curtice named him chief engineer, to replace Bower, who was transferred to Vauxhall in England and later worked at Opel in Germany; but returned to the U.S. before World War II and served General Motors on several defense programs. (Incidentally, Bower lived in retirement in Flint to the ripe old age of eighty-eight. During his last years he was mainly engaged in philanthropic activities, and died in March 1971.) Chayne was a superb engine man himself, and wanted to concentrate his own efforts in the power train area, so he knew he was going to need some good men to develop the Buick chassis. Two of those he found stand out: Mathews and Booth.

Coming to Buick as a chassis engineer in 1927, Verner P. Mathews played a key role in adapting the Cadillac independent front suspension to Buick in 1934. The coil spring rear suspension with torque tube drive was largely his creation, and in 1939 Mathews was placed in charge of all Buick chassis engineering with the title of assistant chief engineer. Up to 1937 Buick had used semi-elliptic rear springs, which carried the load and served to locate the rear axle at the same time. But the rear leaf springs, which had been well matched with the leaf spring front axle suspension used up to 1934, were not compatible with the independent coil spring front suspension. The coil spring rear suspension system was first used on the 1937 Century (Model 61), and then adopted across the board for 1938.

James H. Booth joined Buick as a chassis engineer in 1936, after spending the previous six years as a member of the Duesenberg engineering staff in Indianapolis. He came from the Philadelphia area and had studied engineering at Pennsylvania State College. In 1939, Booth was placed in charge of steering and suspension development.

Buick exterior body design was dominated by one man, Harley J. Earl, who had become director of GM Styling, with responsibility for all models of all divisions. He had a growing staff of assistants who submitted their ideas in sketch form and built scale models of those approved by Earl, under his guidance. Divisional studios were soon set up, to preserve make-and-model identity and to avoid similarity between the makes, any more than the general sharing of basic Fisher bodies rendered necessary. Where did Harley Earl come from, and how did he get to head GM Styling? His story sounds like fiction, but that's just the sort of miracle that could and did happen in the automobile industry.

Harley Earl was the son of a carriage manufacturer in Los Angeles where he was born on November 22, 1893. After breaking off his studies at Stanford University, he returned to the family business in 1918. He soon became general manager of the Earl Carriage Works, and began to take orders for special car bodies built to his own designs. He developed a technique of making detailed scale models, which he could show to a customer. This was just the thing for Hollywood celebrities, and soon the local Cadillac distributor, Don Lee, took over Earl's business and placed Harley in charge of the new Don Lee Coach & Body Corporation. One day in 1925 Lawrence P. Fisher, one of the Fisher brothers, who was then general manager of Cadillac, paid a visit to Don Lee and was shown the special body shop. Fisher was so impressed with the models and with the main features of Earl's designs that he arranged for Earl to come to Detroit as a special consultant to Cadillac in 1926. Fisher then arranged for Earl to meet Alfred P. Sloan, president of GM. And together they agreed to engage Earl to design one specific car for Cadillac. That was the 1927 La Salle. After that, Fisher and Sloan realized that Earl possessed the genius they needed for all GM cars, and in June 1927, they established a new department, the Art & Color Section, which became GM Styling in 1934.

Reputedly, Harley Earl himself had the idea for the 1936 Buick. The 1937 Buick, on the other hand, was mainly the work of Paul Meyer. Bill Mitchell had a lot to do with the 1939 cars, and the overall body shape for the 1941/42 models stemmed mainly from sketches by George A. Jergenson. The 1942 fender lines and the whole front end with its low, wide grille were taken from the Y-Job, a Buick prototype built for Harley Earl's personal use in 1938 and mainly designed by George Snyder. The Y-Job was a three-passenger convertible built on a Buick Super chassis with its wheelbase stretched to 123 inches. It had a power-operated top that folded and stowed away under a metal cover on the rear deck, ahead of the trunk lid, making the car look like an open roadster. The most striking thing about the Y-Job was its low build. By using thirteen-inch wheels, the whole chassis was brought closer to the ground. Harley Earl liked long hoods, as he thought they made the car look more powerful, and nothing was done to disguise the height of the Buick straight-eight. The hood on the Y-job towered over the fenders, which held concealed head lamps. The lids were opened and closed by electric motors wired into the light switch. The Y-Job had a hood ornament that was referred to as a machine-gun sight at the time and was the forerunner of the gun sight ornament used on the postwar Buicks. Its door handles, however, were never copied on a production Buick. The handles were flush with the door panels, and were arranged to pop out when pressed in, by a spring-and-ratchet mechanism.

The world first learned of the Y-Job's existence in April 1940, when Buick sent out a press release. Harley Earl used the car for his personal transportation during the 1942-44 period, but then retired it. It was stored in the GM Styling garage for a while, and then brought out and face-lifted in 1947. The concealed head lamps were replaced by standard Buick units, and a new type of push-button door handle was fitted. Also, the original bumpers were replaced by production-type 1947-model front and rear bumpers. The car is still in existence, and forms the nucleus for a permanent GM Styling museum yet to be created.

As can be seen, there were many influences in the styling of the 1946 Buick, though none as strong as that of Harley Earl himself. With the arrival of Ned Nickles, who became chief designer of the Buick studio in 1945, that began to change. Then thirty-seven years old, Nickles was something of a phenomenon. He had started to draw cars at the age of five, but did not pursue his formal schooling beyond high school in his native Wisconsin. He came to GM Styling in 1940 after working for a paper company, and spent the war years developing camouflage techniques and materials. He was as-

signed to the Chevrolet studio for a while, and worked on styling proposals for the Comet small car project which never went into production. Like several of his colleagues at GM Styling, his head was swimming with jet fighter plane shapes and other high-flying ideas when the war ended, and his influence was to show up in the 1947 models.

The silhouette of the 1946 Buick was basically the same as it had been in 1942. There were two styles for four-door sedans—notchback and fastback. All two-door sedans had the fastback 'sedanet' look. All convertibles were two-doors, and the Estate Wagon had four doors and a tailgate. Buick had built its last four-door convertible as a Roadmaster (Model 71C) in 1941. Buick's 1946 body retained the long hood from 1942, and capped it with a gun sight type of ornament at the nose. The grille was practically unchanged, too, with a number of curved vertical bars set in a semi-oval frame. A change from 1942 was that the frame section bearing the BUICK EIGHT inscription was raised and given extra emphasis. Headlights were positioned, as in 1942, at the front of the fenders, with turn signals directly below them. The bumper was a curved-face bar with a centerstrip along its full width, curving around the fender tips at both ends, with a taller face section near each end. Two overriders supported a horizontal cross bar carrying a bulb with the Buick crest. There were valleys between the tall hood and the front fenders, and the hood was a one-piece shell, hinged on both sides, and arranged to tip sideways, as the hinges were unhooked on one side or the other. This type of hood design had been adopted in 1940. On either side of the cowl was a stylized 'bomb' with a series-identification label. The front fender line on the Super and Roadmaster was swept back to meet the rear fender, well above hub level. This fender line had been used on the Super sedanet and convertible in 1942, while all other 1942 models had front fenders ending halfway into the front door. Only the Special continued the short front fender line which lasted into the 1948 model year. All 1946 models had rear fenders with spats that covered most of the hub caps and wheels. The fuel filler neck was concealed under a small lid in the left rear fender panel. Below and behind it was a small reflector. The 1946 Special had a heavy chrome molding at the lower fender edge, and double wide chrome moldings on both front and rear fenders. The other series had a more discreet tapered molding, a little above hub level along front and rear fenders.

All 1946 models had doors hinged at the front and opening at the back end. Exterior door handles were massive pieces with old-fashioned arms that had to be bent down to release the lock. Inside door handles were smaller levers curved to fit the hand. The door lock buttons on the window sill, used on the 1942 models, had been discarded in favor of combining the lock with the handle. Doors were locked by pushing the handle to a

stop beyond the closed position, and released by merely pulling the handle back. The 1946 windshield was divided, with two panels of straight glass, meeting at a chrome bar at the edge of the vee. Four-door notchback models had vent windows in the front doors, and similar separations in the rear door glass to enable the window to be fully lowered. Four-door fastback models had one-piece rear door windows, plus a fixed rear-quarter window. Two-door models also had vent windows in the doors, and a single-piece type of rear side window was used. All models had undivided rear windows.

The 1946 instrument panel was almost symmetrically laid out, with a circular speedometer set in a pod in front of the driver and an equal-size dash clock above the glovebox. Other gauges were placed at a lower level, on both sides of the steering column. The steering wheel was an eighteen-inch three-spoke design with a large hub and a full-circle horn ring. The spokes were evenly spaced. The push-button radio was positioned in the center, with the loudspeaker directly below it. The pedal arrangement in 1946 had a long and fairly narrow accelerator pedal, hinged at the floor along the rear and connected to the throttle linkage near its front. Clutch and brake pedals had rectangular rubber pads, and stood side by side on curved stems extending from the floorboards. At the extreme left was the parking brake pedal.

Vacuum-operated windshield wipers were standard, switched on and off by a knob centrally located on top of the instrument panel. Twisting the knob beyond the on position gave variable speed control. But as always with vacuum-operated wipers, they failed to maintain speed when the engine ran under high load, and tended to over speed on coasting. The first Buicks to use vacuum wipers were the 1932 models, and the last were the 1958 models. Then Buick went to electric wipers. A windshield washer was made optional in 1947. The washer worked when the driver twisted the wiper button fully to the left, against a detent spring, and held it against the spring tension for three to five seconds. Turning the knob to the right would then start the wipers in time for the water jet. This was modified in 1949, when the knob was equipped with a small button. Depressing the button for a few seconds would open the water supply. On release of the button, a jet of water was squirted from the nozzles, which were mounted at the wiper arm bases. Buick's heating and ventilation system was known under the trade name Weather Warden. All models had dual air intakes at the grille, the left admitting fresh (cool) air to the interior, and the right leading fresh air to the under-seat heater core, via a fan located low down on the cowl. The defroster did not work with fresh air, but had a separate blower which gathered interior air and directed it at the windshield through one outlet on each side. Each outlet was no more than four inches wide.

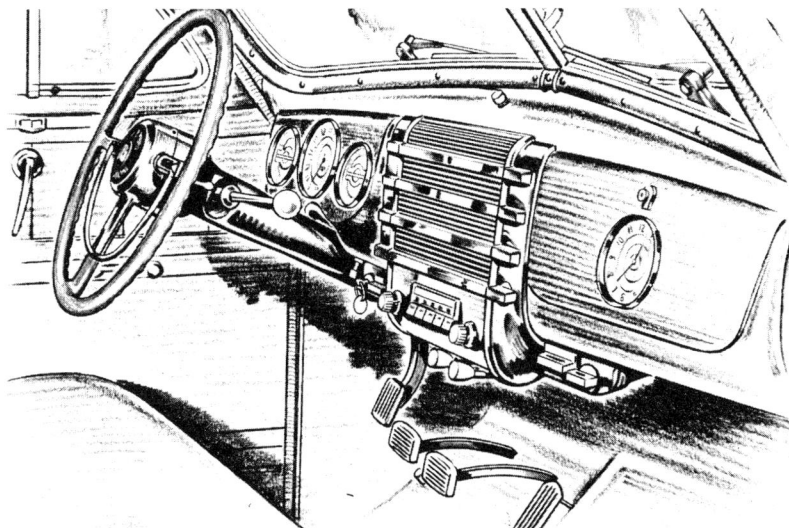

DRIVING COMPARTMENT—SERIES 40

The 1948 Special had simpler interior trim and instrumentation than the Super and Roadmaster, but all basic controls were the same throughout. All series had step-on parking brake and starter motor operated by accelerator pedal.

Dynaflow automatic transmission was optional for the 1948 Roadmaster, which permitted the axle ratio to be lowered from 4.1:1 to 3.9:1, with a 3.64:1 ratio optional. The extra cost for Dynaflow was $125, which caused a lot of people to say, "I can do a lot of shifting for $125."

At the wheel of the 1946 Buick Roadmaster, the driver looked out over a hood that seemed immensely long. An outline of the left front fender was visible, but the right one was completely out of sight. This was normal at the time, and not a particular handicap. The gun sight hood ornament helped the driver place the car relative to lane markings and other traffic.

Cruising at 60 mph, the Buick was remarkably quiet. At that speed, the engine was loafing at about 2100 rmp, giving off a steady purr. Wind noise was low, even with vent windows partly open. And road noise, on good pavement, was just a gentle murmur from the tires. On bad roads, the ride

was soft, and the body and chassis relatively rattle-free. The ride motion was boatlike, the car progressing in a series of heaves, according to speed and road roughness. With its all-coil springs, the Roadmaster was free of pitch motions, except when crossing a humpbacked bridge or similar constructions at low speed.

The engine usually started with a roar, for the starter switch was connected to the accelerator linkage, and was engaged by depressing the pedal beyond its full-throttle position. When the pedal was released, the engine settled into a smooth idle, its beat absolutely regular instead of throbbing like the V-8's of the Cadillac, Mercury and Ford. Of course, the Buick engine was noisy on full-throttle acceleration, but most Buick owners accepted this happily. Noise spells performance, and it seemed natural that use of its full power should be accompanied by a rising roar. And the acceleration

30

was indeed impressive, especially for a car in the Roadmaster's weight class. It would reach 60 mph from standstill in about fifteen seconds, and cover the standing quarter-mile in about eighteen seconds, with a terminal speed of about 72 mph.

First gear had a low 2.39:1 ratio, which would take the car to about 40 mph before shifting into second. The steering-column gearshift was a rugged device, free of play, with a solid feel and capable of withstanding energetic movements of the lever. Throws were rather long, with the lever down about four o'clock in first, and up at one o'clock in second, but the gate was very well defined. Second gear was good for speeds up to 65 mph. The engine was so tractable, the car could actually be started in second gear on level ground, and pull strongly in top gear from about 15 mph. The clutch was truck-like, the pedal standing high off the floor, but it had a gentle action, free of chatter and grabbing. Gear noise was loud in first gear, moderate in second, and inaudible in top gear.

Steering response was quite slow, as was common for all American cars at the time, and the handling characteristic was a firm understeer, which could be upset by braking too late into a curve. That would often shake the rear axle loose, which was easily overcome by getting off the brake and making steering corrections with the wheel. Steering was slow-geared, but remarkably light for such a heavy car. Body roll seemed slight, and this Buick did in fact have a flatter ride on curves than most cars of its day. On hard cornering, tire squeal gave audible warning to slow down.

Brakes? The pedal was relatively hard, but smoothly progressive in action. Braking stability was about average, far below what is demanded to-day, but tolerable then. The slightest maladjustment would lead to side pull, and the self-energizing effect of leading shoes could also provoke uneven braking. Even without a power servo, the brakes were immensely powerful, and capable of locking all wheels in a panic stop.

To sum up, the 1946 Buick had better road manners than most of its rivals, combining high power with a chassis that was well equipped to handle it, all in a package of balanced good looks.

The 1947 models received a modified grille, with fewer but more accented vertical bars, still with a convex curve and a beefed-up grille frame. At the same time the BUICK EIGHT lettering went back on the grille frame, while an enlarged chrome molding above it carried the triple-shield medallion. Every year Nickles added more chrome to the cars, first at the top of the line, and working it gradually onto the lower-priced models. He felt that chrome was symbolic of a return to the good old days, to prosperity, to a sort of fulfillment of American ideals. Chrome had been reserved for the defense industries during the war, and was still in short supply for a couple of years afterwards.

As General Motors got back into car production, only Chevrolet had its own assembly plants around the country. In order to give Buick, Oldsmobile and Pontiac the same benefits, the corporation set up a new organization, the B-O-P Assembly Division, which operated a number of plants. In short order, the Buick was assembled in B-O-P plants located at South Gate, California; Linden, New Jersey; Kansas City, Kansas; and Atlanta, as well as in Buick's own plant at Flint.

CHAPTER 4
From Wiles to Ragsdale

IF THE TITLE of this chapter brings to your mind the old cliche 'from rags to riches' we can only apologize for misleading you. The success that Buick had enjoyed in the thirties and forties was not to continue through the next decade. For Buick, the 1950's was a difficult period, during which the division went the opposite route, from riches to rags. The fact that the general manager who held the reins at Buick during its decline happened to be named Ragsdale is one of history's coincidences, the cruel fates mingling irony with tragedy.

Harlow H. Curtice had led Buick towards the top. Through 1946 and 1947 Buick maintained its hard-won fourth place in the sales race, with only Chevrolet, Ford and Plymouth, the low-priced three, selling more cars. Buick's sales volume was running better than one-third of Chevrolet's and handsomely ahead of both Oldsmobile and Pontiac. Domestic sales soared from 126,322 Buicks in the 1946 calendar year to 246,115 during 1947. That year, Buick held a 7.77-percent share of the U.S. car market. Curtice was regarded as a miracle man, and in retrospect it's a wonder that Buick was able to hold on to him for so long, since he was obviously destined for higher office at the corporation. In November 1948, when Curtice was appointed executive vice president of General Motors, shortly after Buick had

built its five-millionth automobile, Ivan L. Wiles became general manager of Buick. Under Curtice's management, Buick had built 2,250,000 cars.

Wiles was an accountant who had worked for Marmon and Oakland before coming to Buick. In his first year at the helm of Buick, the U.S. car market expanded from 3.5 to 4.8 million units, and Buick participated fully in the growth, with a total of 372,425 cars registered during the 1949 calendar year. That gave Buick a 7.7-percent share of the market and fourth rank behind Chevrolet, Ford and Plymouth. It was also in 1949 that Ragsdale became general manufacturing manager of Buick. His automotive career had started in 1916 when he joined Maxwell as a tool designer. Edward T. Ragsdale had been at Buick since 1923, when he left a job in Buffalo, New York, as body designer for Pierce-Arrow, to move to Flint as a draftsman. By 1935 he was working as a body engineer at Buick, and in 1939 he was made assistant chief engineer for bodies, under E. F. Reynolds.

On the engineering front, Charlie Chayne was still very much in charge. Under his guidance, the Buick product had continued to develop, year by year. But the spectacular success won during 1949 was certainly due to styling more than engineering. Here was the first Buick with a true postwar look, designed by Ned Nickles. GM Styling and Fisher Body came out with

Buick Roadmaster Riviera of 1949 was the first of the Fisher Body hardtops, creating quite a sensation in the market and in the industry. It also introduced the Riviera name, which was to be used for an outstanding car many years later.

a totally new C-body for 1949, and it was used for the Buick Super and Roadmaster. Naturally, Buick had to share it with the Oldsmobile 98 and Cadillac 60, 61 and 62. Strangely, the 1949-model Buick Special continued unchanged from 1948, but was suspended in December 1948, to be revived for 1950, when Fisher Body had engineered a new B-body, which Buick had to share with the Oldsmobile 88. Chevrolet and Pontiac used the Fisher A-body, which was also new for the 1949 model year. This sharing of bodies meant that the cars would have a common styling theme—a GM look. Buick was locked into many of the same dimensions as Oldsmobile and Cadillac, and the cowl position, windshield base and angle, roof length

and certain other fixed points could not be altered. But the Buick studio had freedom to shape the 'skin' of the car, the outer body panels, and was to design the entire front and rear ends, superimposing a Buick look on top of the GM look.

The 1949 Buick silhouette was lowered considerably. Though the hood was shortened as much as the length of the straight-eight engine would allow, it still looked impressively long. The hood line remained tall and

Buick Super Sedanet (Model 56-S) of 1949 had an all-new body with fastback styling. This was the year of the full-width grille and the ventiports. All Buick engines were still straight-eights, and Dynaflow was optional in all series.

straight, and the deck lid acquired greater emphasis. The front fender line was raised to meet the top of the rear fender, which was a separate design element, emerging behind the door on two-door models, and springing out of the rear door panel on four-door models. In each front fender skirt, near the top, was something new: a neatly arranged, horizontal row of little round holes. They were 'ventiports,' which were to be a Buick trademark for the next twenty-five years. It was a gimmick that Nickles had put on his own car, a 1947 Super convertible. He actually put little lights in them and wired them to light up in sequence to simulate fire and exhaust. He did the same thing to a 1948 Roadmaster, and when Curtice saw it, he made an on-the-spot decision to put ventiports on every Buick. Without the lights, of course, which would have made it too expensive. In accordance with Curtice's decree, there were three ventiports on each side for the Super and four on the Roadmaster. At first, Buick claimed they actually served to ventilate the engine compartment, but that's something of an exaggeration, since their effect was negligible. They were a styling device, described in Buick's sales literature as "striking a smart nautical note," which was not what Nickles had intended at all.

The 1949 grille was widened so that its ends lined up with the head lamp center lines on both sides. The turn signals were moved into streamlined housings on the fender tops, trailed by a chrome molding. The grille frame faithfully carried the BUICK EIGHT lettering, surmounted by a large

Buick emblem, with a diamond-studded belt crossing diagonally from upper left to lower right, the left field being occupied by a Greek cross and the right field by a hart's head with antlers. The bomb-sight hood ornament was shortened but helped emphasize the Buick identity of the car. Taillights were blended smoothly into the rear fender shape, inserted at the point where the fender line began its tighter arc down to bumper level.

Though the 1949 body continued with a split windshield, it also introduced curved windshield glass, which permitted the A-post to be set back even more. The V-point in the roof was very slight, hinting at the coming disappearance of the center divider. The A-post is body engineering slang for the windshield pillars. The B-post is the pillar between the doors on a four-door model, or the center post on two-door models. The C-post is the sheet metal that links the roof to the lower body at the rear end, often called rear quarter panels or sail panels. This explanation is important, for in 1949 Buick took the drastic step of eliminating the B-post on one model—an industry 'first' which gave birth to a whole new body style, the *hardtop*.

The idea was to provide convertible-type styling for a closed car, and Ned Nickles pulled off a spectacular *coup* with the Roadmaster Riviera hardtop coupe, as the first one was called. The new roof had a very slim-based C-post, with a wraparound rear window, supported by two thin pillars at both sides of the flat section in the rear. About 1945 Nickles had built a scale-model of this type of body, and when Curtice saw it, he wondered if it could be produced. Curtice was always receptive to new styling ideas, but this one involved body engineering at the basic level, and Ragsdale was called in to give his expertise. He was sure it could be produced, with no great cost penalty, and Curtice gave the order to go ahead. Stories have been told of how Ragsdale invented the hardtop because his wife wanted a closed car that looked like a convertible, but that's not the way it happened. Ragsdale had a lot to do with tooling up for it, but the design idea had been born in the styling studio several years earlier.

Another styling feature introduced on the 1949 Riviera was the sweepspear, which was to become as much a part of the Buick look as the ventiports. It was a chrome molding that started in the front fender and ran horizontally back into the door panel, then swept down while becoming fatter and fatter, ending at the base of the rear fender. It traced an imaginary front fender line, imposing itself on the body shell no matter what its shape. It was highly visible, and gave the car its individual character. The 1949 Riviera also had Buick's first power windows. Each door had its own switch—push down to open, up to close. In addition, a panel on the driver's door had four buttons, so that the driver could open and close any window without moving from his seat. The new instrument panel for 1949

The Riviera sedan of 1950 was a Road-master built on a 130-inch wheelbase. It was a regular pillar-type sedan; not a hardtop. This year the grille formed part of the bumper, with teethlike protrusions across the bumper face.

Combined grille and bumper of the 1950 Buick Super was not well received. It was a costly assembly of individual bars, and was discontinued at the end of the model year. Straight-eight engine necessitated tall hood line.

was described as 'pilot-centered' because the speedometer was made larger and raised higher, still mounted straight ahead of the driver, with the other instruments grouped around it. The design was taken from the 1938 Y-Job, almost without change. Space for a radio was provided near the middle (slightly offset towards the passenger side), with a large grille for loud-speaker mounting below it. The dash clock was moved away from the glovebox area to join the other instruments. Full-width bench seats were standard on the 1949 models. The steering wheel was a new three-spoke design, with two spokes running through the hub as a straight bar, and the third linking the hub to the rim at right angles to the other two spokes. A semi-circular horn ring was set in the lower half of the wheel. The pedals stood on a pivot shaft located below floor level, and the accelerator pedal was hinged at the heel, and attached to the throttle linkage near its front end.

The steering on the 1949 models was the same 'Permi-Firm' design that had been used since 1946. The Super had a steering ratio of 24:1 and the Roadmaster 29:1. The Roadmaster steering wheel needed a full five turns from full left to full right, while 4½ turns would do it on the Super. An im-proved Weather Warden heating and ventilation system appeared on the 1949 models. As before, two fresh-air intakes were mounted at opposite ends of the grille, but the blower was moved up behind the wire-mesh filter

that was part of the right side inlet. At standstill and low speeds, the blower would force the air in; at higher speeds, the air rushed in by ram effect. The air was ducted to the heater core, and led to the car's interior. As in the 1948 model, the second duct was for fresh air only, and discharged directly into the passenger compartment. The defroster had a separate heating core and drew fresh air from the duct with the blower. Defroster outlets now ex-tended for the full width of the windshield.

A new B-body (for the revived 1950 Special—Series 40) shared some elements of the larger C-body, and Buick used the same front and rear ends on all series. The frontal design was totally new for 1950. The wide grille was maintained, but it was now integrated with the front bumper, and in fact, overlapping the bumper face. The vertical bumper bars were separate parts, each one detachable, and Buick claimed this would be an important factor in reducing repair costs after low-speed impacts. Instead of replacing the whole grille, it would be possible to replace the bars singly. But some-

35

Sweepspear accent line, as used on this 1951 Super convertible, was to become a Buick trademark, along with the ventiports. Power top was hydraulically operated. Built on a 121.5-inch wheelbase, this Model 56-C weighed 3,700 pounds.

thing had been forgotten. It was a complicated assembly, expensive to produce. What's more, the bars were not all the same size and shape, and this led to a proliferation in parts numbers and complicated ordering, stock control and store-keeping. The following year, Buick reverted to the one-piece grille, and pulled it back behind the bumper. Two pods carried on the bumper overriders contained the parking lights and turn signals. There was no ornamentation on top of the fenders. The fender sides, on the other hand, were decorated. A tapered chrome molding (not a sweepspear) went

straight back, a little above bumper level, from the right fender skirt to the rear bumper. If the 1950 silhouette did not change much, the accent lines certainly did. First, the front fender line was pulled down, sweeping lower and lower through the door, and permitting a giant kickup before the rear wheel, becoming a rear fender line. A crease in the rear fender panel dipped down at the kickup and then went straight back to curve into the bumper near the tail. The big difference from the 1949 style was that both front and rear fenders went to the full body width in their entire length. The year before, the front fenders had tapered into the body sides making the car narrower in the door area, and then becoming wider again as the rear fenders jutted out ahead of the rear wheels.

Body details that were new for 1950 included the one-piece curved windshield, oval ventiports and push-button door handles. The windshield glass was nearly flat in the center, but curved around with a diminishing radius towards the corner posts. The new push-button exterior door handles provided a full grip, with a push-button for the thumb. Ventiports had been set in the fender panels in 1949, but on the 1950 models were moved up into the side of the hood. They were changed from circular to oval, which put paid to the idea of using nautical symbols on a road vehicle, but remained the same in number, four for the Roadmaster, and three for the other series. In 1951 they were made round again, with smaller holes set in a semi-spherical ornament. They were moved back to the fender skirts at the same time, extending the overall car width.

Priced at $1,925, and three inches shorter in length than its predecessor, the 1950 Special was competing directly against the Dodge, Hudson Pacemaker and the eight-cylinder Pontiac. The Super cost about $230 more, and the Roadmaster started at $2,528. The Special series for 1950 included two body styles and three models—a four-door sedan, a two-door sedan and a two-door business coupe. All 1950 two-door sedans were fastbacks, while four-door sedans were available either in fastback or notchback style. The Riviera coupe was, of course, a notchback, following the convertible profile. In the four-door fastback sedans, the rear quarter window had disappeared, and rear doors received a vent window, as on the notchback models. Notchback sedans had three-piece wraparound rear windows, while the fastback models continued with single-piece glass behind the back seat. The 1950 Roadmaster series included six models: four-door Tourback sedan on a 126.25-inch wheelbase (Model 71); four-door Tourback sedan on a 130.25-inch wheelbase (Model 72); two-door Jetback Sedanet (Model 76S); two-door convertible (Model 76C), two-door Riviera coupe (Model 76R); and four-door Estate Wagon (Model 79).

Use of the Riviera name plate was extended to include a four-door notchback sedan in the Super series. Far from being a hardtop, however, it was a long-wheelbase sedan with one-piece glass in the rear doors and swing-out rear quarter windows in the sail panels. Two-door Riviera models, in both Super and Roadmaster series, were to continue as hardtops in 1951 and 1952. The 1951 grille remained wide, as in 1949 and 1950, but the frame was made crisper, and the bumper face had a kicked-down center section, giving added emphasis to the vertical bars, which now had a slight convex curve. On top of the grille frame you could still see the BUICK EIGHT lettering, but the crest-type emblem was replaced by an oval. The gunsight hood ornament was retained. The parking light pods were moved apart, becoming separated from the bumper overriders, and looked like the front ends of little turbojet engines emerging from both sides of the grille.

Taillights were now built into a vertical red lens unit with a chrome frame, standing in the rear fender tails. But the most obvious styling change was a prominent sweepspear on all models.

In the 1951 instrument panel, the speedometer was moved down and set at the right-hand side of the steering column. It remained a big, circular dial, however. The other gauges were grouped on the left. Radio and loudspeaker were brought into the center, and a dash clock filled the small panel that separated the loudspeaker grille from the glovebox lid. This arrangement did not last long. The instrument panel on the 1952 models had a very large speedometer placed directly ahead of the driver, with a big round dial set in a pod that rose out of the top of the dashboard. Lower down on each side were gauges for oil pressure, coolant temperature, battery charging, and fuel tank content. A shift lever extended from the right-hand side of the steering column, and the P-N-D-L-R indicator was conveniently placed, extending from the steering column behind the hub of the steering wheel.

The 1951 Special series included a four-door Tourback (Model 41); four-door Deluxe Tourback (Model 41D); two-door Riviera coupe (Model 45R); two-door Tourback business coupe (Model 46S); two-door Tourback sedan (Model 48); and a two-door Deluxe Tourback sedan (Model 48D). A new Custom Special (series 44) was added in the 1951 model year. It shared the basic Special chassis, with the 121.5-inch wheelbase, but had some body panels from the Super, which stretched overall length to 206.2 inches (from 204.8 inches). The 1951 Super series had six models: four-door Tourback (Model 51); four-door Riviera sedan (Model 52); two-door Riviera coupe (Model 56R); two-door convertible (Model 56C); two-door Jetback Sedanet (Model 56S); and the four-door Estate Wagon (Model 59). There were only four Roadmaster models in the 1951 model year; a four-door Riviera on a 130.25-inch wheelbase (Model 72R); a two-door Riviera on a 126.25-inch wheelbase (Model 76R); a two-door convertible (Model 76C); and a four-door Estate Wagon (Model 79R).

Styling changes for 1952 were hardly visible and centered around the side decor. However, all fastback models had been discontinued at the end of the 1951 model year. Buick stagnated under Wiles' money-minded management, as engineering innovation and excellence lost emphasis. A former Buick engineer told us how Wiles had approached him when he first took over at Buick: "He came to my office and said he did not know the first thing about engineering, so he was going to leave the product to us. But within six months, he was back, telling us how to do our jobs." Wiles has also been blamed for committing grave errors involving Buick's manufacturing programs. Former Buick personnel told us that he authorized putting up a whole new building for making Buick bodies, instead of buying them all from Fisher. When the body plant was finished, Wiles told his executives that they weren't going to get any bonus that year, because it cost Buick $15 per car more to build its own bodies. When Wiles finally passed the order to try and take some of the cost out of the bodies, it was too late. With two months to go, there was not enough time left before production startup to make any important changes. "At the same time," said a retired Buick official, "he ordered change-overs in the bodies for several series at the same time, something that we had never done before at Buick, so the tooling bill was really, well, up to the moon!"

On September 1, 1949, Buick built its one-millionth postwar car, the six-millionth Buick was assembled in mid 1950. Buick boosted its market share to 8.47 percent in 1950 with sales of 535,807 cars, coming within 12,000 cars of knocking Plymouth out of its traditional third spot. As the United States became increasingly involved in the United Nations police action in Korea, materials shortages began to hit the auto industry, while the auto makers were simultaneously invited to bid on defense contracts. Buick received defense contracts for the production of J-65 Sapphire turbojet engines and an automatic transmission for tanks. These activities took up a certain amount of Buick's manufacturing capacity, and car output was curtailed. At the same time, the domestic market for new cars suffered a decline, from 6.3 million units in 1950 to five million in 1951 and 4.16 million in 1952. Throughout this period, however, Buick maintained its share of the market in the 7.5- to 8-percent bracket. Buick built its seven-millionth car on June 13, 1953. In the meantime, Buick had got a new chief engineer.

Chayne left Buick in 1951, to take over the position of vice president in charge of the GM Engineering Staff, as head of a group of 1,200 technical personnel. Before leaving Buick, he had presided over the engineering of the 1954 models. Among his many other achievements can be counted the introduction of the Dynaflow automatic transmission in 1948, and the adoption of power steering in 1952 and power brakes in 1953. He directed the design of a new version of the straight-eight engine, with 263-cubic-inch displacement, which was standard on the 1950-model Buick Super. And the new Buick V-8 was designed under Chayne's guidance. It was Verner P. Mathews who took his place as chief engineer of Buick. He was known as a first-class design engineer, but his talents as a coordinator and administrator were to fall short of the demands his new duties placed on them. As the man who held final responsibility for the product, he was blamed for design flaws and material defects alike. Customer complaints rose drastically as quality control slipped. Buick built too many cars, too fast, in 1955 and 1956. Buick was building 600,000 to 700,000 and more cars a year in a plant designed for about 400,000. The factory did not have capacity for

fixing sloppy assembly work and it shipped defective vehicles, hoping that the dealers would put things right during delivery preparation. This was too much to ask, particularly in view of the ever-increasing volume of cars to be handled and the rising frequency and growing severity of repair work required on brand-new cars.

Ragsdale, who was the general manufacturing manager, was obviously guilty of failing to uphold Buick's standards. He was rewarded by being promoted to general manager of Buick in 1956, when Wiles was transferred to a corporate office assigned to work with dealer contracts and relations in the GM Building in Detroit. As for Wiles, one of the men who worked under him at Buick said: "He should get credit for being a good accountant, but Buick got in trouble because of his poor judgment." Buick had displaced Plymouth from third place in 1954 with sales of 513,497 cars, raising its market share to 9.28 percent. The following year Buick set an all-time record with sales of 737,879 cars, taking a 10.3-percent slice of the total domestic market. On the face of it, 1956 was a good sales year for Buick, with a total of 529,371 registrations in the U.S. That kept Buick in a strong third place, behind Chevrolet and Ford, with a 45,000-car lead over Plymouth and a 90,000-car lead over Oldsmobile, who were fourth and fifth. The drop in volume could be dismissed because the total car market shrank from 7.2 to six million units. Buick's market share was still an impressive 8.89 percent. But the day was inexorably approaching when the quest for increased sales, regardless of what was happening to product quality, would come to take its toll of Buick's fortunes. In 1957, Buick's domestic sales tumbled to 394,553 cars, which allowed Plymouth to jump ahead into third place in the market. Buick's market share had been cut from 8.89 percent to 6.59 percent within twelve months.

Bespectacled and balding, with a small moustache, Ragsdale was worried. He decided to get a new chief engineer. Mathews was relieved of his duties at Buick before he was sixty-two and forced to take early retirement at the end of 1957. Oliver K. Kelley came in as chief engineer on the first of September 1957, and Mathews spent the last four months of his professional career in limbo, though he was carried on the payroll as an engineer on special assignment to Ragsdale. Mathews settled in Tucson, Arizona, where he died at the age of seventy-five in 1970. While he had been chief engineer of Buick, a number of other men had left greater marks on the product. For a long time they fought a losing battle against the effects of corporate policy, which led to cars that steadily increased in size and weight. This placed higher and higher demands on the brakes. And the brake system had hardly evolved since 1936.

One of the basic facts about brake systems is that they work by converting energy into heat. Any moving car has a certain kinetic energy stored in

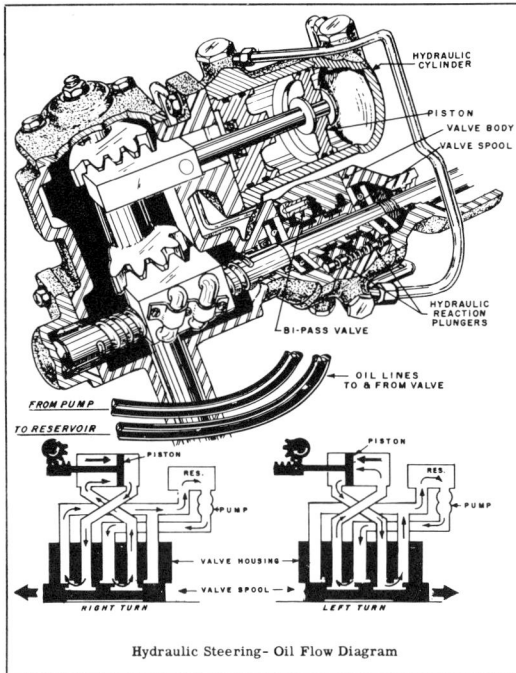

Hydraulic Steering- Oil Flow Diagram

Left, diagram of power steering gear for the 1952 models shows how the hydraulic cylinder provides additional steering effort to supplement input by driver. Hydraulic power was supplied by a separately mounted pump, belt-driven from the engine. Roadmaster Riviera sedan of 1952 (Model 72), right, was first Buick available with power steering. Its straight-eight engine was America's first to use a four-barrel carburetor. Brake system began to suffer due to heavy weight of 4,285 pounds, with its 12-inch cast-iron drums.

it. To stop it, the kinetic energy must be overcome. You cannot throw it out of the window. But you can convert it into heat. This is done by the friction between the brake drum and the shoes inside it. Friction is a force that restricts movement between two objects at their contacting surfaces—or interface, as the engineers like to say. The amount of kinetic energy to be absorbed depends on the weight of the car. The heavier the vehicle, the greater its kinetic energy, and the greater the amount of heat to be dissipated. This heat is first stored in the brake drum and brake mechanism. Then it is dissipated into the air. The rate of heat dissipation sets a limit to what the brakes can do. The mass of the drum and the airflow around it are more important than the size of the friction area. Provision for brake cooling is one of the most important elements in brake engineering. If brakes overheat, they fade. Fade is a loss of braking effect caused by the bonding agents in the friction material rising to the surface and reducing the coefficient of friction between the brake lining and the drum. Buick was begin-

ning to run into brake fade problems in the early 1950's. Normal brake action is proportional to pedal pressure. When fade sets in, the effect of increased pedal pressure is reduced, until, with extreme fade, no amount of pedal pressure can produce any help in slowing the car. To the driver, it feels as if his brakes had been oiled.

"In 1950 we developed test vehicles for brake research," Frank Daley explained to us. "That was when the SAE (Society of Automotive Engineers) brake standards started. We looked at a number of things, such as heat transfer characteristics, the pouring of cast iron, the compounds of the linings, and the whole structure of brakes. We also developed holes in the

39

wheels to promote brake cooling, something that was considered counter-productive by the styling department." Daley was one of two top men in Buick's brake engineering section. The other was Charles D. Holton. Holton was the senior partner, having joined General Motors in 1932. He started as a test engineer at the GM proving grounds, and worked almost exclusively on brakes. It was he who developed the brake system for the Buick Hellcat in 1942. He remained with Buick for the rest of his career. Frank Daley came to GM at the age of 26 in 1945 with a bachelor's degree in chemistry from the University of Massachusetts and was assigned to Chevrolet as assistant resident engineer. He made brakes his specialty and was transferred to Buick that same year as a staff engineer on chassis. Walter Boehm was responsible for the metals development in the Buick foundry, and worked very closely with Charlie Holton. For friction material development, a major contribution was made by Berlin B. Brambaugh, who was the top engineer on brake lining composition at Inland Division of General Motors, in Dayton, Ohio. Of course, these men knew how to make better brakes. But under Wiles, a financial man, there was great pressure on the engineering department to keep down the cost of every part. Consequently the first improvements were modest and followed the path that involved the least expense.

For the 1952 models, Chayne approved Holton's recommendation to widen the linings, which of course also meant using wider drums, with a thicker flange to prevent distortion. The greater mass improved their heat-sink capacity. The drums were made by an efficient low-cost centrifugal mold technique and had good heat dissipation characteristics. On the Special and Super, brake lining width was increased from 1.75 inches to 2.25 inches. On the Roadmaster, lining width was increased to 2.50 inches. Power brakes were introduced on the 1953 Roadmaster. That was an answer to a problem of increasing pedal effort that had resulted from the year by year weight increase in the cars. It was a joint development between Buick and Delco. The idea was borrowed from a Bendix truck brake system called Hydrovac, which consisted of using a vacuum power cylinder, drawing vacuum from the engine's intake manifold, to increase the pedal effort going into the master cylinder. But the power brake system was rushed into production before it had been adequately developed. A problem soon popped up. The rubber O-ring that sealed the master cylinder from the vacuum cylinder would fail, and this would open a path for the brake fluid to leak into the vacuum line to the manifold, and from there into the engine, where it would be burned with the gasoline. When this happened, the car had no brakes. It was total brake failure. Ralph Nader in his book *Unsafe at Any Speed* made a big issue out of the way Buick tried to keep the problem quiet instead of urging all owners to bring their cars in for modification, as

soon as an improved O-ring had been produced. Service bulletins were sent out to dealers, with instructions to replace the O-rings on all 1953 Roadmasters brought in for other work, but there was no full alarm, and no sincere follow-up.

After the installation of V-8 engines in all 1954 models, Buicks became both faster and heavier, and brake fade problems became more obvious. Frank Daley tells the story: "We developed the tortuous West Virginia mountain cycle for testing brakes. That was about a 1,000-mile trip, starting in Dayton and going east in Ohio, across the Ohio River, then south into West Virginia on U.S. 252, to a place called Catawbra, then going back and forth over a couple of the big mountains down there. We would go back to Dayton by Route 60 and Route 35, after a pretty full three days of running. When we first started out with this test, about 1950-51, there were days when we had hardly crossed the Ohio River before the first brake failures occurred. By 1957-58, cars could go around the whole trip, on winding mountain roads, at maximum safe speed, back to Dayton and be ready to do another one. This difference in performance between the beginning of the tests and the end was proof of our success."

All the time this research and development work went on, Buicks were leaving the factory with inadequately fade-resistant brakes. The results of Holton's, Daley's, Boehm's and Brambaugh's work did not get into production until 1957—for the 1958 models. By this time, at Kelley's powerful insistence, Ragsdale loosened the purse strings. Buicks must have better brakes, at any cost. And the system that Holton and Daley had developed was the same kind, with finned aluminum drums, that was then used by European racing cars such as Ferrari and Maserati. Buick's work on brake linings and the advances made in metallurgy were shared throughout GM, and the lessons from Buick's tests were to benefit the other divisions as well. But Buick alone standardized the finned aluminum drums. Chevrolet used them on the 1957 Sebring Corvette (not a production model), but it was Buick that developed them for mass production. Since aluminum is lighter than iron, the drum mass could be dramatically increased without adding weight. Aluminum is also a better conductor—about three times better than iron. The fins were roughly triangular in shape, rising from the inside edge of the periphery to a point near the outside edge, then maintaining full height for about one-fourth inch and ending flush with the open edge. Maximum fin height was about one-third inch. Each drum had forty-eight fins, evenly spaced around its circumference. They were designed to stimulate turbulence in the cooling air and increase the drum's surface area in contact with the air.

But aluminum is a bad friction material. Softer than iron, it would wear faster. Therefore Buick put a cast iron liner inside the drum, as a rubbing

Bolt · Flange Gasket · Wheel Cylinder · Adjuster Link · Brake Shoe · Adjuster Actuator · "O" Ring · Cover · Wheel Mounting Bolt · Axle Housing · Backing Plate · Pawl · Bearing Retainer · Oil Seal · Bearing and Grease Seal Assembly · Cover Gasket · Flanged Axle Shaft · Brake Drum

Because the rear wheels do only one-tenth to one-third of the braking, Buick found it could obtain adequate improvement by merely adding cooling fins to the drums on the rear wheels. This exploded view, left, shows the whole rear brake assembly. Right, Buick's finned aluminum brake drums gave vastly improved heat dissipation and practically eliminated fade as an everyday problem. Thin cast-iron insert worked as friction surface against the brake linings.

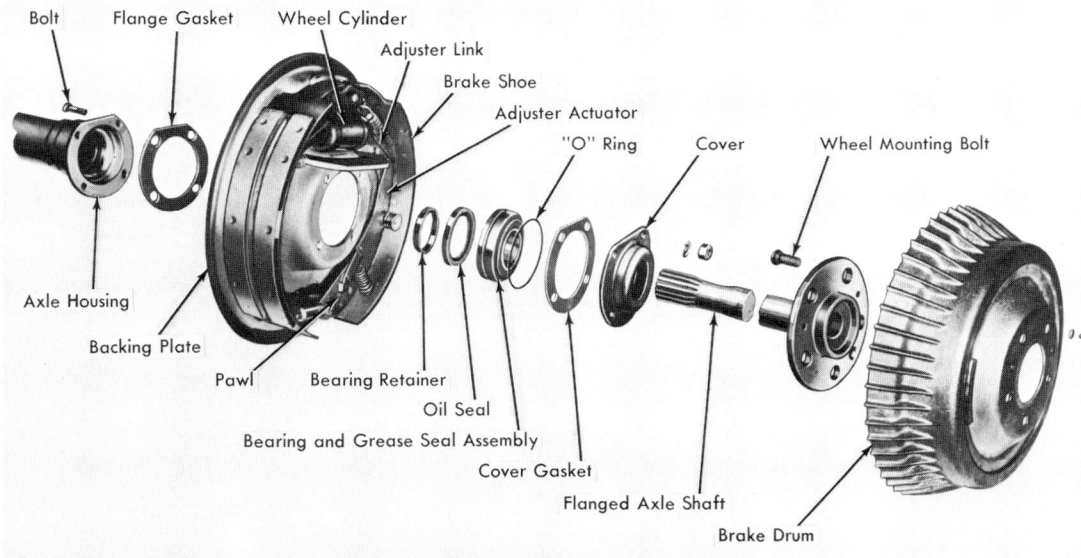

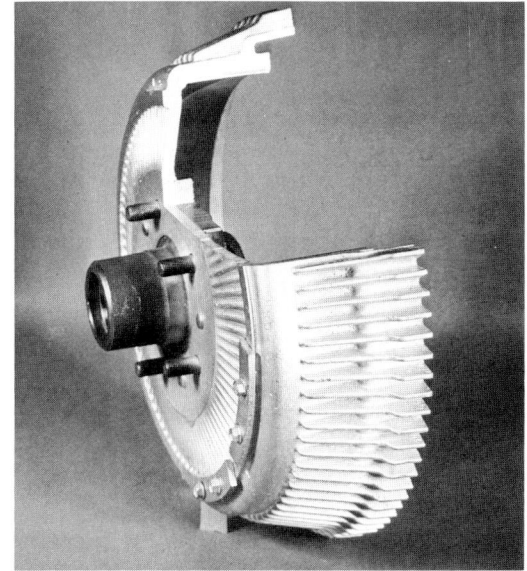

surface for the brake linings. The liner was bonded to the drum. Actually, the liner was made first, and three rows of holes were drilled through it. Then the drum was molded around the liner, with the light alloy filling the holes and locking the two components together. Later, a simpler bonding technique was developed. These bi-metal drums were used only on the front wheels, for they do two-thirds to nine-tenths of the braking, depending on conditions. The rear drums remained unchanged for 1958, but the following year, they had fins, too. They were made of cast iron, built in a sand mold with automatic molding equipment, so that Buick got a big improvement for a small increase in unit cost. At the same time Buick changed to a new master cylinder of simplified design, and relocated its mounting under the hood.

From having had one of the poorest, if not the absolute worst, brake systems in the industry, Buick suddenly had the best by far. "By 1960," recalls Frank Daley, "I finally caught hell from somebody because we had a group of cars that would consistently go over 100,000 miles before they needed any consideration for the brakes. That was considered a combination of over-design and great achievement." Worth noting, however, is the fact that the 1958 Special never received the bi-metal front brakes. It retained the plain cast iron drums until the end of its production run. This had

to do with pricing. There was no way to hold the low price of the Special if it were to be equipped with finned aluminum drums. Of course, the Special brakes had also benefited from the strenuous test and development program, and had linings with at least twice the fade resistance of the materials used for the 1953 models.

Another product development that was directly related to the weight increase in Buick cars was power steering. The greater the weight on the front wheels, the more effort was needed to steer the car. The effort could be reduced by raising the steering ratio, but Buick felt that any slower response than used on the current models would introduce other problems. The answer was to provide power assist and lower the steering ratio. Power steering was first offered as an extra-cost option for the 1952 Roadmaster. For power-steered cars, Buick reduced the steering ratio from 29:1 to 26:1, which speeded up the response. Wheel motion between extreme left and

Skylark was a new name in 1953, introduced to celebrate Buick's 50th anniversary. It shared the Roadmaster's new V-8 engine and featured genuine wire wheels. The Skylark was built only as a convertible and was listed at $5,000.

right steering angles was reduced from five turns to 4½. The change was kept small, not because the power system could not handle the load of speeding up the response beyond that, but because General Motors felt that drivers were conditioned to slow steering, and that it could be a hazard to offer faster gearing.

The Saginaw integral power steering unit used a recirculating ball-type of worm and nut gear, with the nut also acting as the servo piston. Movement in the nut was transmitted to the drop-arm shaft via a rack and sector. The control valve assembly was placed between the steering wheel and the reduction gear, which gave the most direct operation of the valve for fastest possible response. The control valve was a rotary type, fitted around a steering stub-shaft, and rotated by the stub shaft through a spherical-ended driving pin. The steering-wheel shaft was connected directly to the stub shaft through a torsion bar link. The valve was surrounded by a sleeve, which contained oil-flow ports and was fixed to the worm, so that it turned when the worm turned. The worm and valve assembly, being attached to the stub shaft, turned when the steering wheel was turned. The presence of the torsion bar, however, assured that the worm and valve sleeve would lag slightly behind the stub shaft and rotary valve. This lag enabled longitudinal grooves machined in the valve to line up with the ports in the sleeve, opening the way for oil to flow to one side of the servo piston and give assist to the steering effort. It was the torsion bar that, by being twisted, produced the centering force for the valve. The engineers could make changes in assist force and its action by merely making small changes in torsion bar diameter and valve port location. Fluid pressure on the servo piston began to build up at one-fourth-degree of steering wheel movement and reached 1,000 psi at two degrees. After the installation of a new steering linkage on all 1954 models, power steering became optional for all Buick series.

For the 1954 models, the power steering gear ratio was changed from 26:1 to 24:1 to speed up the steering response. The steering gear ratio is defined as the ratio between the number of degrees rotation in the steering wheel necessary to turn the pitman arm shaft one degree. Lowering the steering gear ratio, without making any other changes, would cause an increase in the steering effort. In order to limit the steering effort to the same four pounds as on the 1953 models, the hydraulic valve centering spring-loading was lowered.

Buick went to 12-volt electrical systems when switching from straight-eight to V-8 engines. That change was effective from the start of the 1953 model year for the Super and Roadmaster, and beginning with the 1954 model for the Special. The Century series was revived in the 1954 model year (series 60). The new Century shared the 122-inch wheelbase with the Special, but was powered by the Roadmaster engine. As in the original concept, it combined the lightest chassis and body with the most powerful engine. The Roadmaster had been downgraded in 1953, now sharing the Super chassis with the short wheelbase, and the same body. But the Riviera sedans available in both Super and Roadmaster series, continued with the long wheelbase from the old Roadmaster. The 1953 Super and Roadmaster Estate Wagons were the last Buicks to use real wood in the bodywork. The 1954-model wagons had all-metal bodies.

By 1953 General Motors was overdue for new B- and C-bodies. The existing ones had been in production, with annual facelifts, since 1949. The change came with the 1954 models, which also had new chassis. One practical body change had been made the year before. The hood on the 1953 models was of the alligator type, replacing the side-hinged design that had been used since 1940. Hinged at the cowl, the new hood extended further down towards the fenders, permitting easier access to the engine. Buick had used an alligator hood on the 1938 Y-Job, but it was to take fifteen years to get it into production.

The year 1953 marked Buick's fiftieth anniversary, and Buick celebrated it by introducing a new model known as the Skylark. It was a new name for Buick, and its inspiration was probably poetical or lyrical, from Hoagy Carmichael's immortal composition. The 1953 Skylark was based on the Roadmaster chassis, and the body received its own styling touches by Ned Nickles. It was not a new body, but a modified Roadmaster convertible. The belt line was lowered, with the cowl and windshield base a full four inches lower than on the Roadmaster convertible. A prominent chrome sweepspear was supplemented by a belt line that was kicked up aft of the doors. Wheel openings in the rear fenders were rounded out to match the front fenders. Genuine Carlo Borrani wire wheels imported from Italy, with knock-off hub caps, were used as standard Skylark equipment.

The 1954 Skylark was a different car altogether. No longer based on the Roadmaster, it was built on the Century chassis. This change reduced the wheelbase by 3.5 inches and overall length by 5.3 inches. The resultant weight saving was fifty-five pounds. The two-door convertible (Model 100) was built on a 122-inch wheelbase and was powered by a Roadmaster engine matched up with Dynaflow drive. Standard equipment included a power-operated top, power radio antenna, power steering and power brakes. Buick delivered 1,690 Skylarks in 1953 and 836 in 1954.

For the 1954 Special, Super, Century and Roadmaster, the silhouette was boxier, the hood shorter, and the deck lid longer. Glass area was considerably increased, giving a greenhouse effect to the passenger compartment. The slab sides were highly dependent on accent lines, of which there were several, usually in conflict with each other. The main theme was the sweepspear, running from the top of the front wheel opening to the start of the rear wheel opening, then being kicked up to follow the rear wheel opening curve to its acme and leaving in a horizontal line towards the tail. The front fender line blended into the belt line at the windshield base. The belt line went horizontally back to the rear fender kickup, well ahead of the wheel opening, and then was kicked up again behind the wheel opening, suggesting the start of a tail fin.

Nickles had revised the grille, so that it was now even wider than the 1953 edition, and looked more refined, with a greater number of vertical bars, still with a slight convex curve. The grille frame formed a lip extending from the sheet metal, and the panel above it again received a new type of Buick emblem. Parking lights and turning signals on the 1954 models were integrated with the headlight design, placed at the bottom of a vertical-ellipse chrome frame at the head of each fender. The frame profile was not even, but extended towards the top, giving the effect of a hood over the head lamps. The valley between the hood and the fenders began to disappear, as the hood was lowered to fender level. Ventiports on the 1954 models were set in the fender skirts, close to belt-line level, and were oval in shape. They had an eccentric cavity, as if to hint at pipes from inside coming out at an angle. Taillights were two separate round lenses on each fender, emerging from flutes in the fender skirts like streamlined head lamps going in the wrong direction.

Panorama windshields were used on the 1954 models, with the dogleg

A-post intruding on the door opening. This was a styling device that was eagerly seized by the men in charge of Buick, and adopted for the B-bodies against Cadillac's protest. But Buick, with far greater sales volume, had more clout. From a safety-engineering viewpoint, the change was indefensible, for it reduced front roof support strength to about twenty percent. All models had small rectangular vent windows in the front doors. The Riviera sedan (Model 72-R) had rear quarter windows in the sail panels, with one-piece rear door glass, whereas all other four-door sedans had vent windows at the rear edge of the rear doors. Riviera two-door hardtops were available in the Super, Century and Roadmaster series. Rear side windows rolled down into the body panels, and a one-piece curved-glass rear window wrapped around to a very thin C-post. Buick's 1954 models went to a horizontal-gauge speedometer, placed in a cluster at the top of the instrument panel, immediately in front of the steering wheel. Other gauges were set below it in three round dials. The wheel remained the typical Buick three-spoke design with a full horn ring.

Engineering changes for 1954 centered on the front suspension. Revised geometry aimed at reducing the steering effort, which was a vital factor for cars not equipped with power steering, still an extra-cost option. Of course, Buick compromised here, and made the steering hard enough to make sure a lot of customers would order the power steering. Basic suspension principles were unchanged, but new telescopic shock absorbers replaced the lever-type in the front suspension. Kingpins were still retained, though General Motors had been experimenting with ball joint mounting for years, and Buick was to go that route a few years later.

Ned Nickles was working two to three years ahead of production, and could not learn of public reaction to a new design until he was committed for another two or three years beyond its introduction. This lead-time hampered his work, especially in the mid-fifties, when GM cars were beginning to look more and more alike. Harley Earl seemed to have set his mind on one style for all, and to let the divisional studios do the rest with surface ornamentation and other cosmetic effects. The Buick studio did not make the most of these opportunities, small as they were, and the result was a bland-looking run of cars, particularly for 1955 and 1956. But public acceptance, as we have seen, was excellent both years.

In Buick's grilles for 1955 the vertical bars were replaced with a tight mesh. The grille frame blended with the bumper, whose corners were raised and held two torpedo-like cones on the sides of the grille. A horizontal bar with a circular emblem in the middle provided some degree of balance to the whole. The panel above was part of the hood, and carried the letters BUICK on a slight arc. Circular head lamp bezels were slightly hooded and were placed to mark the top of the fender line. Turn signals were mounted

separately below the head lamps. Taillights were shaped like a delta-wing airplane banking at right angles. This assembly filled the entire fender tail, with three separate lenses—one on the 'fuselage' in the middle, and one above and below, in each 'wing.' The rear fender lines were straightened out, with the second kickup suppressed. Front wheel openings began to sport a rakish lack of symmetry, almost following the contour of fender lines. Instead of closing in on the wheel, the skirt would be opened at a slant. Rear wheel cutout styling differed from model to model. On four-door sedans, the fender panel came down to a horizontal line almost down to hub level; but on two-door bodies, it was a full and symmetrical opening, though with a much larger radius than the wheel, giving a tight fit on top and open space front and rear.

Buick's 1956 styling theme continued the previous year's. The accent lines on the slab-sided bodies were similar, and the head lamps dominated the front fenders, with a slight kickup to mark the rear fender, and extra emphasis on the ventiports, now more egg-shaped than oval. The grille and bumper assembly was modified in several ways. First, horizontal lines replaced the mesh pattern. Secondly, the torpedoes were redesigned as jet-plane engine pods. The long-familiar gunsight hood ornament was replaced by a winged sculpture semi-countersunk into the hood, obviously inspired by something from the world of aviation. On 1955 models, the gunsight hood ornament had been streamlined, but was still recognizable.

New frames appeared on the 1956 models, along with a revised front suspension, and modified rear suspension. Telescopic shock absorbers were now also fitted on the rear. Frames were the same type as before, with deep cross-bracing in the middle, and right-angle cross members at both ends, at front and rear suspension mounts, aft of the engine, and at the front end of the torque tube. The side members were spaced farther apart than before, approaching full body width in the center section within the wheelbase. Brake system modifications for 1956 were restricted to a suspended brake pedal and improved weather sealing. A new Perimeter heating system was introduced on the 1956 models. It distributed warm air throughout the car by ducts from the heater element to both front and rear seating areas. The power steering gear was dramatically improved for 1956 models. Now the overall steering ratio was reduced to 19.8:1 for a turn diameter of forty-three feet. Power steering was made standard on the Super and Roadmaster, optional on Special and Century, whose standard steering gear gave an overall ratio of 29.2:1.

There were six models in the Special series: four-door sedan (Model 41); two-door sedan (Model 48); four-door hardtop (Model 43); two-door Riviera coupe (Model 46R); two-door convertible (Model 46C); and four-door Estate Wagon (Model 49). The Super series had no station wagon, but

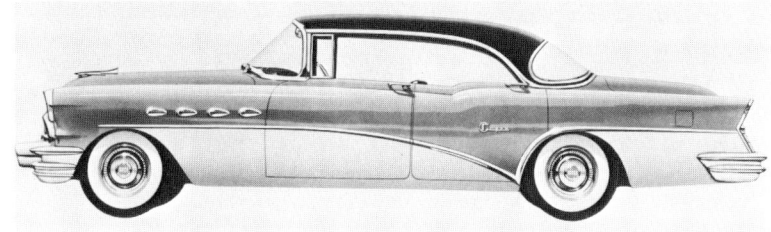

included four other models: four-door sedan (Model 52); four-door hardtop (Model 53); two-door Riviera coupe (Model 56R); and a two-door convertible (Model 56C). Four models were listed for the 1956 Century: four-door hardtop (Model 63); two-door Riviera coupe (Model 66R); two-door convertible (Model 66C); and a four-door Estate Wagon (Model 69). At the top of the line, there were four Roadmaster models: four-door sedan (Model 72); four-door hardtop (Model 73); two-door Riviera coupe (Model 76R); and two-door convertible (Model 76C).

Buick had fully restyled bodies again in 1957. All new were a lower silhouette, a more extreme panorama windshield and smoothed-over body sides with rear fenders maintaining their full height to the tail end. The sweepspear moldings that had been so prominent on the whole line in 1955 and 1956 were modified for 1957. The line did not dip all the way to the base of the rear wheel opening, but ended ahead of the rear wheel opening at a point corresponding to rear bumper level, where it was kicked up in the usual arrangement, and ran horizontally back to the taillight assembly from the wheel cutout apex. Front wheel openings extended into the fender skirts, continuing the asymmetrical look that had been pioneered in 1955. This was not repeated in the rear wheel openings, however. The rear fender kickup was moved forward from the rear wheel and given greater emphasis. A slanting accent line, leading down towards the rear wheel, was still there, as a crease in the sheet metal, but the vertical crease was almost erased. On two-door models, the kickup began right at the door edge, and on four-door models, the rear fender kickup extended beyond the halfway point. The top of the rear fenders was a straight line all the way to the taillight assembly, which had been redesigned, with frames now extending

upwards and backwards from the bumper. It was rather like an A-frame in rear aspect, with an odd oval lens in the center. The 1957 grille reverted to vertical bars, with a large number of very thin-sectioned bars separated by narrow and almost imperceptible slits. The grille frame was visually separated from the bumper, being set back. The bumper bar was very low and had a straight face with two small overriders flanking the license plate, and turn signal/parking lights enclosed in large pods at the extreme ends. The chrome surface stretched back to the wheel opening, reinforcing the turbojet engine pod theme. Headlights were set in round bezels at the fender tops, slightly hooded.

The 1957 Riviera hardtop coupe had a reverse-slant C-post, extending from the fender kickup to the rear edge of the roof. This theme was also applied to the Riviera four-door sedan, with the C-post being split at an angle between the rear door and the roof panel. Most of the C-post was actually part of the door. Other hardtops, both two-door and four-door, had a conventionally contoured C-post, with a roofline sloping gently from where the B-post would have been to the top of the rear fender. Wraparound rear windows gave a V-profile to this C-post, with a narrow base and wide top. Three-piece rear windows were used, with thin pillars linking

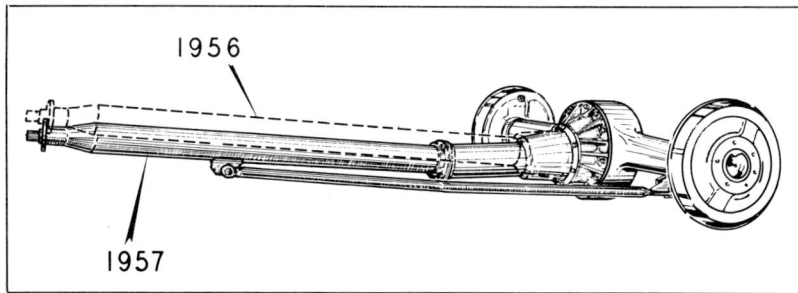

1956

1957

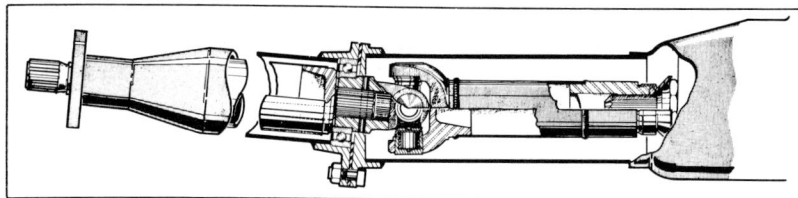

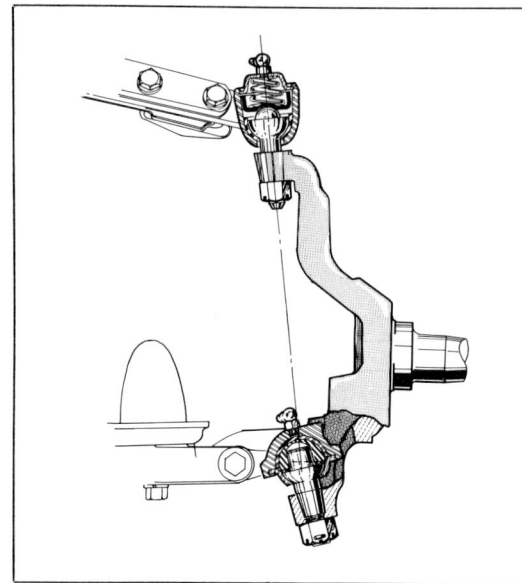

For the 1957 models, Buick redesigned its torque tube with a kink in it, to lower the drive line and the floor tunnel. The stay running diagonally on the left partners one on the right (not shown) and assists in locating the rear axle.

A simple universal joint on the propeller shaft enabled Buick to bend the torque tube. The joint worked at a constant angle but did produce minute variations in velocity. It was Buick's last attempt to modernize its torque tube drive system.

Buick's 1957 models adopted ball-joint front suspension to replace the kingpins that had been used on all earlier models. Ball joints reduced steering friction and were easier to lubricate.

the roof to the rear deck inside of the fender panels. Even the Special series included a hardtop wagon in 1957—the Riviera Estate Wagon, with four doors and a tailgate. The sedan-type C-post was retained, curving into the rear fender. The regular Estate Wagon had straight B-posts and the same curved C-posts. Tailgate glass was curved at the edges giving an eave effect to the roof.

Engineering changes on the 1957 models included a revised front suspension system with ball joint mounting. This eliminated the kingpin, as the steering knuckle assembly now included two arms with provision for ball joints, linking them to the upper and lower A-arms. There was also something new in the drive line. A two-piece bent torque tube was used on the 1957 models. The new design consisted of a short tube extending forwards from the rear axle and was actually an extension of the differential nose-piece, containing a lengthened pinion shaft. At the front end of the pinion shaft was a universal joint, also enclosed in the short tube. Ahead of it, the short tube was bolted to the main torque tube at an angle, which meant that the rear universal joint was operating at constant angularity. The flange was the lowest point in the system, as the main torque tube pointed down to the back, and the short one pointed down to the front. This was done to lower the transmission tunnel while still allowing adequate freedom for the axle to move up and down during spring deflections. New engine mounting systems were introduced, with four-point suspension for Century, Super and Roadmaster, and three-point suspension for the Special, due to its different transmission design. The new systems were based on the fact that any vibrating body has points that are practically free of vibration. These are called nodal points. Buick's idea was to locate the mounts near the nodal points and thereby reduce the vibration transmitted to the frame. In addition, the mounting blocks were placed at an angle in order to exploit the

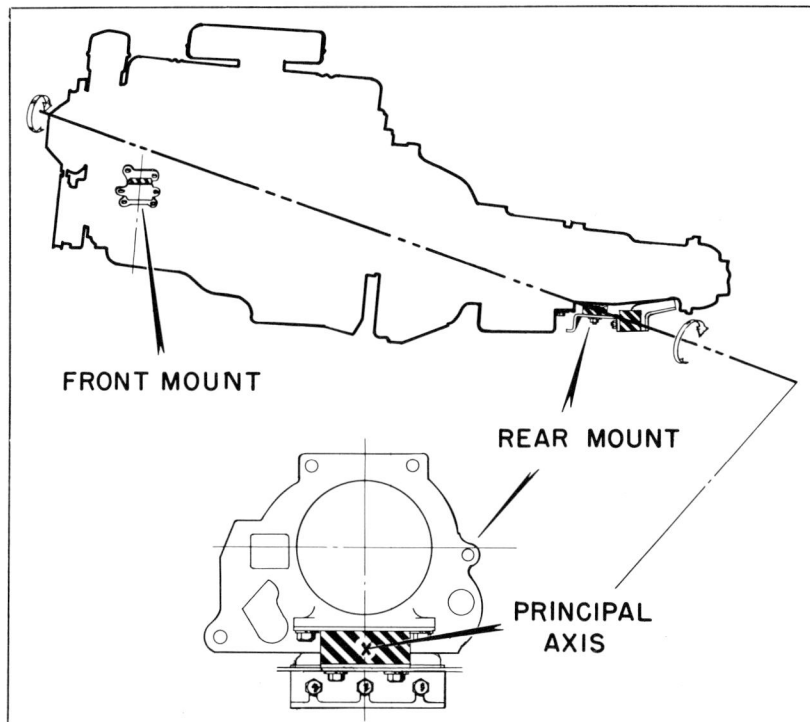

FRONT MOUNT

REAR MOUNT

PRINCIPAL AXIS

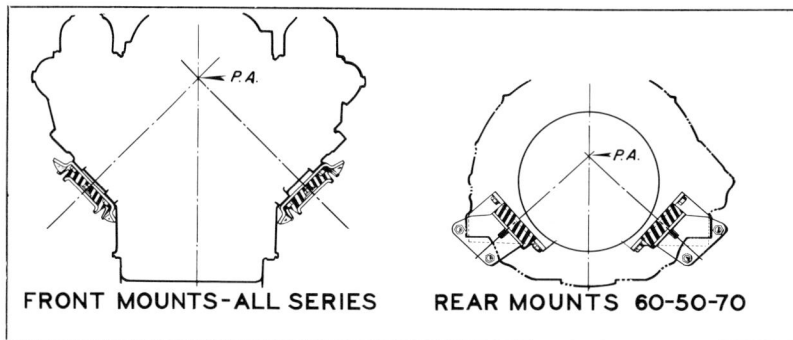

FRONT MOUNTS-ALL SERIES   REAR MOUNTS 60-50-70

Making the Buick V-8 smoother was solved mainly through the installation of better motor mounts. Their position was carefully calculated for maximum steadying effect. Torque reactions tend to rotate the engine around its principal axis.

Wide-based motor mounts well spaced out at front and located closer in at the back were coordinated with the principal axis so that the motor mounts absorbed a maximum of engine vibrations without transmitting them further.

low shear rate and high dampening coefficient of the rubber in controlling torque reactions, and to increase the engine's lateral stability.

On the 1958 models, air springs became optional. The air spring system was a Cadillac development that had been in the experimental stage from 1951 to 1957. It consisted of a double bellows, made of rubber, containing air under pressure. Air pressure was controlled by valves, which were arranged to maintain a constant level. This unit occupied the same space normally reserved for the coil springs. A rod rising from the rear suspension radius arm had a piston at its top end. The piston acted against a diaphragm inside the bellows, which then reacted to restore the balance. Few Buick buyers opted for the Air Poise, as it was called in the sales brochures, but those who did usually found trouble. The system tended to leak. And loss of air meant loss of springs. Buick quickly dropped the Air Poise option. For 1959 Buick no longer listed the four-point air suspension as an option, but

instead offered a new self-levelling rear suspension system, using air bellows. This option was no longer available in 1960, however.

Buick also revived the Limited (Series 70) for 1958. It was built on a lengthened Roadmaster frame, and was available as a Riviera sedan (four-door hardtop), Riviera coupe (two-door hardtop) and two-door convertible. The four-door hardtops in all series had vent windows in both front and rear doors, while the two-door hardtops had rear quarter windows that lowered into the body panels. The four-door sedans had one-piece rear door glass. Front doors had vent windows at the leading edge, matching up with the A-posts. One-piece wraparound rear windows were used on all closed bodies, including station wagons. Both hardtop and pillared versions of the station wagon body continued in 1958. The Riviera hardtop station wagon was available in the Special series only. When the same body was used in the Century series, it was renamed Caballero.

All models had bodies with partly new skin and a surfeit of brightwork on the body sides. The silhouette was not changed from 1957, but from any angle the 1958 models had a totally new look. Front fender openings reverted to a closer-to-symmetrical design, and rear wheel openings were pulled down, presenting a low aspect with a horizontal line breaking the full circle of the hub cap. The sweepspear was a chrome molding that started

Edward T. Ragsdale, left, was in charge of Buick during the decline of the 1950's, which cost Buick its reputation as a high-quality car. Century series, revived in 1956, included a Riviera hardtop in 1957, right. This Model 66-R was listed at $3,270 and came with a 300-hp V-8 and Dynaflow transmission as standard equipment. But Buick found it was a glut on the market.

on the head lamp brow, ran horizontally for the full length of the front fender, swept down across the doors, and came to a sharp point at hub level in the rear fender, from where it was kicked up and blended with the rear fender chrome trim. Rocket-inspired sculptures appeared on the rear fenders of all series. They had various horizontal chrome inlays, or inlays in second-color paint, according to model and color combination. The Limited was different from all others, as the rocket sculpture was covered with three sets of five simulated louvers, tilted back to line up with the taillight assembly. In addition there was a chrome-plated gravel shield filling the entire space between the wheel opening and the rear bumper.

The 1958 grille was made up of four rows of small chrome-plated squares, extending the full width of the body, framed at the top by a horizontal bar, coming to a subtle point in the center, and continuing around the fender corners to the wheel openings. The bumper bar had provision for a license plate in the middle, with a raised lip above it. Two overriders were spaced farther out and supported torpedo-like nose cones. Turn signals and parking lights were built into long chrome-plated pods at either end of the grille. Side-by-side dual head lamps were used for the first time, with a sheet metal hood lined with a chrome strip above them. The 1958 hood ornament was a plain chrome molding running down the center of the hood. Instead, the gunsight theme was revived for two standup fender ornaments on the head lamp hoods. The hood panel surmounting the grille carried a huge circle with a V-emblem—to symbolize the fact that Buick now had V-8 engines—with two horizontal chrome strips on each side. There were no ventiports on the 1958 models.

A new instrument panel was heavily sculptured, repeating the rocket theme of the rear fenders, decorated in chrome and brushed aluminum. Instrumentation was obviously a secondary consideration. The horizontal speedometer was retained. A rectangular dash clock was set on the far right, and the glovebox was moved towards the center. The steering wheel, which had become slightly dished in 1956, with three spokes and a full horn ring, was changed for 1958. Apart from deeper dishing, the wheel received a new arrangement for the three spokes. Instead of being evenly spaced at 120 degrees, the two principal spokes rose at a slight angle from the hub to the rim, while the third one ran straight down.

The cars Buick had to sell were of a brand-new and spectacular design. Buick had the best brakes in the industry, the most advanced automatic transmission, and one of the most reliable and long-lived engines. There was nothing wrong with the Buick product, but it was not what the American public wanted. The U.S. economy was recovering from a brief slump, and in fact the car market expanded from 4.65 million units in 1958 to six million in 1959, where it had been before the brief recession. But GM's share of the market fell from forty-six to forty-two percent. Buick's penetration declined from 5.68 percent in 1958 to a despondent 4.07 percent; its sales had slipped from 263,981 cars in 1958 to 245,909 in 1959. Other GM cars also took a beating in 1959, but none worse than Buick, which fell from fifth to seventh place, behind Chevrolet, Ford, Plymouth, Rambler, Oldsmobile and Pontiac. Buick production was running at about two-thirds of planned capacity.

Yet the situation in 1959 was not similar to that other fateful year, 1933. That time Buick was in the doldrums because of an unimaginative model policy and marketing methods that failed to present the Buick car as the outstanding value it truly was. Everywhere the Buick name was held in high esteem, and Buick's welfare was considered essential to the corporation. But this time Buick was down because its repute had been lost, its fame tarnished. The Buick name had been disgraced. The very image of the Buick car had been destroyed. The division's integrity as a car maker was in

Ventiports disappeared while sweep-spear continued on 1958-model Buicks. This is the Super Riviera sedan—a four-door hardtop—219 inches long and weighing 4,500 pounds. But this year Buick had the best brakes in the industry.

doubt. This time, the corporation's top management must have debated whether it would not be best to kill off the Buick. Faced with failure after failure, Ragsdale retired in the spring of 1959, and went to live in Sarasota, Florida, where he died in June 1971, at the age of 74.

CHAPTER 5

Buick Develops the Dynaflow

BUICK BECAME A PIONEER in the field of automatic transmissions almost against its will. Neither Chayne nor Mathews, Buick's chief engineers in the 1936-1957 period, was enthusiastic about automatic drive. But it was in this period that the industry as a whole adopted automatic transmissions. Buick could not refuse to go along without losing popularity and sales, and the corporation would not allow Buick to operate under such a handicap. Its hand forced by market conditions, Buick did go along, but on its own terms. Buick chose to develop its own automatic transmission, using principles different from all other automatics then in use for American passenger cars.

Actually, Buick's experience with automatic drive goes further back than that of any other GM division. In 1928 the GM research laboratories became interested in a transmission system patented by Frank Anderson Hayes, an inventor living in Middletown, New Jersey. The Hayes patents described a stepless toric drive, relying for its functioning on a double ball thrust bearing with a set of rollers. The double ball thrust bearing was composed of three parallel races, mounted axially in line. Between each pair of races ran three rollers carried on stationary spider shafts. The front and rear races were connected to the engine flywheel, and the center race to the propeller shaft. Thus, the power flowed through both sets of rollers. Gear ratios were continuously variable by changing the angle of the rollers, whose spider shafts could be tilted by a linkage to a hydraulic pump. Hayes

was invited to Detroit and designed a transmission for installation on a 1928 Buick. The unit was built, installed and tested. And rejected.

It was 1937 before Buick had any further automatic transmission activity. It was not a Buick project, and it was only because of its manufacturing capacity that Buick got involved. The project had started at Cadillac in 1932. The design consisted of two planetary gear sets driving four forward speeds, with automatic shifting carried out by hydraulic pistons that worked brake bands and clutches that locked or released the elements in the planetary gearing. Shifts were timed by a simple centrifugal governor. In 1935 the project was transferred from Cadillac to the GM Engineering Staff, and shortly afterwards Oldsmobile became interested in it. Oldsmobile began a very active development program, and in 1936 it was cleared for production. But the Olds plant in Lansing did not have the capacity to build the transmission, and came to Buick for help. In Flint, Buick quickly tooled up, and began to manufacture semi-automatic transmissions for Oldsmobile in June 1937.

Oldsmobile hoped greater production volume would bring the price down, and invited Buick to use the semi-automatic transmission on its own cars. Buick offered it as an option for its 1938 Special only.

To operate, the driver moved a lever mounted on the steering column from N (neutral) to F (forward). There were only three positions, the third being R (reverse), arranged in a prophetic R-N-F pattern. But the driver still

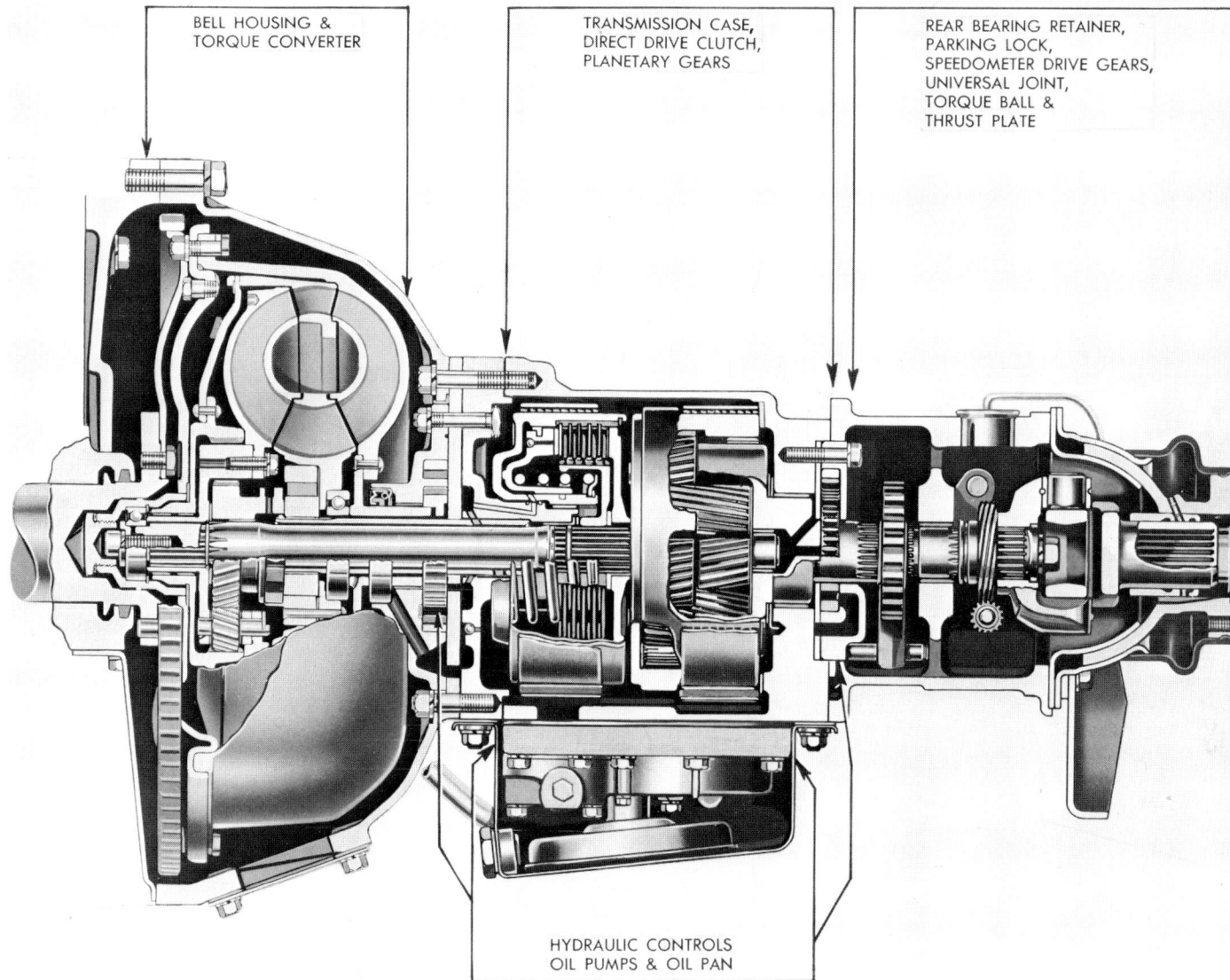

BELL HOUSING &
TORQUE CONVERTER

TRANSMISSION CASE,
DIRECT DRIVE CLUTCH,
PLANETARY GEARS

REAR BEARING RETAINER,
PARKING LOCK,
SPEEDOMETER DRIVE GEARS,
UNIVERSAL JOINT,
TORQUE BALL &
THRUST PLATE

HYDRAULIC CONTROLS
OIL PUMPS & OIL PAN

The Twin Turbine Dynaflow of 1953 reversed some of the theories behind the Dynaflow in terms of torque converter arrangement, but it continued on the road towards eliminating the gearing and doing more with hydraulic means.

BELL HOUSING &
TORQUE CONVERTER

TRANSMISSION CASE,
DIRECT DRIVE CLUTCH,
PLANETARY GEARS

REAR BEARING RETAINER,
PARKING LOCK,
SPEEDOMETER DRIVE GEARS,
UNIVERSAL JOINT,
TORQUE BALL &
THRUST PLATE

HYDRAULIC CONTROLS
OIL PUMPS & OIL PAN

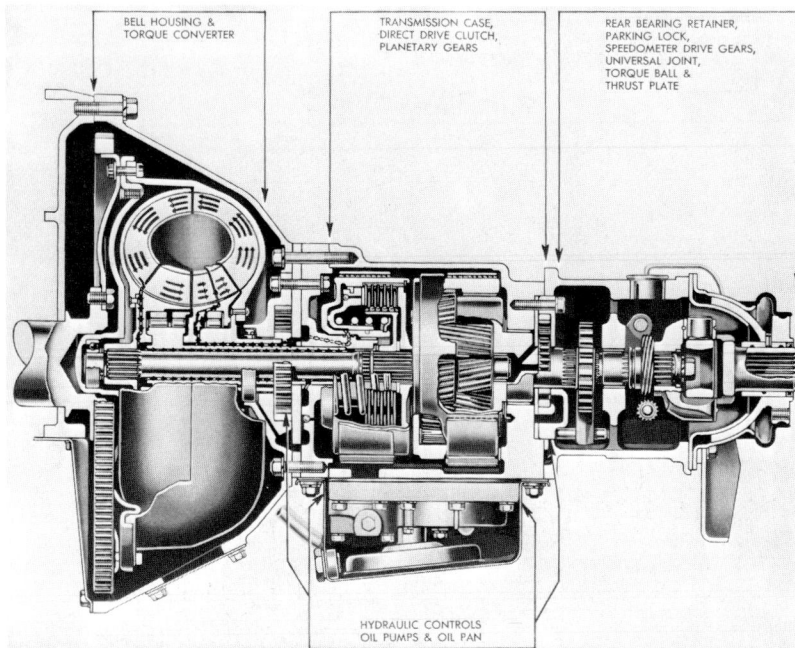

Sectioned view of original Dynaflow
transmission shows five-element torque
converter and two-speed planetary gearing. This design was defeated by over-
complicated and inefficient hydraulics
to obtain mechanical simplicity.

needed a clutch, for starting and stopping, and shifts between F and R. It is
estimated that Buick built about 40,000 of these semi-automatic transmissions before production stopped in September 1939. The 1940-model
Buicks had no alternative to the three-speed synchromesh transmission.
Oldsmobile, on the other hand, introduced the HydraMatic. It was based on
the semi-automatic, using the same planetary gearing. But the friction-plate
clutch had been replaced by a hydraulic coupling. Oldsmobile had introduced two-pedal control—one for go and one for stop. To manufacture the
HydraMatic, the corporation organized the Detroit Transmission Division.

Cadillac adopted the HydraMatic on its 1941 models, but Buick did not
want it mainly because it was difficult to combine with Buick's torque tube
drive. Jolts were felt throughout the car when it shifted gears, because of the
direct connection to the rear axle. On Cadillac and Oldsmobile, the springs
would absorb the jolts, and shifts would be fairly smooth. Then came the
war, and Buick was called upon to manufacture another type of automatic
transmission. It was a hydraulic torque-converter system, for use on the
Hellcat.

The torque converter differs fundamentally from the hydraulic coupling,
yet the torque converter will, under the right conditions, function as a hydraulic coupling. The hydraulic coupling consists of two vaned rotors inside
a casing filled with an oil-based fluid. The housing is shaped more or less
like a doughnut. The rotors are assembled to close tolerances but do not
touch. They are mounted on separate shafts, and there is no mechanical
connection between them. They constitute, instead, a fluid coupling. One of
the rotors works as the driving member. It's called the impeller. The driven
member is called the turbine. The impeller shaft is driven from the engine,
and the turbine shaft takes the drive to the gearbox. The impeller has a
number of radial vanes attached to its inner surface, and the turbine is provided with vanes facing those of the impeller, but one or two less in number. When the impeller begins to rotate, some of the oil on its vanes spin
around with it. As speed increases, the rotational flow changes due to centrifugal force and goes into a spiraling motion, called vortex flow, from the
impeller to the turbine at the periphery and back to the impeller at the other
end. This results in a transfer of the impeller's rotation to the turbine, but
with a certain degree of slippage. Compared with a clutch, the hydraulic
coupling is smoother in action and relieves both engine and transmission
from shock loads. It will prevent damage in case of stalling.

Now for the torque converter. First, it differs from the hydraulic coupling in having at least three internal members instead of two. The extra
members are stators (vaned stationary rings). Secondly, the vanes are curved
(hypoid), not straight and radial. In the hydraulic coupling, as we have seen,
the fluid flow follows an unbroken line from one rotor to the other and
back again. This is not the case in the torque converter. Once the fluid gets
between the blades of a stator, the smooth flow pattern is destroyed. The
fluid leaves the stator in a straight, axial, flow pattern and then returns into
the impeller. There the fluid is picked up and returns to vortex flow.

What the stator member does is to increase the torque load on the turbine by pure hydraulic means. This is accomplished by the curvature and
pitch of the stator and turbine vanes. The exit flanges of the turbine vanes
curve sharply backwards, which makes the fluid spin backwards as it is discharged. The fluid then hits the stator, which is interposed between the turbine exit and the impeller entrance. Its curved blades are shaped to receive
the backwards-spinning fluid and redirect it to rotate forwards. The return
flow to the impeller will therefore tend to accelerate the impeller. The result

is torque multiplication. Naturally this involves additional friction and slippage losses. There is no magic. It's just another way to change speed and torque, and this can be a useful means to simplify the mechanical gearing in a transmission system.

We mentioned that the torque converter could function as a hydraulic coupling. It does this automatically when little torque multiplication is required, generally under steady-state, light-load conditions. That's when its slippage is lowest and its efficiency highest.

Both the hydraulic coupling and the torque converter originated in Germany. The first hydraulic coupling was made in Stettin in 1903 by Dr. Hermann Föttinger (1877-1945) and patented in 1905. He built the first torque converter in 1909 and patented it in 1910. Both were used in ships before the automobile industry became interested in hydraulic transmission systems. Several German and British pioneers built experimental cars with hydraulic couplings in the 1920's. The Daimler car, made in Coventry, England, was first with a production model, in 1930. By 1934 a brilliant Swedish engineer, Alf Lysholm, had perfected an automotive torque converter, which Spicer adopted in 1938. The Spicer Models 90 and 91 hydraulic transmissions were introduced in the 1938 GMC Model 740 coach. In addition to the hydraulic torque converter, the Spicer 90/91 units included direct drive and countershaft reverse, output bevel gears, electro-pneumatic shift control and fully automatic range selection. It was this transmission system that became the basis for the Buick-built Hellcat drive. This experience gave Buick an invaluable background in torque converters, while Cadillac, using a giant HydraMatic in its M-24 tanks, did much to advance the technology of hydraulic couplings and automatic shift mechanisms.

Hydraulic torque converters were also the subject of a major study being made, starting in 1942, by a special transmission development group at the GM Engineering Staff. The head of the group was a man of exceptional inventive talent named Oliver K. Kelley. Born in Finland in 1902, he emigrated to the United States in 1921. He worked his way through school, graduating from the Chicago Technical College with a bachelor's degree in mechanical engineering in 1925. Next, he studied for two years at the Massachusetts Institute of Technology, and joined Cadillac in 1927. About five years later he was transferred to the corporate engineering staff to work on advanced projects. In his forty-year career with General Motors he took out eighty-two patents in his own name, plus another thirty-three with coinventors. This was the man who was mainly responsible for the creation of the Dynaflow.

Kelley's basic idea was to simplify the automatic transmission, and reduce its mechanical complexity by exploiting the properties of the torque converter. He looked askance at the four-speed planetary gearing in the

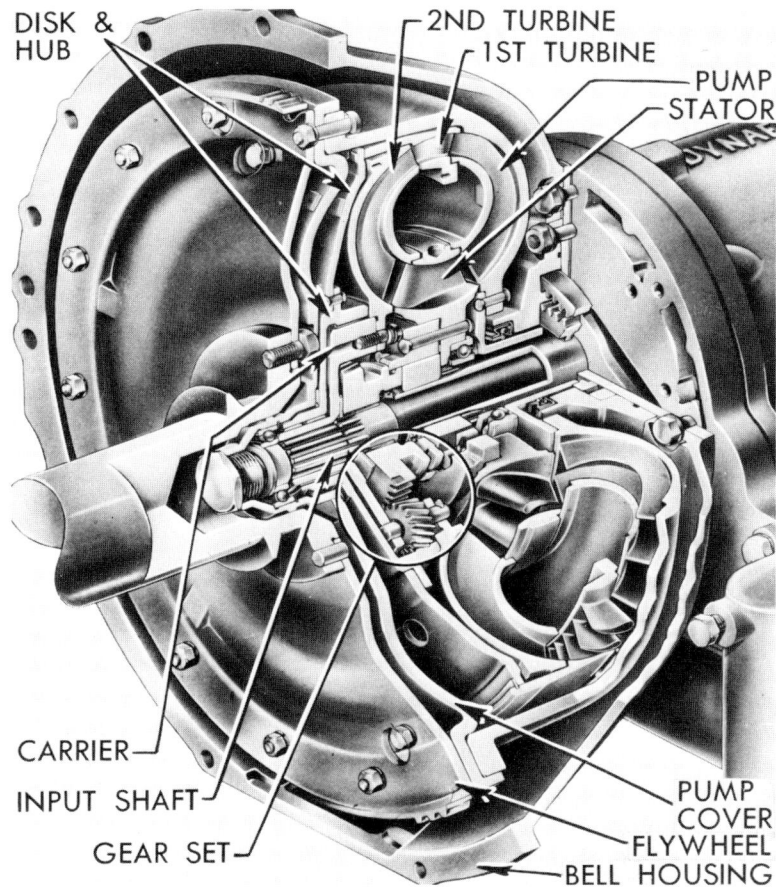

Turbine positions in the Twin Turbine Dynaflow show that impeller delivers fluid to primary turbine, while secondary turbine feeds into the stator member. The planetary gearing follows behind the torque converter.

HydraMatic, and set his mind on eliminating gear changes while obtaining all the torque multiplication by hydraulic means. But success was to come slowly. To work with such a simple mechanical system, Kelley found himself forced to complicate the torque converter. At the experimental stage, he was ready to tolerate this, as part of the learning process. But when the first prototype Dynaflow was built and tested in February 1946, it contained a far more complex torque converter than the Spicer and Hellcat transmissions had used. Still, it was judged to be ready for production and handed over to Buick for final development. It had two-speed gearing with all normal driving done in Drive range, but an emergency Low range was added as a precaution. The basic novelty of the Dynaflow lay in the hydraulic parts, of course.

The five-element polyphase torque converter was made up of two impellers, two stators and one turbine. The fluid flowed from the primary impeller. On leaving the turbine, the fluid flow entered the first stator, and then passed into the second stator. After discharge from the second stator, the fluid was scooped up by the secondary impeller.

The secondary impeller was driven via a one-way clutch so that it could freewheel but never lag behind the primary impeller. At low rotational speeds, it would overrun the primary impeller, but at higher speeds it became simply an extension of the primary impeller.

The two stators were locked to the housing during periods of torque conversion, but went into a freewheeling mode as the need for torque multiplication diminished—first the secondary stator, and finally the primary stator. When both stators were freewheeling, the torque converter was acting merely as a hydraulic coupling.

This changeover between torque conversion and basic coupling action could be very sudden in three-element torque converters, and Buick used twin impellers in order to minimize this problem.

In the first production-model Dynaflow, the maximum torque multiplication ratio, at stall, was 2.25:1. The term stall refers to the maximum input before the turbine begins to rotate, i.e. the point where the impeller reaches the highest speed possible with the turbine held stationary. This point is where *stall torque ratio* is reached. Output torque is at a peak the moment the turbine starts turning, and torque multiplication gets lower as the turbine speeds up to match impeller speed (minus a margin of slippage). The higher the torque multiplication, the greater the slip, and the lower the unit's efficiency. It may seem paradoxical, but it is an indisputable fact that the torque converter is least efficient when working at what it alone can do, and most efficient when doing what the hydraulic coupling can also do.

Because of the range of torque multiplication by hydraulic means, the two ratios in the Ravigneaux-type planetary gear train that completed the Dynaflow transmission were not referred to as gears but as 'ranges.' Drive range was direct, so that the propeller shaft turned at the speed of the turbine. Low range had a gear reduction of 1.82:1. Kelley had reached for originality in designing the planetary gearing and came up with impressive

innovations that assured simplicity, light weight and low cost. The most notable feature was a set of long pinions that made multiple engagements. The input shaft was splined to the driving sun gear. It had thirty-three teeth and meshed with three long planet pinions, each with twenty-one teeth. These long pinions in turn meshed with three short ones of thirty teeth each. The short pinions engaged a reaction sun gear with twenty-seven teeth. They also meshed with an annulus that had eighty-seven teeth. When the twenty-seven-toothed sun gear was held stationary by a servo-operated brake hand, power flowed via the three short pinions, which then revolved as an assembly to the annulus, which turned at a slower rate than the input shaft, giving a Low-range reduction of 1.82:1. When the annulus was held stationary, power flowed via the long and short pinions, reversing the direction of rotation to give a Reverse-range gear reduction also of 1.82:1.

It was Harlow H. Curtice who made the decision to go into production with Dynaflow. This was a major decision, for it required a separate plant with totally new tooling. The Dynaflow transmission was announced as a $200 option for the 1947 Roadmaster in January 1947. Then it became standard on the 1948-model Roadmaster and optional for the other series. It was, of course, combined with Buick's torque tube drive. And it was smooth, because there were no shifts in ordinary driving.

In the meantime, Cadillac, Oldsmobile and Pontiac had obtained an improved four-speed HydraMatic, and Chevrolet was working on a simplified torque-converter transmission which emerged in 1950 as their Powerglide. In 1948, Buick's sales literature proclaimed that ''Through the Dynaflow unit, the power plant *adjusts itself* to give quick, strong drive for fast starts, extra pull for acceleration or hill-climbing, and smooth, easy power delivery for cruising. . . .You move from standstill to road speed in one velvety build-up of power without going through fixed gear changes. You take hills with extra thrust such as second gear might give—without ever having any gears shift.''

Reality was quite different. While the engine responded very well to the throttle and accelerated immediately, there was a sadly prolonged lag while the Dynaflow transmission worked to catch up. While the driver could hear the engine race, there was no acceleration until seconds later. The driver got a feeling that the engine had been disconnected from the drive train. During deceleration, this feeling was reinforced. Because the torque converter was unidirectional, there was practically no braking effect from the engine. The transmission also had a set of subdued noises of its own during all this action, but it was mainly engine noise that was heard inside the car. The sound effects were interesting enough for big-band leader Stan Kenton to record a jazz composition entitled ''Dynaflow'' in 1950. Push-starting was authorized with the 1948 Dynaflow, but the instructions warned that a speed of 30 to 35 mph would be required before moving the lever from N to D.

No major changes were made in the Dynaflow transmission for several years. Despite its performance shortcomings, it was accepted by the public. Its most serious service problem was leakage. This was traced to faulty assembly, and the quality control people rejected an atrociously high percentage of the units that came off the line. First, the engineers came down to the line to train the workers, but they ended up revising the assembly methods so that less mechanical skill was needed to put together a leak-free torque converter. Most of those who bought Dynaflow-drive Buicks found it perfectly reliable, and were glad their days of having the clutch adjusted or relined or replaced were over. By 1950, about seventy-five percent of Buick's output came with automatic transmission. In 1951 Buick produced 325,386 Dynaflow transmissions. The following year it was less, 274,259 units, as total car output fell by twenty-five percent.

After that came the first revision in the Dynaflow design. It was mainly the work of Rudolf J. Gorsky, who had come to Buick in 1939. He worked in many areas, but specialized in drive-train engineering, and in 1951 was named staff engineer for transmissions. Gorsky was promoted again in 1956, receiving the new title of executive transmission engineer. At the same time, Charles S. Chapman joined Buick's engineering staff and was assigned to future transmission projects, and Kenneth W. Gage was transferred from Detroit Transmission Division to Buick. Gage had developed the 1952-model Dual-Range HydraMatic, and together with P. J. Rhoads designed the split-torque 1956 HydraMatic with a hydraulic coupling. The new Twin Turbine Dynaflow replaced the original version in 1952, for the 1953 models. It was standard on the Roadmaster and Skylark, and optional in other series. The new design was a four-element polyphase torque converter, combined with the same two-speed planetary gearset that was used earlier. As the name indicated, it used two turbines. It had a single impeller and a single stator. This was the result of new research and development work by Kelley's group at GM Engineering Staff, and really meant a reversal of earlier theory.

Why twin turbines? The idea was to split up the torque multiplication duties between the first-stage and second-stage turbines. The second-stage turbine was a wide-bladed wheel, in the usual position. The first-stage turbine was a narrow-bladed wheel straddling the center section of the converter, and getting the benefit of the full diameter. It was geared to the output shaft through a planetary stepup whose action was gradually phased out as the car gained speed. This was an ingenious method of making use of the mechanical gearing to overcome torque-converter deficiencies. The first-stage turbine received the fluid flow from the impeller, and drove the an-

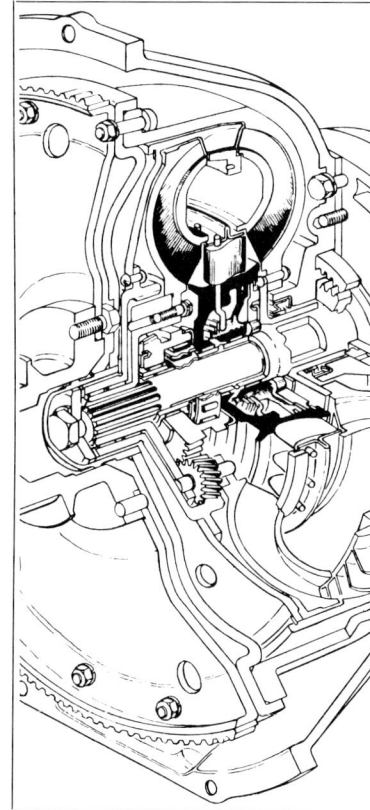

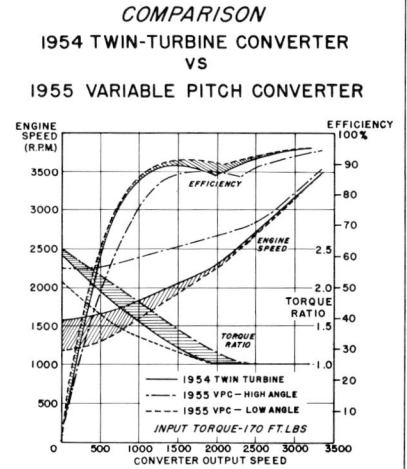

COMPARISON
1954 TWIN-TURBINE CONVERTER
VS
1955 VARIABLE PITCH CONVERTER

Left, Variable-Pitch Dynaflow of 1955 introduced a stator member with variable blade angle. It was a two-position arrangement, not infinitely variable, as was the Flight-Pitch developed later. Mechanical gearing remained a two-speed set of planetary gears. What the variable-angle stator accomplished was mainly to provide two different sets of torque conversion characteristics according to requirement. Efficiency gains, shown at right, were significant throughout the speed range.

55

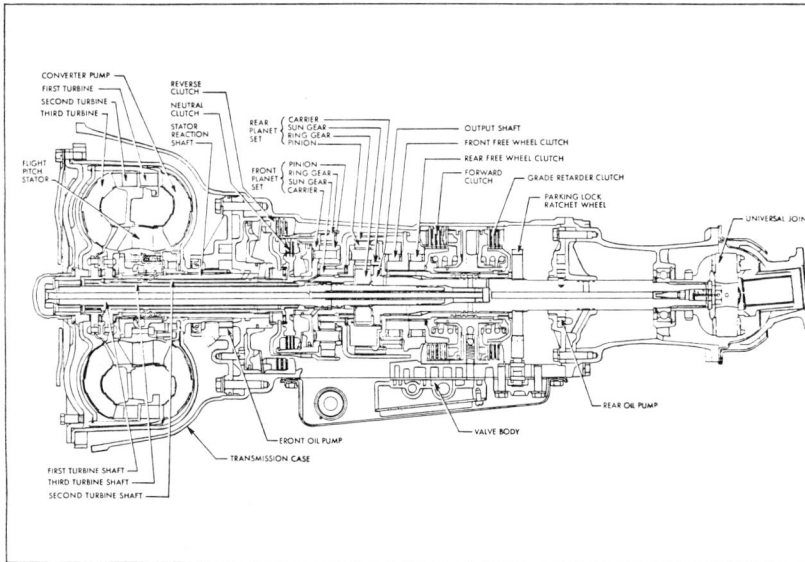

Flight-Pitch Dynaflow torque converter included three separate turbines, and mechanical gearing got more complex due to need for automatic selection of the ideal power flow path. Buick and HydraMatic soon fell in line on joint development of future transmissions.

nulus in the planetary gear set. The second-stage turbine was bolted to the planet carrier, which in turn was splined to the converter output shaft. Thus, its function was to supplement the power flow from the first-stage turbine. The stator was mounted on an overrunning clutch which connected it to the planetary sun gear. Repeated changes in the direction of the fluid flow through the converter imposed certain forces on its various elements. The impeller energized the fluid and delivered it to the first-stage turbine. Here its flow was redirected from the entrance to the exit of the blade, which imposed a driving force on the turbine. This driving torque was multiplied by the planetary gearing before it was fed into the converter output shaft, and the fixed-blade stator then redirected the fluid flow so that it would enter the second-stage turbine at an angle which provided a driving torque for the turbine. As the fluid escaped from the second-stage turbine, it en-

tered the variable-pitch stator, where it was redirected before re-entering the impeller.

At low speeds, all the power was transferred via Low range, with additional torque multiplication in the first-stage turbine. At increasing speed, with lower load, the gearset shifted into Drive range, while the first-stage turbine continued to perform all the torque multiplication. Gradually the torque conversion rate diminished in the first-stage turbine, while the second-stage turbine increased its torque multiplication rate. At high speed, it was the second-stage turbine alone that transmitted all of the driving force. The Twin Turbine transmission had a maximum stall torque ratio of 2.45:1, or about ten percent higher than the earlier five-element converter.

By 1954 about eighty-five percent of Buick cars were equipped with automatic transmission, and Dynaflow production that year reached 479,802 units.

As the next step of progress, the variable-pitch stator was introduced in 1955. The rest of the torque converter remained the same, with a single impeller and twin turbines. Due to the new stator design, Buick renamed its transmission Variable-Pitch Dynaflow. The stator blades could swing from high to low angles, but could only operate in the two end-positions. In other words, it was a dual-pitch arrangement, with no intermediate stages. At low angle, the maximum stall torque ratio was 2.10:1. At high angle, the stall torque ratio could reach 2.50:1. The pitch was altered automatically by a mechanical linkage when the throttle was opened wide, and when the accelerator pedal was released. The variable-pitch stator was intended to provide some measure of extra torque multiplication, accompanied by a rise in engine speed, while avoiding a change in mechanical gearing. This was possible because a high stator-blade angle meant greater change in the direction of fluid flow than with low stator-blade angle, and resulted in higher torque multiplication.

By controlling the pitch of the stator blades, the best angle for the prevailing conditions could be adopted, whether the aim was acceleration, cruising or economy. With the fixed-blade stator, a compromise angle had to be chosen. Each of the twenty blades of the variable pitch stator assembly was mounted on an individual crank pin, which was actuated by the stator piston. Oil pressure applied on one or the other side of the piston would move the blade to either low angle or high angle position. Low angle was for cruising, with low engine speed in relation to road speed, and optimum fuel economy, while high angle was for acceleration. The stator blade angle depended on throttle position. The throttle linkage actuated a valve in the high accumulator body. At all throttle positions, from idle to full throttle, oil under high pressure was routed through this control valve to the front side of that stator piston. Since this pressure would be greater than the converter charging pressure, the piston would move to the rear of the stator unit, and the blades would be positioned at their low angle. This would give the converter a low stall speed and keep the torque ratio at a low level. High stator blade angle was obtained under wide-open-throttle operation. This was accomplished by incorporating over-travel in the throttle linkage, which then mechanically moved the control valve. This valve movement closed off the high oil pressure and assured evacuation of the oil from the front side of the stator piston. Converter charging pressure would then be higher, and act on the rear side of the piston to push it over into the high-angle position. This action would swing the blades approximately seventy-five degrees from the low-angle position, with the result that stall speed and torque multiplication would increase. During Low-range and Reverse operation, the stator blades would automatically go to the high-angle position.

This table shows the effects of the engineering changes made in the Dynaflow from 1952 to 1955:

	Stall speed rpm	Drive range torque ratio	Low range torque ratio
1952 Dynaflow			
Special	1800	2.25	4.10
Super	1800	2.25	4.10
Roadmaster	1600	2.25	4.10
1953-54 Twin Turbine			
All series	1700	2.45	4.46
1955 Variable-Pitch			
All series			
Low angle	1400	2.10	N.A.
High angle	2600	2.50	4.55

For the 1956 models Buick extended its newest design concept by inserting an additional fixed-blade stator to separate the first-stage and second-stage turbines, while retaining the variable-pitch stator between the second-stage turbine and the impeller nearest the converter core. By installing the fixed-blade stator between the two turbine stages, maximum stall torque ratio was increased from 2.45 to 3.5:1. The first-stage turbine was connected through the planetary gearset as before, and the fixed-blade stator was carried on a hub with an overrunning clutch that would allow it to freewheel when it was no longer needed for torque conversion. This revised transmission was called Flight-Pitch Dynaflow and relied on hydraulic

torque multiplication throughout the car's speed range. The intermediate turbine (or fixed-blade stator) did not begin freewheeling until the car reached 88 mph, which corresponded to an engine speed of 3800 rpm. The Flight-Pitch Dynaflow was very expensive to manufacture. It was inefficient and wasted a lot of fuel. It was slow to respond, and gave drivers the impression of lacking speed control. In 1958 Flight-Pitch Dynaflow was standard in the Roadmaster and Limited series, and optional in the other series. Variable-Pitch Dynaflow remained in production and was standard on the Super and Century series, and optional for the Special, which still had a three-speed synchromesh transmission as standard. At this time Buick decided that the Dynaflow name had outlived its usefulness, and Twin Turbine became the new name for the Variable-Pitch Dynaflow starting with the 1959 models.

At the same time, the Flight-Pitch Dynaflow was renamed Triple Turbine, and got the benefit of two years' development work. The first-stage turbine was connected to the sun gear in the planetary transmission. The second-stage turbine was connected to the annulus, which determined whether it was to function as a stator or as a turbine. The third-stage turbine was connected to the front and rear planet gear carriers. By this arrangement, the total gear reduction was determined by the relative speed of the turbines. The first-stage turbine had a narrow set of vanes designed to receive the fluid discharged from the impeller. The second-stage turbine received the fluid expelled from the first turbine, and also had a narrow set of vanes. The third-stage turbine had a much wider crescent-shaped set of vanes, and received the discharge from the second-stage turbine. The variable-pitch stator had been developed so that the helical attitude of the blades was now continuously variable between high- and low-angle positions. The Triple Turbine converter had a maximum stall torque ratio of 4.7:1, with input shaft speed at 3200 rpm. Twin Turbine was standard on the Invicta and Electra series for 1959, and Triple Turbine was optional only on the Electra. From 1960 to 1963 these transmissions were merchandized under the name of Turbine Drive, and no further changes of importance were made until the arrival of the Super Turbine. Turbine Drive was used on all the senior-series Buicks and the Riviera.

When Buick was preparing its first compact car, which was to be launched as the 1961 Special, there could be no thought of outfitting it with the expensive Twin Turbine transmission. Instead, the corporation had a new unit available. In 1957-58 the Detroit Transmission Division of General Motors developed a small lightweight automatic transmission. It was designed to suit the lower power and torque of the new compact cars then being developed by Buick and Oldsmobile. This transmission went into production as the HydraMatic 61-05. Oldsmobile used it for its F-85 under

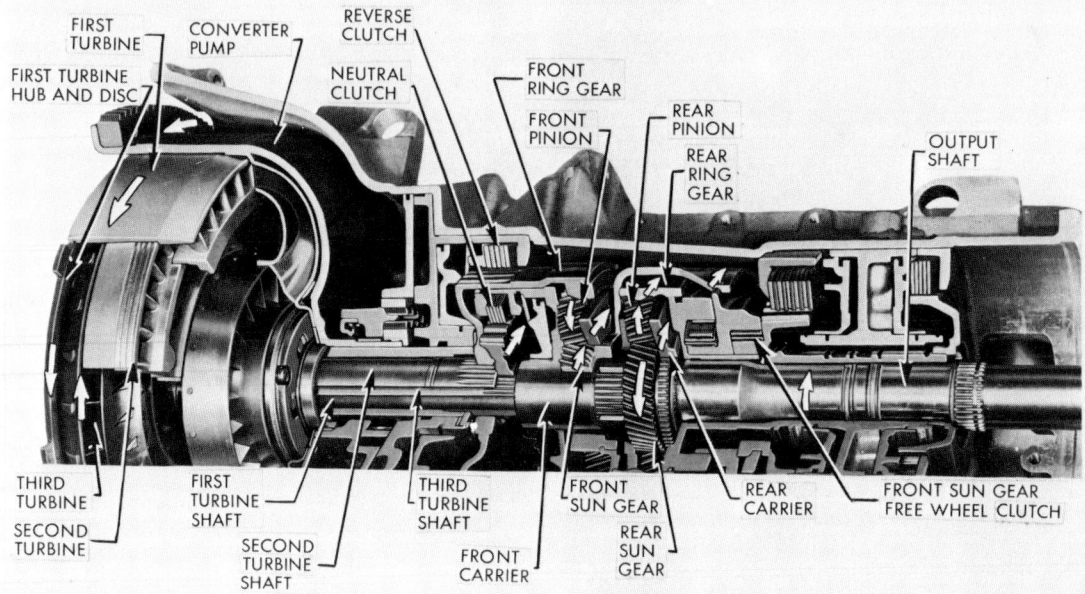

Left, Rudolf Gorsky, a veteran Buick engineer, has played a key part in the evolution of Buick's automatic transmission systems over the years. His work has produced a steady flow of small but significant improvements. Right, this view of the Flight-Pitch Dynaflow transmission shows the disposition of the three turbine elements in the torque converter and the complexity of clutches needed to control the very simple planetary gearing.

that name, but Buick renamed it Dual-Path for use on the Special. It was engineered from a concept by Jack W. Qualman, then assistant chief engineer of Detroit Transmission Division, a post he had held since 1956.

The Dual-Path combined a hydraulic torque converter with three-speed planetary gearing, thus showing that Detroit Transmission (soon to be renamed HydraMatic Division) had recognized the value of Buick's pioneering work in torque converters, but was inclined to rely more on mechanical speed reduction. The use of three speeds enabled the Dual-Path system to use a type of converter with a very low stall torque ratio of 1.3:1. As a result, Dual-Path had improved converter efficiency without sacrificing road-load economy. The most interesting and innovative feature of the Dual-Path transmission was its torque division device, which consisted of an automatic clutch that, in Drive range, split the engine torque along two separate but

parallel paths, one hydraulic and the other mechanical. The input torque was split in a 64/36 percent ratio at a predetermined speed, dependent on throttle opening and vehicle speed, with the hydraulic part taking thirty-six percent of the torque and the mechanical part sixty-four percent. In practice, this meant that slippage losses were reduced by about two-thirds. In S range (for Super) the clutch was engaged and the drive was transmitted one hundred percent mechanically, with the torque converter drained of fluid and rendered inoperative. Upshifts were automatic as long as the selector lever was left in D position, but selection of S position would prevent upshifting. In Low range, the converter was filled and the clutch disengaged for smooth starts. In this mode, torque transmission between the engine and the planetary gearing was purely hydraulic.

The torque converter was a small-diameter unit with three members: impeller, turbine and stator. But unlike Buick's torque converters, this one had straight radial vanes, like a hydraulic coupling. The stator was a ring containing nineteen fixed-angle blades of curved cross-section, located at the converter core. Converter efficiency depends a great deal on size—the bigger, the better. In the case of the Dual-Path, small size was accepted,

58

because of the restricted reliance on hydraulic torque multiplication. The Dual-Path design was also unusual in that the impeller was positioned next to the engine, whereas all previous Buick transmissions had the turbine next to the engine. This was done because of the manner in which the gearing was arranged. The turbine was splined directly to the shaft feeding the power to mechanical section, and this would not have been so easy if the relative position of the impeller and turbine had been reversed. Two gear sets were used to provide three ratios: 1.00:1, 1.58:1, and 3.03:1. The entire unit weighed only ninety-five pounds, including oil (eighty-four pounds dry), which was ten pounds lighter than the synchromesh transmission used on the Special. This was mainly due to the use of aluminum for the main castings. Since it was air-cooled, the weight of a heat exchanger was eliminated. Dual-Path was used on Special and Skylark through the 1963 model year—the time during which they were compact cars.

In about 1960 the corporation decided to streamline its automatic transmission program. Instead of having Buick and Chevrolet producing their own torque-converter transmissions, while Oldsmobile, Cadillac and Pontiac used the HydraMatic (hydraulic coupling and four-speed gearing), plus another variant for the Buick and Oldsmobile compacts; it was decreed that all cars within each size category, regardless of the division that built them, would share the same transmission. At the outset, two sizes of the same basic transmission were planned to satisfy all models made by a GM car division. This was planned to come into effect for the 1964 models and Buick had no objection; neither did Pontiac, Oldsmobile or Cadillac. Chevrolet had one car that required a unique transmission—the Corvair, which was allowed to continue with its own version of the Powerglide.

A multitude of different transmissions were eliminated in this process. Buick discontinued the two versions of its Turbine Drive. HydraMatic stopped production of the four-speed units with hydraulic coupling as well as the Type 61-05 (Dual-Path). Chevrolet, with some delay, began to phase out the Turboglide, which had been used on the standard-size cars since 1957. All were replaced by one of the two new designs: Turbo-HydraMatic 300 or Turbo-HydraMatic 400. Installed in Buick cars, they were marketed as the Super Turbine 300 and Super Turbine 400.

Both Turbo-Hydramatics originated at Buick and were developed to the pre-production stage by the group Charles Chapman headed. When these units were selected to become the new corporate transmissions, HydraMatic was brought into the picture, and HydraMatic's chief engineer Jack R. Doidge and his assistant, Jack Qualman, played an important part in its subsequent development. Having succeeded so brilliantly in the transmission field, Charles Chapman was given wider responsibilities in 1965, with the title of assistant chief engineer of Buick. He wielded a great deal of influ-

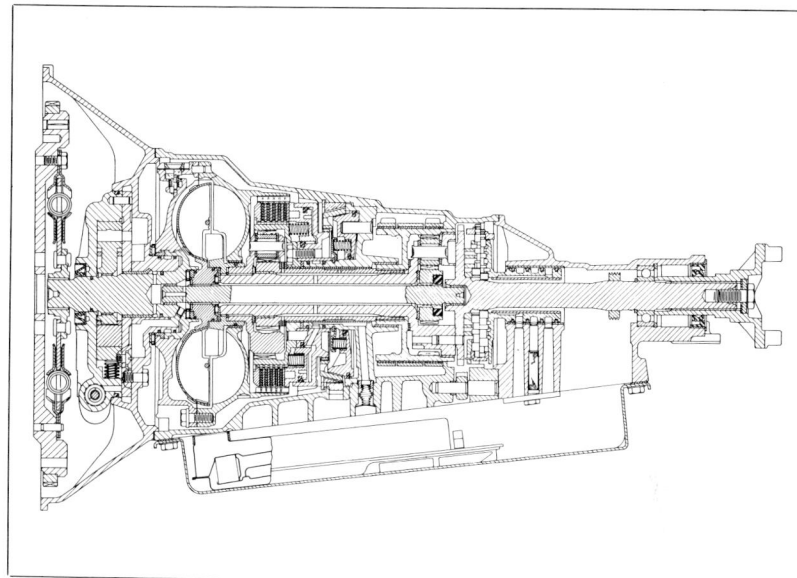

Automatic transmission used in the 1961 Buick Special was a HydraMatic—not a Dynaflow—and incorporated a dual-flow system of dividing torque between hydraulic and mechanical power flow paths.

ence over the engineering of future Buicks for two years, but in 1967 left Flint to go to Germany and take over the post of chief engineer of Opel. He stayed at Opel till 1975 when he was named general manager of GM-Holden's in Australia.

Super Turbine 400 represented a marriage between Buick principles and HydraMatic practice. Buick's steady development of the torque converter triumphed over HydraMatic's age-long adherence to the hydraulic coupling. On the other hand, HydraMatic's use of multi-step mechanical gearing won out over Buick's earlier insistence on a single-step gear reduction (for Low range). The combination used in the Super Turbine 400 was a three-element torque converter and three-speed planetary gearing. In 1964 it was identical to the Turbo-HydraMatic 400, but the following year Buick incorporated in it one exclusive feature in the form of the well-known variable-pitch stator. Maximum stall torque ratio was 2.1:1. The impeller was located next to the

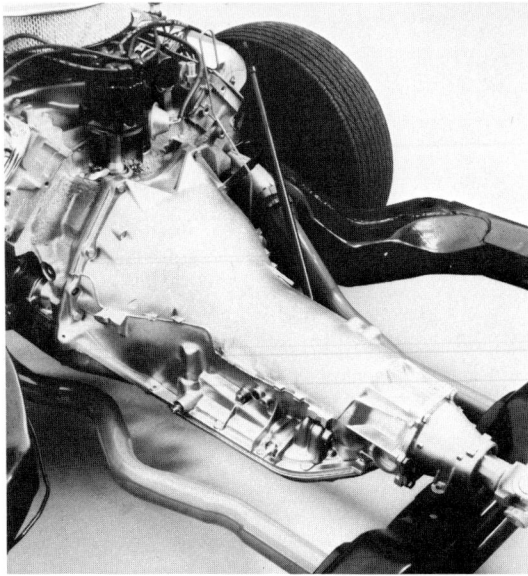

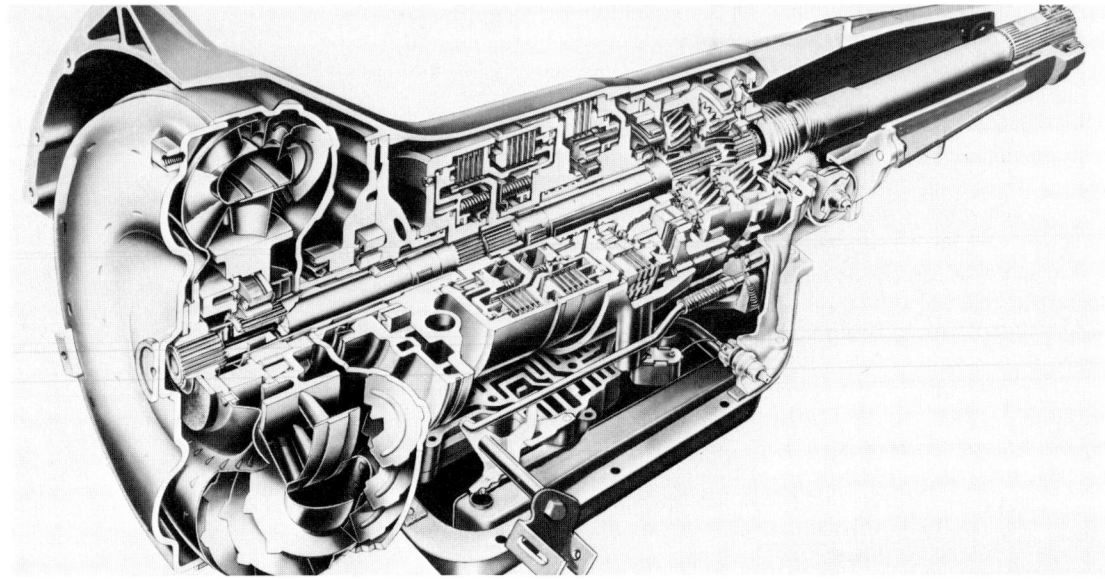

Left, Super Turbine 300 replaced the Dual-Path when the Buick Special went from compact to intermediate size in 1963. It's a three-element torque converter with a two-speed planetary gear set. In 1964 Buick went to the Super Turbine 400, right, for its senior-series cars. It consisted of a variable-pitch three-element torque converter and a three-speed planetary gear set. Four years later the variable pitch idea was abandoned.

planetary gearing, with the turbine closest to the engine. A flex-plate bolted directly to the crankshaft was connected to the outer surface of the impeller. The turbine hub was splined to the main transmission shaft which drove the planetary gear train via the forward clutch.

Compared with the 1963 version of Buick's Turbine Drive, the new Super Turbine 400 gave a forty-three percent increase in thrust at the driving wheels, due to greater reliance on mechanical reduction. Super Turbine 400 had three ranges, with direct drive in Drive, and downgearing with a 1.48:1 ratio in Second and a 2.48:1 ratio in Low range. This was accomplished by one compound planetary gear set (which serves as two sets in one) of the Simpson type, with a double sun gear, a planet carrier with four pinions and an annulus. In Drive range, the entire system revolved as a unit. In S range (second) the sun gears were locked in stationary position, with the planets 'walking' around them, transferring motion to the output shaft via the planet carrier. The front unit was inoperative, but the rear unit

was connected to the shaft, running at a 1.48:1 ratio. In Low range, both front and rear units were engaged. The rear sun gear turned and rotated the pinions, while the planet carrier was held stationary. Since the two sun gears were made as a unit, they turned at the same speed. In the front unit, the planet carrier was also held still, so that the pinions drove the annulus, which in turn transmitted its motion to the output shaft in a 2.48:1 reduction ratio.

Buick claimed that Super Turbine 400 gave better acceleration, reduced creep and roughness at idle, increased braking effect on downhills, improved fuel economy and gave greater reliability and longer life than Turbine Drive.

Super Turbine 400 became standard on all the senior-series Buicks for the 1964 model year. Super Turbine 300 was made optional for the 1964 Special and Skylark, which had a three-speed synchromesh transmission as standard. Made by HydraMatic Division, the Super Turbine 300 was identical with the Turbo-HydraMatic 300 which was used by Chevrolet, Pontiac and Oldsmobile. Olds called it the Jetaway transmission, Pontiac named it Tempestorque, and Buick chose to identify it as a small version of the Super Turbine 400, though it was really a different type of transmission. Super

Turbine 300 had a three-element torque converter based on the Dual-Path design, with near-radial vanes in the impeller and turbine. The stator was a two-position variable-pitch design with an easy curvature on the blades. But Super Turbine 300 did not incorporate the split-drive feature of the Dual-Path. It was only a two-speed unit, and borrowed from the original Dynaflow the idea of long and short pinions for the planetary gear set. The mechanical gearing gave a Low-range reduction of 1.765:1. Gear width and helix angles were increased to provide the same overlap (number of teeth in contact) as on the 1963 Dual-Path. Compared with Dual-Path, it was a much simplified transmission, with the number of parts reduced from 443 to 295. In contrast with the air-cooled Dual-Path transmission, the Super Turbine 300 was water-cooled, like its bigger brother. It also received the aneroid bellows to assure smooth shifts regardless of altitude.

Super Turbine 400 was manufactured up to the end of the 1967 model year, and Super Turbine 300 was kept in production for one year longer. In the 1968 models, the senior series Buicks went to the Turbo-HydraMatic 400 with its fixed-angle stator member in the torque converter. Along with this change, the electrical control system was simplified by eliminating the idle switch and one transmission solenoid. A self-adjusting downshift switch, mounted in the instrument panel, replaced the previous double-circuit switch that was mounted on the engine. Super Turbine 300 was replaced by the Turbo-HydraMatic 350 for the 1969-model junior-series Buicks. It was a joint Buick-Chevrolet development, to be manufactured by both divisions. Instead of basing its design on the Super Turbine 300 it was practically a scaled-down edition of the Turbo-HydraMatic 400, with a three-element torque converter using curved vanes in the impeller and turbine, but having a reduced torque converter diameter to suit the torque characteristics of the 350-cubic-inch V-8 engines. It had three-speed planetary gearing, with some minor improvements in shift control.

In 1973-74, HydraMatic Division developed a smaller unit for four- and six-cylinder engines, which went into production as the Turbo-HydraMatic

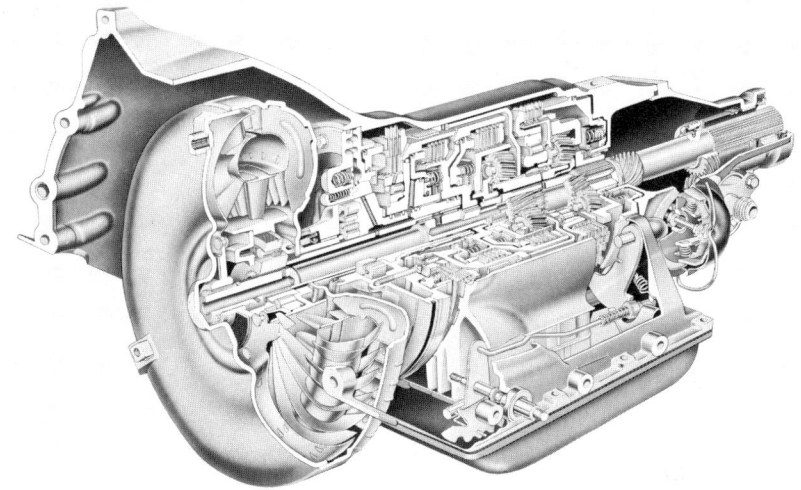

Turbo-HydraMatic 350 became available for the Buick Skylark Custom, GS 350 and Sportwagon models in 1969. It's a scaled-down version of the Super Turbine 400, with fixed-angle stator blades.

200. It is basically a scaled-down THM 350, with three-speed planetary gearing, lighter and more compact, and with reduced torque-input capacity. THM 200 is now used in such cars as the Buick Skyhawk and Skylark.

CHAPTER 6

Buick Goes to V-8 Power

BUICK HAD MANY reasons to switch from the straight-eight to a V-8 engine. The in-line power plant was getting long in the tooth, and Buick was overdue for a new and more modern engine. Rather than incorporate all the technological advances that Buick had been developing into an all-new straight-eight, it was decided to make a V-8. Why? Primarily for styling reasons.

Styling? Yes, because General Motors was planning its next generation of auto bodies with lower and shorter hoods, which meant there would not be room for anything longer than a six in-line and nothing so tall as Buick's long-stroke straight-eight. The old Buick eight would not fit in the future cars that were being planned for all divisions. Cadillac, of course, had *always* had a V-8 (to the purists, the term always in this context means since 1914). All GM divisions were told in 1945 to develop V-8 engines. Oldsmobile dropped its straight-eight and went to V-8 power in its 1949 models. Buick followed, four years behind. And V-8 engines were made available in Pontiac and Chevrolet for 1955.

Buick's experience with V-type engines can be said to date back to 1903, if one considers the horizontally opposed twin as a V-2 with the cylinders splayed 180 degrees apart. Shortly after all two-cylinder units were phased out, Buick's engineering director, Walter Marr, designed both V-6 and V-12 engines in 1915. Prototypes were built and installed in experimental cars. They ran, and ran well. But they never got into production.

Buick's first serious work with V-type engines was done in 1931, when an experimental V-12 was designed, tested and evaluated as a possible companion for the straight-eight, the same way that makes like Packard and Auburn offered both straight-eights and V-12's, or Cadillac made V-8's, V-12's and V-16's side by side. But in the years that followed, Buick ran into a lot of other problems, and the V-12 was never developed.

A development program on a high-compression V-8 began in 1944, and went on without interruption until 1950, when the first V-8 design was approved for production. Under Joseph D. Turlay a special department was set up to study basic engine configurations, different V-angles, crankshaft arrangements and combustion chamber designs. During this period, ten different types of V-8 engines were built and tested, and over a hundred experimental models were made. One was a staggered eight, with cylinders lined up in zig-zag formation in one single block, with a very narrow angle of 22 ½ degrees between the cylinders. Such eight-cylinder engines had been built in regular production in Italy by Lancia during the twenties and early thirties, and the Buick staggered eight proved to be a very exciting, compact and lightweight engine. It was actually in the process of being prepared for production when it began to give problems. There were balance problems and manufacturing difficulties. So that design was shelved. Another V-8 design with a narrow angle of thirty-five degrees between the banks was very promising, in terms of both power and smoothness, but had

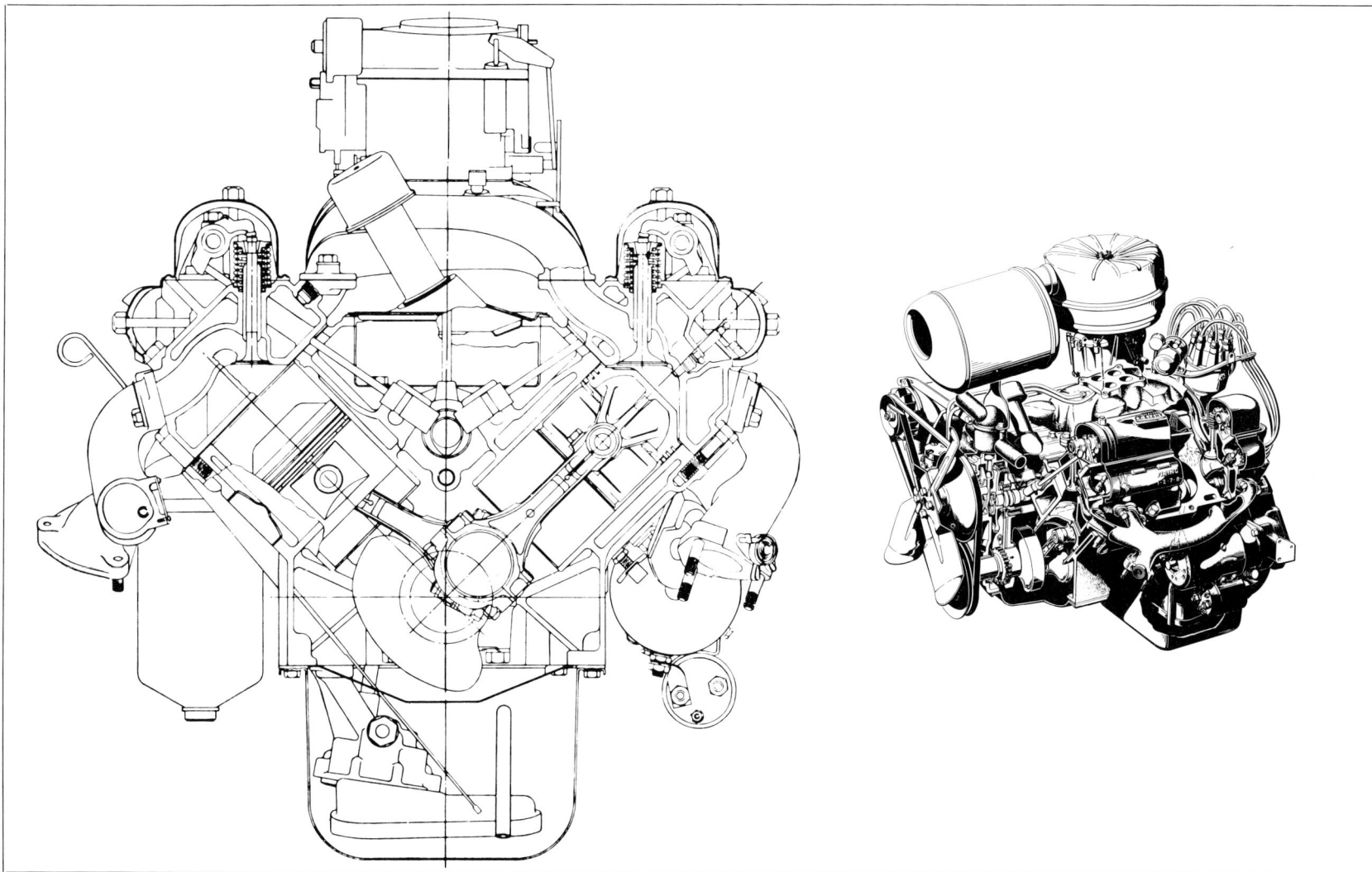

Left, cross section of first Buick V-8 shows emphasis placed on restricting overall width, with valves standing straight up and exhaust passages making sharp curves. Crankcase is integral with cylinder block, in true Buick tradition. Buick's first V-8 engine, right, had a piston displacement of 322 cubic inches and delivered 188 hp at 4000 rpm in the Roadmaster and 170 hp in the Super. All cylinders were inclined, and all valves were vertical.

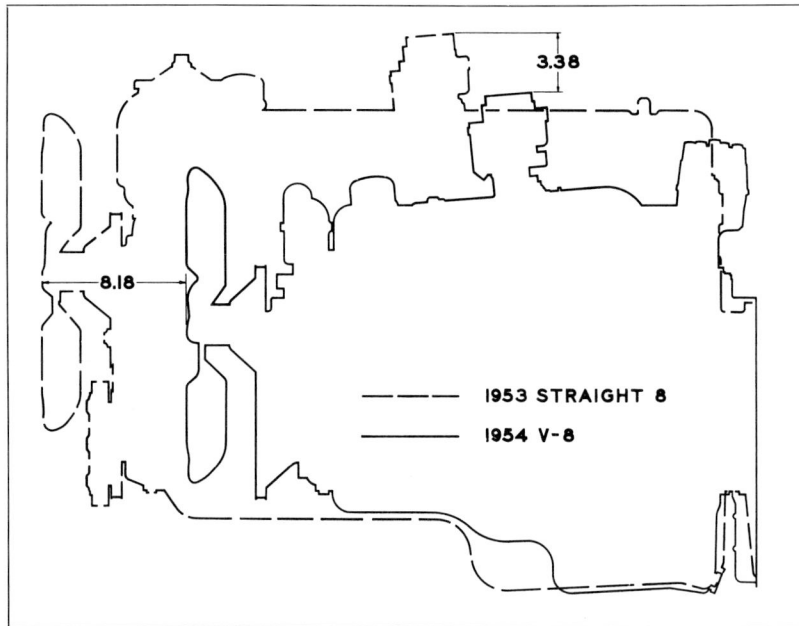

3.38

8.18

- - - - - 1953 STRAIGHT 8
———— 1954 V-8

Not only was there a considerable weight saving in adopting the V-8 engine, but the installation package was over eight inches shorter and nearly 3½ inches lower. Displacement and power output were increased. These drawings show Special engines.

to be abandoned because of packaging considerations. The carburetor height could not be reduced sufficiently to clear hood levels then projected for future models. In fact, the space allocated to the engine by the stylists became one of the most important, if not *the* most important, factor in determining the exact configuration of the Buick V-8.

Of course, the ninety-degree V-8 was not the lowest of all engines, for a horizontally opposed eight is a form of pancake engine, and angles of 120 and 135 degrees also give very low height. But Buick found that the wide-angle V-8's became too wide and could not be accommodated in the chassis without interfering with other vital organs. By process of elimination Buick finally settled on the ninety-degree V-8, as had Cadillac and Olds-mobile, Ford and Chrysler. That's sort of anticlimactic, after all the unusual

designs that had been under consideration. The amazing thing is that Buick came so close to actually producing the staggered eight.

Final design of Buick's first production-model V-8 began in March 1950, while Chayne was still chief engineer. Joe Turlay was in charge of the design, and a new man, Cliff Studaker, was soon to join this group as a student engineer. Studaker was to have enormous influence on future Buick engines. He had graduated from Michigan State University in 1949 and worked for Chevrolet in the resident engineers' laboratory from June 1949 to August 1950. After the end of the student course which took about a year, Studaker joined Turlay in the special projects group to work on engine design and development. Studaker recalls that when he joined the group in 1951, the V-8 was already undergoing dynamometer tests. Joe Turlay had joined Buick about 1928, and had always worked in power train engineering. He started in transmissions, and gradually came to do more and more work on engines, until, in 1945, he was Buick's top engine designer. He had seen the Cadillac and Oldsmobile V-8's, and he had access to everything that the GM Engineering Staff had been doing since their designs were frozen. He was as familiar with engine manufacturing and installation problems as anybody in the business.

Turlay's V-8 was boldly new in some ways, but very conservative in others. Malleable cast iron was chosen for the main parts—cylinder block and cylinder heads. The block was a Y-type construction, extending below the crankshaft center line, but did not go as deep as the crankcase on the straight-eight. The Buick V-8's stroke/bore ratio of 0.8:1 was the lowest then used in an American production engine. The bore was four inches and the stroke 3.2 inches, giving a displacement of 322 cubic inches. The short stroke assured lower piston speed and reduced the crank throw, which translated into a more rigid crankshaft. It reduced crankpin bearing loads and improved crankcase rigidity. It made possible a genuine weight saving in the block, contributed to a lower engine profile and gave the engine a higher rpm potential. It also reduced cylinder bore and bearing friction, to improve the engine's mechanical efficiency and reduce wear. The big bore assured vastly increased piston area, which is a main criterion of the engine's accelerative power. In the straight-eight, aggregate piston area was a modest 74.2 square inches. In the V-8 it had been increased to 100.5 square inches, which is more than twenty-five percent better. But this accelerative power was not available at low rpm. By shortening the stroke, Buick had given up some of the tremendous low-end torque of the straight-eight, in favor of better performance at higher crankshaft speeds.

With the bigger bore, there was a greater risk of irregular and abnormal combustion. The compact shape of the combustion space threatened to become a low-roofed cave, spread out radially in all directions, with a quench area of such great expanse as to cause incomplete combustion, which means a waste of fuel, and therefore a loss of power. Turlay avoided this problem entirely by adopting a pentroof design, with a conical piston crown matching up against the combustion chamber recess in the cylinder head and a spark plug positioned right opposite the piston center. The port and valve configurations, gas flow direction and turbulence, and the overall combustion-chamber shape were developed from a design invented and tested at GM Research by a group headed by Darl F. Caris, a scientist trained by years and years of working as an assistant to C. F. 'Boss' Kettering. The combustion chamber was fully machined. It could be described as a shallow cone, with a flattened top to provide a compact combustion space with a minimum distance of flame travel from the centrally located spark plug to the extreme edge of the effective portion of the combustion chamber. The close clearance around the raised crown cone assured high turbulence for faster and more complete combustion, while the short flame front travel allowed higher compression ratios with no increase in octane requirement. The piston design featured a transverse slot and a divorced full-skirt. The wrist pin bores were centrally located. Pistons were made of aluminum alloy, cam-ground and anodized. They carried two compression rings and one oil control ring.

Intake valve-head diameter was enlarged from 1.75 inches to 1.875 inches, while exhaust valve-head size grew from 1.25 inches to a 1.50-inch diameter. They were operated via a pushrod and rocker-arm mechanism from a centrally located camshaft, driven from the crankshaft by a short duplex chain. The camshaft was a steel forging and ran in five bearings. It drove the fuel pump via an eccentric driven from the front sprocket, and a skew gear at the rear end drove the near-vertical shaft for the oil pump and ignition distributor. Hydraulic valve lifters were standard, and the lubrication system included a triple oil gallery which metered oil to the lifters and ensured uniform lubrication of all moving parts. The valves were arranged vertically, i.e. vertically to ground level, but at a forty-five-degree angle relative to the cylinders. All valves were positioned in a single straight line, in typical Buick fashion. Both intake and exhaust valves were therefore on the same side of the cylinder—on the intake side, which meant that the cylinder head castings contained long exhaust passages leading from the exhaust ports to the manifold which was bolted on, outside of the block.

The valve-gear layout was influenced by considerations totally unconnected with the engine's inner workings, however. When Buick decided to go with the ninety-degree V-8, both chassis and body engineers found the reduced height and length of great value, but the increased width, compared with an in-line engine, gave them a serious problem. In Buick's case, there was a critical point in getting clearance between the engine and the

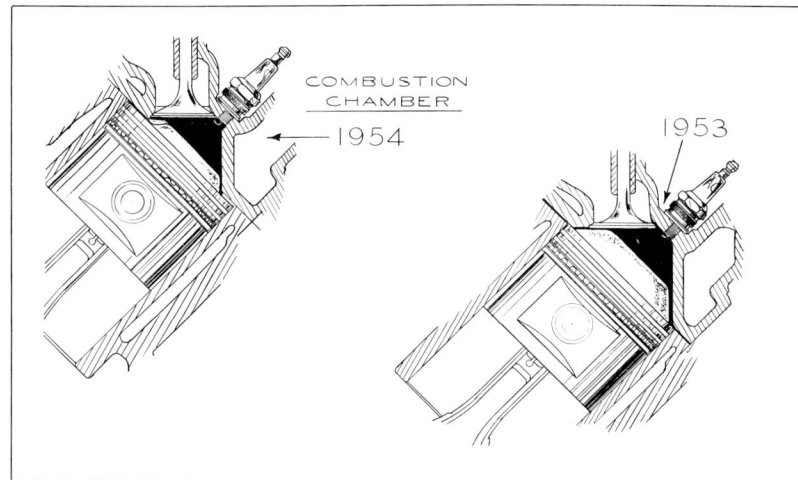

Pentroof combustion chamber of 1953 V-8 engine was modified for 1954, with larger intake valve heads and a lowered piston dome. Crevice areas that quench the combustion were reduced by half.

steering gear, and frame members. This consideration had a lot to do with the choice of vertical valves, which gave a narrower engine cross section than a design with valves in line with the cylinders, or valves splayed to opposite sides. The vertical valve position, however, necessitated the use of a valve gear in which the pushrods passed through bosses drilled in the cylinder heads. The pushrods crossed the valve guides, with the rocker arms doubling back to open the valves. This arrangement worked well enough but imposed restrictions on valve and port sizes. Valve timing was fairly 'hot,' with an intake valve opening duration of 282 degrees and sixty-seven-degree overlap. The intake valves opened twenty-five degrees before top dead center and closed seventy-seven degrees after bottom dead center. Exhaust valves opened seventy degrees before bottom dead center and closed forty-two degrees after top dead center.

The intake manifold was a two-level design fitting inside the valley between the two banks. It carried the carburetor at its center—a two-barrel one for the Super and a four-barrel one for the Roadmaster. Two passages through the cylinder heads led the exhaust gases to outer chambers in the intake manifold in order to heat the divided sections where the fresh mixture was led in. Heating the mixture during engine warm up assisted vaporization and gave more even fuel distribution in the mixture. Each exhaust valve had its own individual port and branch to the manifold, instead of the siamesed exhaust ports of the straight-eight. The new design eliminated interference between exhaust charges from adjacent cylinders in the port areas, where it could cause valve burning.

The forged-steel crankshaft was a conventional two-plane design, with the connecting rods from opposite cylinders paired on the same crankpin. Because of the ninety-degree angle between the banks, this gave even spacing between firing impulses, at ninety-degree intervals. The firing order was 1-2-7-8-4-5-6-3. As the crankshaft was fully counterweighted, the engine had no unbalanced primary forces, but like all other V-8's, it had an unbalanced secondary rocking couple* that was due to the swinging action of the connecting rods. Their motion was not perfectly symmetrical, and that gave rise to this rocking couple. Its effects were minimized by developing a new engine mounting system that confined the rocking to the engine itself and avoided transferring vibration to the frame and body. The harmonic crankshaft balancer was eliminated, but a small amount of counterweighting was carried in the crankshaft fan-belt pulley and in the flywheel. This soon proved inadequate, and a harmonic balancer was added as a running change halfway into the 1953 model year. The design was based on Cadillac practice, using a rubber grommet as an absorbing member (instead of the leaf-spring type used on the Buick straight-eight). It also contained a cast-iron inertia member, and the previous sheet-metal flange was replaced with a cast-iron flange.

The crankshaft ran in five main bearings of 2.50-inch diameter, and had crankpin journals of 2.25-inch diameter. It was the fifth main bearing that took the end thrust, and it had a width of 1.765 inches, while the front main was only 1.22 inches wide, and the intermediate bearings had a width of 1.25 inches. Connecting-rod center-to-center distance had been reduced to 6.00 inches. The lowered connecting rod reduced the length-to-bore ratio from 1.91:1 in the straight-eight to 1.875:1 in the V-8. The use of cam-contoured counterweights enabled the Buick engineers to shorten the block and crankshaft, and leave minimum clearance between the counterweights and the pistons without cutting away the piston skirts.

The V-8 was 180 pounds lighter than the straight-eight, and more than one foot shorter. It was also about seven inches lower, and Buick disclosed it cost about seven percent less to manufacture. The V-8 weighed 623.93 pounds complete with starter motor and generator. The block and crankcase

scaled 176.52 pounds, which meant a weight saving of over seventy-two pounds compared with the 320-cubic-inch straight-eight. However, the use of two cylinder heads instead of one caused a weight gain of 12.65 pounds. Each cylinder head for the V-8 weighed fifty-three pounds. Despite the use of two separate rocker arm shafts and two valve covers, the V-8 gave a net weight saving of 3.2 pounds in these parts. In addition there was a seventeen-pound weight savings in the camshaft, camshaft drive, valve lifters and valve springs. This was mainly due to the shortening of the camshaft itself, plus the shortening of the pushrods. The short crankshaft weighed only 55.91 pounds, or less than half of the straight-eight crankshaft. At the same time, the flywheel was reduced from 12.05 pounds to 9.44 pounds, and the crankshaft harmonic balancer (13.68 pounds on the straight-eight) was eliminated. On the other hand the V-8's front cover was heavier, at over twelve pounds compared with less than seven pounds for the straight-eight. That weight gain was canceled out by using a lighter water pump on the V-8, weighing 7.66 pounds against 13.25 pounds on the straight-eight.

"By reducing engine weight, the steering effort is reduced, while car balance, handling and performance are improved," said Verner P. Mathews. "Weight is also a major factor in production cost, but to realize the maximum cost saving, any reduction in weight must be obtained by good commercial design, and not by the use of more expensive materials, or by the adoption of designs which are more complicated and difficult to manufacture." He was very satisfied with Joe Turlay's accomplishments. Production of the V-8 began in the summer of 1952. It was to have started one year earlier, but the Korean war effort created difficulties for the machine tool industry, and Buick's orders had to wait while defense orders took priority.

Buick's first V-8 production engine was introduced in the 1953-model Golden Anniversary Roadmaster and Super series. It had a compression ratio of 8.5:1 and delivered 188 SAE gross hp at 4000 rpm in the Roadmaster series. For the Super, power output was rated at 170 SAE gross hp at 4000 rpm. The difference was due to the use of a four-barrel carburetor on the Roadmaster and a two-barrel carburetor on the Super engine. A 264-cubic-inch version of the same V-8 engine was developed for the 1954 Special. It had a 3.625-inch bore and the same 3.20-inch stroke as the larger unit. With a 7.2:1 compression ratio it delivered 143 SAE gross hp at 4000 rpm for cars with synchromesh transmission. Dynaflow-equipped cars had engines with a higher (8.1:1) compression ratio, which raised power output to 150 SAE gross hp at 4000 rpm. Buick cars switched from a six-volt to a twelve-volt electrical system as they adopted the V-8 engines. The smaller unit had introduced a revised combustion chamber which was rushed into production for the 1954-model 322-cubic-inch V-8. It combined

---

*Engine vibrations stem from two types of unbalanced forces. One type is linear (up and down, side to side), and the other type is revolving. The latter is called a couple because it's combined from two or more components. When a couple appears on and off, it's a rocking couple, tending to rock the engine on its mounts.

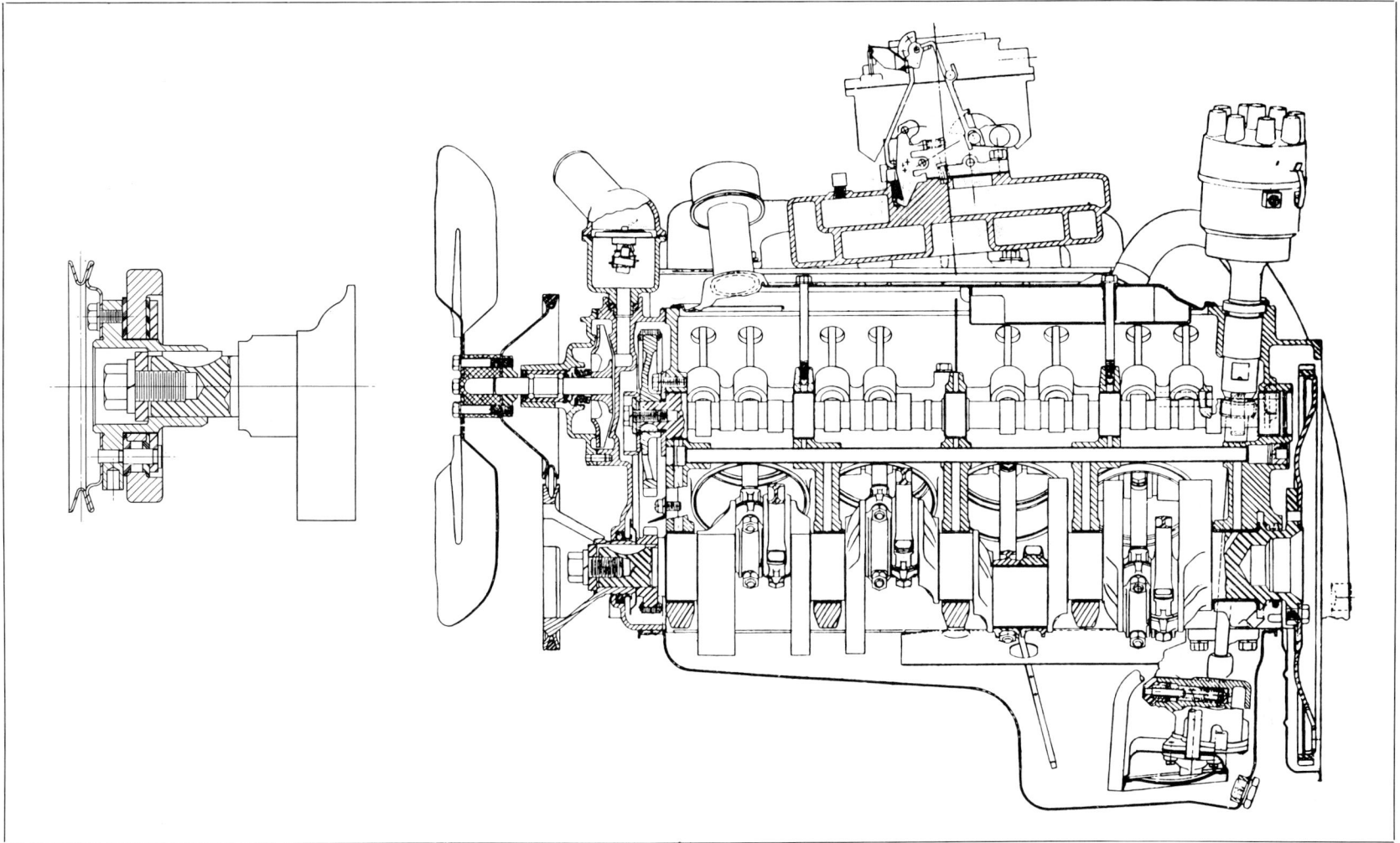

pistons with a new crown design and a cylinder head with redesigned intake and exhaust passages. The dome on the piston was flattened in height and reduced in diameter to conform to the shape of a new smaller cylinder head recess. This resulted in a wide quench area on the outer land of the piston crown, which at top dead center, had the barest minimum clearance

At first, Buick tried to eliminate the harmonic balancer from its V-8, but the engine did not have the required smoothness without one, so for 1954 this balancer assembly, left, was added to the front end of the crankshaft. Side elevation of the 1953 Buick V-8, right, shows closely spaced cylinders, generous bearing dimensions and compact valve gears. Its ultimate limitations lay in the cylinder head design and not in the bottom end (as was the case with the straight-eight).

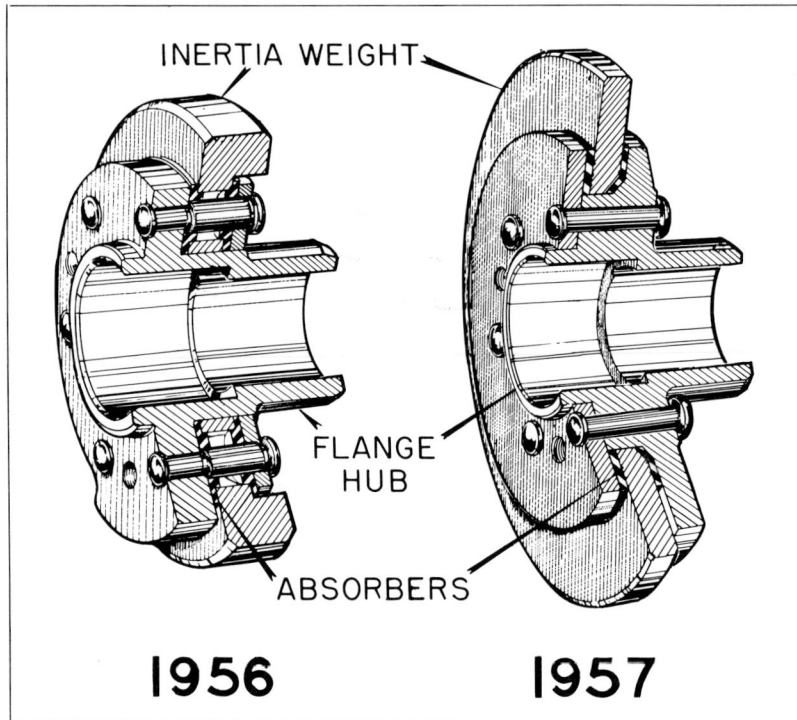

INERTIA WEIGHT

FLANGE HUB

ABSORBERS

1956   1957

An improved harmonic balancer was adopted for the 1957 V-8 engines. With the new design, the inertia weight was better linked to the flange hub, and the mass was rearranged as a larger-diameter disc instead of a small drum.

with the cylinder head base. Power output was stepped up to 200 SAE gross hp for the Roadmaster and 182 SAE gross hp for the Super (with Dynaflow Drive). In addition the Super was available with a lower-compression unit for cars equipped with synchromesh transmission. It had an 8.0:1 compression ratio and put out 177 SAE gross hp.

By 1955 Flint joined the horsepower race in a big way. On the 322-cubic-inch V-8, compression ratio was raised from 8.5:1 to 9.0:1, and exhaust valve diameter was increased from 1.25 inches to 1.375 inches. Crankshaft speeds were raised, and advertised power output was boosted from 200 SAE gross hp at 4100 rpm to 236 SAE gross hp at 4600 rpm. The word 'advertised' is the clue to what happened to horsepower ratings after that. The whole industry was caught up in a battle to offer the most powerful engines. Now, horsepower isn't something that can be calculated on the basis of the engine specifications. It can only be established by testing. The American car makers test in the way prescribed by the Society of Automotive Engineers (SAE). Tests are made on a dynamometer, which is a hydraulic or electric brake connected to the crankshaft. When a load is put on the brake, one gets a reading on engine torque. And from the torque figures, horsepower can be calculated. At that time, the SAE allowed engines to be tested without air cleaners, generators, water pumps and mufflers. The result was what the SAE called gross horsepower. These gross numbers had no relation to the power of the engine as installed in the car.

At first the advertising agencies just put more emphasis on horsepower. Then the sales departments began asking the engineers for higher horsepower ratings. The next step was for the sales people to inflate the figures a little. After a while, gross exaggerations became commonplace. Finally, the sales departments and advertising agencies concocted the horsepower ratings without even telling the engineering department. Buick was no worse and no better than the other manufacturers. The numbers advertised were next to meaningless, but they have historical importance as an illustration of a trend—a passing phase in the evolution of an industry. That's why we are giving you a lot of horsepower numbers while describing how Buick developed its V-8 engines. The 1955-model 264-cubic-inch V-8 delivered 188 advertised (SAE gross) hp at 4800 rpm, with a peak torque of 256 pounds-feet at 2400 rpm, using the 8.4:1 compression ratio cylinder heads designed for the Dynaflow-equipped cars. The base engine continued with an 8.0:1 compression ratio and unchanged horsepower rating. The 1955 Roadmaster engine was advertised as putting out 236 SAE gross hp at 4600 rpm with a maximum torque of 330 pounds-feet, at 3000 rpm.

The 1956 version was refined in the area of combustion chamber design, with larger ports and exhaust valves, along with other evolutionary modifications. They included a new camshaft with a change in valve timing, with a longer intake valve opening duration for pumping a larger volume of fresh mixture into the cylinders. The exhaust valve was streamlined to improve the exhaust gas flow from the combustion chamber into the port area. The former exhaust manifolds were replaced by a new double-Y type manifold, which served to separate the exhaust pulses well into the manifold area instead of mixing the flow from adjacent ports at the start. This kept overlapping pulses from blocking each other, and assisted materially in improving exhaust gas flow. Dual exhaust pipes were standard on the 1956 Roadmaster and optional for all other models.

Buick specifications listed higher compression ratios than ever before. On the Century, Super and Roadmaster engines, the compression ratio was raised from 9.0 to 9.5:1. Compression ratio in the Special engine was raised from 8.4 to 8.9:1. It should be emphasized that compression ratios were also subject to exaggeration. To start with, compression ratios are nominal. They record the theoretical change in volume during the compression stroke, without taking the dynamics of gas flow through partially open valves into account. Advertisements could claim almost any compression ratio the advertiser wanted to. Power output in the 322-cubic-inch V-8 with four-barrel carburetor was advertised as 255 SAE gross hp at 4400 rpm, with a maximum torque of 341 pounds-feet at 3200 rpm. This engine was used in the Roadmaster, Super and Century. The 264-cubic-inch engine was discontinued, and the Special received its own version of the 322-cubic-inch unit, with an advertised power output of 220 SAE gross hp at 4400 rpm (for Dynaflow equipped cars) with peak torque of 319 pounds-feet at 2400 rpm.

It was the Dynaflow that enabled Buick to use engines of this type, with peak torque readings at two-thirds of peak-power rpm rather than one-third of crankshaft speed at the point where maximum power was generated. Using three-speed synchromesh transmissions with such engines would require unacceptably high final drive ratios, or lead to unacceptably high rates of clutch wear. Cylinder displacement was increased from 322 to 364 cubic inches for the 1957 models. The cylinders were bored out to 4.125 inches and the stroke was lengthened to 3.40 inches.

The new 364-cubic-inch engine had wider carburetor throats, larger intake and exhaust valves, and higher capacity ports and manifolds. Valve lift was increased from 0.378 of an inch to 0.423 of an inch, and the new camshaft had cam contours designed with steeper ramp angles for faster opening and closing. Valve opening duration was increased by five degrees for the intake cams and reduced by five degrees for the exhaust cams. A beefed up crankshaft which had thicker cheeks but shorter main and crankpin journals was adopted. The harmonic balancer was redesigned to obtain greater strength and durability. Pilot diameter was reduced by 0.06 inches to increase the hub section by 0.03 of an inch, giving added strength at the keyway section. The method of piloting the inertia weight and absorbers was revised by piloting the absorber directly to the hub flange instead of through the rivets (as in the 1956 design). It was on this engine that Buick first adopted Delco-Remy's new ignition distributor, with the sliding access window for minor timing adjustments. At the same time, spark plug covers were eliminated, and replaced by resistance-type high-tension cables giving higher voltage at the plug, with a stronger spark. A new starter motor was introduced with, for the first time, an enclosed drive to prevent jamming of the mechanism due to rocks, dirt or ice. Different engine versions were fitted in different 1957 models. The Special had the base version with an 8.0:1 compression ratio for cars with synchromesh transmission. Specials with Dynaflow drive had a higher (9.5:1) compression ratio, which gave the engine an advertised power output of 250 SAE gross hp at 4400 rpm, with a maximum torque of 384 pounds-feet at 2400 rpm. All other 1957 models had an engine advertised as having a compression ratio of 10.0:1, and developing 300 SAE gross hp at 4800 rpm, with a maximum torque of 400 pounds-feet at 3200 rpm.

These engines were carried over into the 1958 models without change, but for 1959 a new version with larger displacement was added, while the 364-cubic-inch unit continued as the base engine. The new power plant had 401-cubic-inch displacement, and was a bored-out and stroked edition of the base engine. The 401-cubic-inch V-8 had a bore of 4.1875 inches and a stroke of 3.64 inches. That's a stroke/bore ratio of 0.87, compared with 0.80 in the original V-8 and 0.88 in the 264-cubic-inch unit, and 0.824 in the still current 364-cubic-inch engine. With a nominal compression ratio of 10.5:1, it was advertised as delivering 325 SAE gross hp at 4400 rpm, with a maximum torque of 445 pounds-feet at 2800 rpm. The 401-cubic-inch V-8 was designated Wildcat and became standard for the 1959 Invicta and Electra series, while the LeSabre received the 364-cubic-inch engine. When the 1962 models were announced, the 364-cubic-inch V-8 was discontinued, and the LeSabre received a detuned version of the 401-cubic-inch unit, rated at 280 SAE gross hp at 4400. At the same time, the nominal compression ratio for the Invicta/Electra engine was reduced to 10.25:1.

The horsepower race had petered out and a return to realism began to permeate the industry. But inflation of horsepower ratings and compression ratio figures was still rampant, if only to avoid shocking the public by taking too sudden a step from fiction to fact. It had to be done gradually. Sales executives feared a loss of face, because publishing honest power output figures would have been tantamount to an admission of having advertised mythical horsepower figures in the past.

For the 1963 models, Buick made a still larger engine optional at an extra cost of $50. Displacement reached 425 cubic inches, which was obtained by boring out the cylinders from 4.188 inches to 4.313 inches, while keeping the same 3.64-inch stroke. This represented the limit of expansion possible within the original cylinder block. The cylinder heads were really not capable of handling the air flow needed for such large displacement. Valve size was no longer compatible with cylinder volume, and the power plant was nicknamed the 'nailhead' engine. Actually, the 425-cubic-inch V-8 had an intake valve-head diameter of 1.875 inches, while the exhaust

2 BARREL CARBURETOR
ON SERIES 40
4 BARREL CARBURETOR
ON SERIES 50-60-70

2 BARREL CARBURETOR
ON SERIES 40
4 BARREL CARBURETOR
ON SERIES 50-60-70

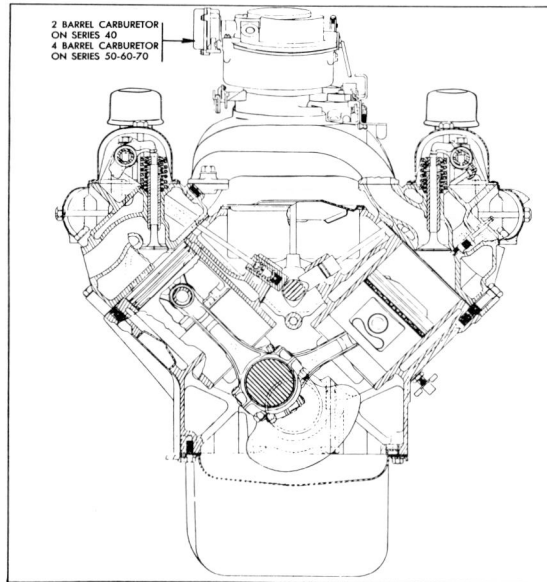

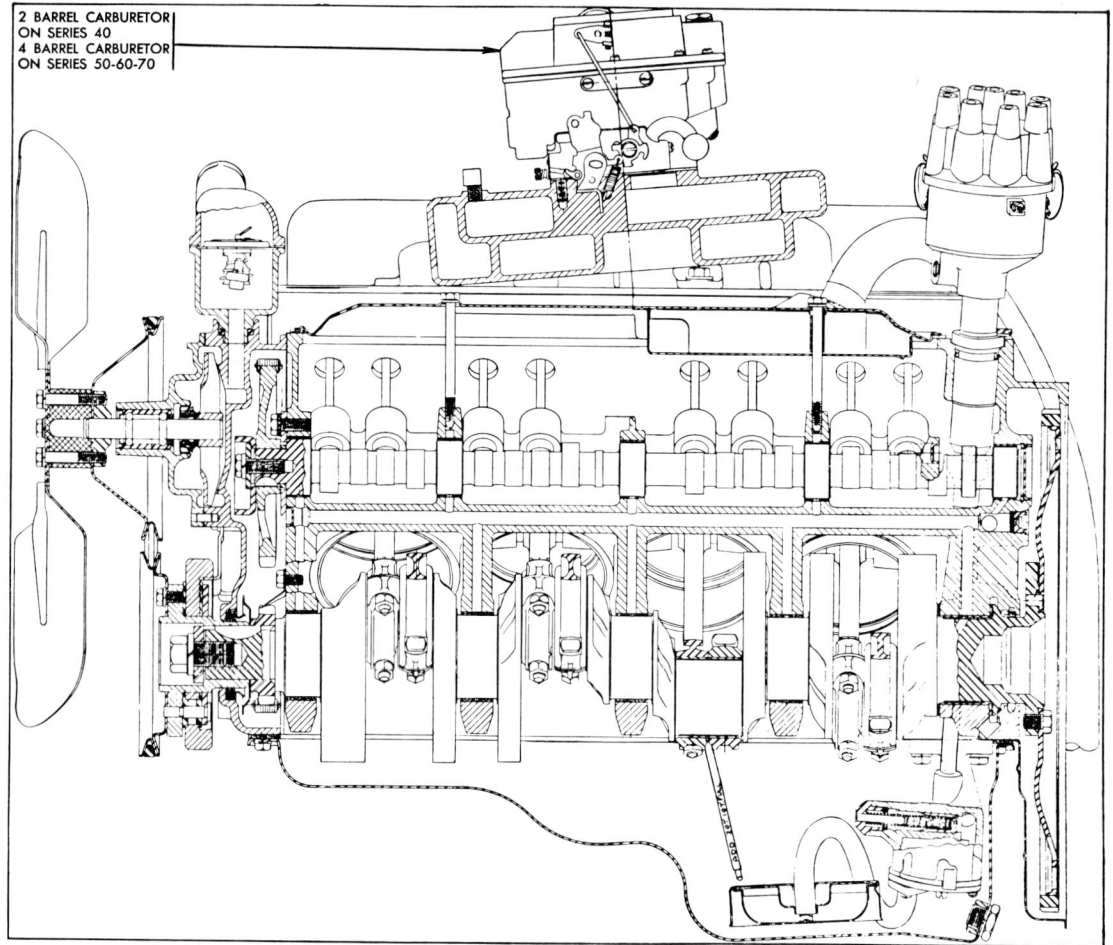

Buick enlarged its V-8 to 364 cubic inches for the 1957 model year, left and right, retaining the central spark plug position and the same valve gear, but altering the valve timing to compensate for the impossibility of increasing valve size. Successive bore and stroke increases were handled without changing bore spacing, crankshaft bearings and valve gear layout. This 364-cubic-inch version was stretched further, first to 401 and finally to 425-cubic-inch displacement.

valve-head diameter was 1.50 inches. The intake valve-head diameter was therefore 43.5 percent of the cylinder bore, compared with an industry average of about forty-five percent. Other companies were still building engines with smaller valves relative to the bore, right down to forty to forty-one percent. But Buick knew that its small valves kept the engine from reaching its potential, and had to make compromises in valve timing that

70

The ultimate version of the original Buick V-8 design was the 425-cubic-inch engine used in the Riviera GS in 1965 and 1966. It was nicknamed 'nailhead' because the valves were too small for the cylinders.

Left, Joseph D. Turlay was Buick's top engine man from the thirties into the fifties, and creator of the Buick V-8's. It was Turlay who designed the aluminum XP-300 engine in 1950. Right, Clifford G. Studaker is now executive engineer for engines at Buick, having devoted practically his whole career to making Buick engines better. The new even-firing V-6 is his 'baby.'

began to hurt the engine's smoothness at low rpm. The main engine modifications, apart from the change in dimensions, were made in the piston rings. Two cast iron compression rings were used, as on the 401-cubic-inch version. But the top ring in the bigger unit was chrome-plated while in the older one, both rings had the Lubrite treatment. The oil control ring for the 425 was chrome-plated steel with a circumferential expander, instead of the uncoated steel ring with hump-type expander used in the 401.

The 425-cubic-inch V-8 was standard in the 1965 Riviera GS and optional in the Wildcat, Electra 225 and Riviera. The Riviera GS engine was equipped with dual four-barrel carburetors and delivered 360 SAE gross hp at 4400 rpm, with a maximum torque of 465 pounds-feet at 2800 rpm. The following year the rating was raised to 370 SAE gross hp—the highest that Buick was ever destined to advertise. The dual four-barrel setup for the

Riviera GS had a progressive throttle linkage that used only the primaries of the front carburetor for all light-load operation, and opened the primaries in the second carburetor at a given speed. For full acceleration, the secondaries in both carburetors opened together. The displacement increase of 103 cubic inches, from the original 322 of 1953 to the final 425 of 1963, was obtained within the basic package size, which had been chosen for compactness rather than its expansion potential. Such design parameters as the cylinder bore spacing, valve spacing, crankshaft-to-camshaft span, main bearing diameter, crankpin diameter and other basic dimensions were unchanged from 1953 through 1966.

CHAPTER 7

During the Rollert Years

BUICK'S ROAD TO RUIN was traced in the fifties. The reasons for the make's loss of its good name were detailed in Chapter Four, and now we can direct our attention to the subsequent recovery.

Rescue was the only possible way out for Buick in 1959. Letting it go down the drain would not be accepted by old-timers with strong links to Buick. Their number included Alfred P. Sloan, GM chairman from 1937 to 1958, who still retained a seat on the board. Harlow H. Curtice, general manager of Buick from 1933 to 1948 and president of General Motors from 1953 to 1958, also sat on the board of directors in 1959. Buick's chief engineer from 1936 to 1951, Charles A. Chayne, was head of the GM Engineering Staff, and not without high-level influence.

Of the new corporate leaders, Chairman Frederic G. Donner and President John F. Gordon, neither were Buick men, but both knew that Buick was not a wreckage. Buick was basically a healthy piece of property. Its good name was what needed restoration, more than the division, its personnel, production facilities, and distribution network. The man chosen to turn Buick around was Edward D. Rollert, who had been general manager of Harrison Radiator Division since 1955. He had been with General Motors since 1934, when he joined AC Spark Plug Division as a student engineer after graduating from Purdue University with a master's degree in chemical engineering. Rollert had advanced to assistant work manager at AC by 1946, when he left GM to become manufacturing manager of the

Elgin Watch Company. Two years later he returned to GM, as production manager for New Departure Division. From 1950 to 1955, he worked in the Buick-Oldsmobile-Pontiac Assembly Division, rounding out his experience to include the complete car.

Back in 1951 General Motors had picked Rollert for the tricky assignment of organizing the company's first dual-purpose plant at Kansas City where output was split between automobiles and military jet planes. This was something that had never been done before. The purpose was to obtain a new dimension in product mix flexibility, with highly diverse products, so that extra capacity would be available for making planes when urgently required, and that with cutbacks in plane orders, there would be additional capacity for building cars. Rollert accomplished this task as smoothly as if the products had been no more different than half-quart and full-quart bottles of beer. Coming to Buick in 1959, Rollert could not make any changes in the basic design and appearance of the cars until the 1963 models went into production. But what he could do was to put mechanical quality back into Buick cars. Extrapolating from his experience of aircraft production, he revolutionized Buick's inspection procedures, test methods, reliability checks, and overall quality control.

From seventh place in 1959, Buick was moved even further down on the ranking list in 1960, as Dodge swept past both Buick and Pontiac to secure sixth place, and Mercury got ahead of Buick, too, putting the Flint-

Buick XP-300 was built in 1951 as a dream car, and was to have considerable influence on the 1959 models. Every part in it was wildly experimental, including engine and chassis, which cannot be said of most subsequent show cars, by Buick or other companies.

based division into an execrable ninth spot. Nevertheless, a few more Americans bought Buicks in 1960, boosting registrations to 267,837 cars, which was not enough to improve Buick's market share but maintained it exactly where it was, at 4.07 percent.

The product was ready-made for Rollert, having been under development for several years. The fact that Buick's recovery was so slow was no reflection on its current cars, but on its past sins. And public opinion, which is instantly swayed by bad news, is slow to react to good news. The 1959 models had been in preparation since mid-1956, when the basic charac-

teristics of all-new Fisher A-, B- and C-bodies were laid down. Buick had to design new frames. Its power train must be adapted to the new models.

Ned Nickles and his design staff had to mold a new kind of Buick identity into the new shapes that all the GM divisions had to share. The first clay models and styling drawings were produced in January 1957. A full-scale mockup was ready in April, and engineering prototypes were ready

LeSabre experimental car of 1951 had same engine as Buick's XP-300 and a different chassis, also built by Buick. Cadillac-type rear fenders clash with sweepspear styling, but the car did have its impact on the design of the 1959 Buicks.

that September. Tool and die orders went out before the end of 1957. Road cars were built and tested during the first half of 1958. Production began in September 1958.

Looking back to the end of August 1957, we see that O. K. Kelley had just replaced V. P. Mathews as chief engineer of Buick. About the same time, Philip C. Bowser was named director of research and development. These two deserve great credit for having carried out the program without a hitch. We have read about the ceaseless efforts of Joe Turlay and Cliff Studaker with their staff to improve the engine, and we have seen how the automatic transmissions evolved under the leadership of Rudolf Gorsky and Kenneth Gage. We know about the tremendous progress achieved in brake engineering by Charles Holton and Frank Daley. One man who had more than perhaps any other to do with tying all the components together into a complete car—and to whom must go more of the honor of making it a *good* car—was Forest McFarland.

McFarland came to Buick in 1954 as assistant chief engineer to work mainly in the fields of automatic transmissions, acoustics and suspension. He was meticulous in his work, and always aimed for perfection. He had an eye for finesse and intricate detail, and worked with extreme accuracy. On top of all that, he had a highly inventive mind. In his career, McFarland took out forty-six patents, involving improvements in engine vibration dampers, overdrives, automatic transmissions, transmission governors, couplings, steering linkages, suspension systems and supercharger drives. Born in 1900, Forest McFarland graduated from Michigan State University in 1921 with an engineering degree, and then took a one-year course at the Michigan State Auto School. Next, he spent two years in an automotive tool shop to get the experience, and in 1924 joined Packard as a draftsman. In his formative years he got the chance to work closely with the guiding genius of Packard engineering, Jesse G. Vincent, and McFarland in turn made his contribution to Packard's excellence over the years. He stayed there until Packard was sold to Studebaker. He had an excellent reputation around De-

troit, and Buick was lucky to get him. Shirrell C. Richey was another assistant chief engineer who helped put his mark on the 1959 Buick. He worked closely with a team of chassis engineers which included Harvey Barkley, H. Mullany, M. E. Weldy, E. G. Peckham, A. C. Lillrose, W. G. Findlater and R. J. Grieve.

A series of Buick 'dream car' prototypes built during the 1950's had considerable influence on the shape and structure of the 1959 production models. First in this series was the XP-300 of 1951. It's significant that Buick was the first GM division to undertake such programs. Ned Nickles says it's because Buick's management has always been more enthusiastic about new things. There was a Buick spirit, almost personified by Harlow Curtice, who was a conservative financial man, but had a wild, uninhibited taste in cars. When GM Styling needed the help of a car division to get something built, Buick was a natural. The men in Flint were always ready to cooperate, and no doubt aimed to benefit from the experience. Compared with Buick, the other GM divisions were introverted, unreceptive, and slow to react. Buick was novelty-oriented. That's why Buick was not only the first to show 'dream cars' publicly, but also built and displayed more experimental cars than Oldsmobile or Cadillac. The initial project actually involved two experimental cars, the XP-300 and LeSabre. Charles A. Chayne took the responsibility for the engineering of both, while Harley J. Earl undertook the styling of the LeSabre, as a task for his personal design office, while the XP-300 was done in the Buick studio under Ned Nickles. LeSabre and XP-300 had the same power train, and the chassis design differed only in detail. Both were built by Buick and both remain strongly identified with Buick.

LeSabre experimental car from 1951 pioneered the panorama windshield and explored new fender lines for cars of very low build. Of its technical features, Buick developed its front suspension for 1957 production, and Opel the rear suspension for 1969.

Cockpit of the 1951 LeSabre prototype is obviously aircraft-inspired and its instrumentation cannot claim to be practical for a car. Umbrella-type handbrake and vertical-slot shift lever have never been used on production-model Buicks.

The XP-300 was a two-passenger open roadster mounted on a 116-inch wheelbase and had an overall length of 192.5 inches. It was 39.1 inches high to the cowl, and 53.4 inches high to the top of the windshield. Ground clearance was 6.6 inches. Total body width was eighty inches. The body had a 28.9-inch front overhang and a rear overhang of 47.6 inches. Its rear track was sixty inches, slightly wider than the 59.1-inch front track. Side by side with the 1951-model production two-door convertible, the XP-300 was nearly two feet shorter and about six inches lower, with about the same width, which made it seem even lower. The frame was a box-type steel structure, with the body welded to it. When the doors were closed, hydraulically operated steel bars slid into place, like the bolts securing the door to a vault, thereby making the doors a structural part of the body and frame assembly. Body panels were heat-treated aluminum panels, which reduced the total weight of the car to 3,125 pounds. The engine was a supercharged aluminum V-8 which will be described in considerable detail in a later chapter dealing with Buick's production-model aluminum engines. The transmission was based on standard Dynaflow components used in a novel arrangement.

Front suspension resembled Buick's standard setup with regard to the use of double A-arms, a long one below and a short one on top. But there the similarity ended. Torsion bars were used instead of coil springs—a design that may have influenced Chrysler. The torsion bars ran straight back from their anchorage points at the lower A-arm pivot shafts to the toeboard frame member. The outer ends of the control arms were secured directly to the steering knuckle via ball joints. This was an idea that Ford was also working on at the time, and placed in production on the 1952 Lincoln, while Buick did not replace its kingpins with ball joints until the 1957 model year.

Rear suspension was of the De Dion type, which can be described as semi-independent. There was no conventional rear axle, but the wheels were connected via a tube that spanned the full width between them, like a dead axle. The drive shafts were open, with double universal joints. Hub carriers were connected to radius arms which ran to anchorage points on the frame cross member ahead of the rear suspension kickup. These radius arms took up the driving thrust. The final drive unit was held in a cast-iron carrier, bolted to the frame, so that driving and braking torque reactions were taken up by the differential carrier first, and ultimately by the frame itself. The Dynaflow transmission was driven via a reduction gear that slowed the rate of rotation by eleven percent relative to engine speed. The final drive ratio was 3.60:1 as the differential combined a pinion with nine teeth and a ring gear with thirty-two teeth. The final drive unit was integrated with the modified Dynaflow transmission, which was attached to the front of the differential carrier. It was an idea called a transaxle, which had never been used on a production Buick but was adopted for the 1961 Pontiac Tempest.

Extra-wide brake drums provided space for double sets of brake shoes. Front brakes were mounted outboard, but the rear drums were carried inboard on the drive shafts, next to the final drive unit. The steering gear came from Saginaw, and was a worm and nut type with recirculating balls, but without power assist. The steering gear had a 17:1 ratio, which gave an overall steering ratio of 18.2:1. The steering column was articulated, with two universal joints and a splined section providing four inches of telescopic adjustment. The steering wheel diameter was eighteen inches, as on contemporary production Buicks. Disc-type pressed-steel 15x6 wheels with standard drop center rims were used, carrying special Firestone 7.10-15 four-ply low-pressure tires. Four hydraulic jacks were permanently installed on the car and operated by an engine-driven hydro-electric system. The jacks were arranged to work in pairs, raising either side of the car, but not both front or both rear wheels.

XP-300 and LeSabre pioneered the panorama windshield. The glass was curved around at the corners so that the A-posts were vertical, and the glass had a tinted band across the top to prevent glare. A Riviera-type rear window could be lowered and raised without folding the soft-top. The top was detachable and meant to be stowed in a separate compartment behind the seat. The rear deck was extremely long, with a sweeping taper leading to a circular tailpiece, resembling the exhaust end of a turbojet engine. But instead of being used for exhaust gases, this circle served to contain a strong backup light. The real exhaust pipes were integrated with two 'bombs' near the center of the rear bumper. A tapered fin was stretched down the center of the deck, concealing the hinges that allowed access to the trunk by side-opening lids, one on each side. The hood and front fenders opened as a unit, tilt-cab fashion, to give access to the engine compartment. The entire front body section was hinged just behind the front bumper, to be raised or lowered by a hydraulic mechanism controlled by the driver.

Louvers on the fenders, filling the panels from aft of the front wheel opening to the rear wheel skirts, were functional. The front section was intended to provide air evacuation from the engine compartment. Louvers on the door were for the extraction of stale air from the interior, and could be opened and closed from inside the car. The grille was inset in an opening in the center of the front bumper, and had vertical bars shaped to present a concave surface. The fender lines were borrowed from the production Buick and modified for a sports car, so that the line dropped steadily from the headlights to the rear bumper. The rear fender flowed out of the body side at a higher level, giving a kickup effect for the rear wheels. The bucket seats could be individually raised or lowered and adjusted forward or backwards by a hydraulic mechanism. Color-matched lap belts were fitted. Hydraulic power side windows were installed, and the doors were opened by push-buttons. Each door contained a storage bin. The instruments were called aircraft-type because they had white figures on a black background—a principle used in night-fighters and known as 'black lighting.' A level-gauge was set to normally show the oil level in the engine sump, but pressing a button would make it give a reading on the fluid level in the Dynaflow transmission.

LeSabre was built from a similar concept, as a two-passenger open roadster, and it had the same panorama-type windshield, and similar di-

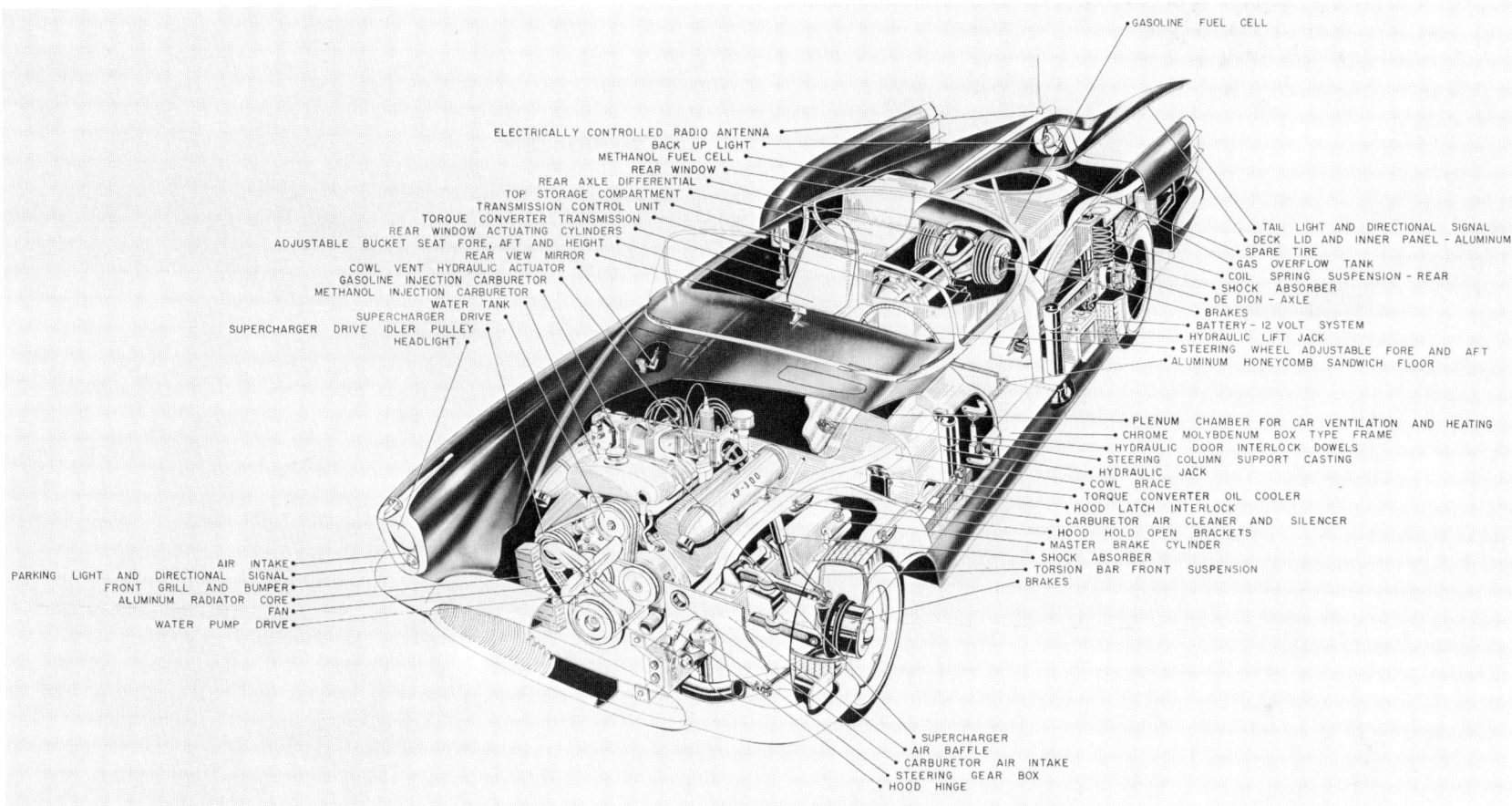

GASOLINE FUEL CELL

ELECTRICALLY CONTROLLED RADIO ANTENNA
BACK UP LIGHT
METHANOL FUEL CELL
REAR WINDOW
REAR AXLE DIFFERENTIAL
TOP STORAGE COMPARTMENT
TRANSMISSION CONTROL UNIT
TORQUE CONVERTER TRANSMISSION
REAR WINDOW ACTUATING CYLINDERS
ADJUSTABLE BUCKET SEAT FORE, AFT AND HEIGHT
REAR VIEW MIRROR
COWL VENT HYDRAULIC ACTUATOR
GASOLINE INJECTION CARBURETOR
METHANOL INJECTION CARBURETOR
WATER TANK
SUPERCHARGER DRIVE
SUPERCHARGER DRIVE IDLER PULLEY
HEADLIGHT

TAIL LIGHT AND DIRECTIONAL SIGNAL
DECK LID AND INNER PANEL - ALUMINUM
SPARE TIRE
GAS OVERFLOW TANK
COIL SPRING SUSPENSION - REAR
SHOCK ABSORBER
DE DION - AXLE
BRAKES
BATTERY - 12 VOLT SYSTEM
HYDRAULIC LIFT JACK
STEERING WHEEL ADJUSTABLE FORE AND AFT
ALUMINUM HONEYCOMB SANDWICH FLOOR

PLENUM CHAMBER FOR CAR VENTILATION AND HEATING
CHROME MOLYBDENUM BOX TYPE FRAME
HYDRAULIC DOOR INTERLOCK DOWELS
STEERING COLUMN SUPPORT CASTING
HYDRAULIC JACK
COWL BRACE
TORQUE CONVERTER OIL COOLER
HOOD LATCH INTERLOCK
CARBURETOR AIR CLEANER AND SILENCER
HOOD HOLD OPEN BRACKETS
MASTER BRAKE CYLINDER
SHOCK ABSORBER
TORSION BAR FRONT SUSPENSION
BRAKES

AIR INTAKE
PARKING LIGHT AND DIRECTIONAL SIGNAL
FRONT GRILL AND BUMPER
ALUMINUM RADIATOR CORE
FAN
WATER PUMP DRIVE

SUPERCHARGER
AIR BAFFLE
CARBURETOR AIR INTAKE
STEERING GEAR BOX
HOOD HINGE

XP-300

Cutaway view of the XP-300 shows the drastically different chassis, with ball-joint front suspension and De Dion-type rear end. Dual-fuel idea has not yet proved practical but is coming closer to reality every day.

mensions. Overall length was fractionally above 200 inches, and overall width was 76.75 inches. The body was 36.25 inches high to the cowl, and the height with raised top was fifty inches. It had Cadillac-type rear fenders, though in deck lid design it resembled the XP-300. The grille was a small oval, set high up at the nose, and blending right into the hood line. An air intake was recessed below the grille. A chrome molding extending from the grille frame ran horizontally above the concealed headlights, curved around the fender, and described an arc right back to the rear wheel opening—a fairly typical sweepspear. As we can see, both LeSabre and XP-300 used

styling elements that were to be repeated in production-model Buicks. The LeSabre chassis had a 115-inch wheelbase. The frame was essentially the same as on the XP-300, but the LeSabre had quite different front and rear suspension systems. At the front end, rubber springs (working in torsion) were used. At the rear end, LeSabre had tapered single-leaf semi-elliptic

Wildcat name was first used for this roadster, which was an experimental car with plastic body, built in 1953. Buick never followed up with an all-plastic-bodied production car, while Chevrolet introduced the Corvette that same year.

Buick Wildcat II appeared in 1954 and was another styling experiment with a plastic body. Smaller and lighter than any postwar production-type Buick, it was built on a 100-inch wheelbase. Its V-8 engine carried four carburetors.

Buick's 1956 Centurion show car introduced another name that would be used for a later production model. It was a plastic-bodied four-seater coupe with practically standard Buick engine and chassis. Rearview mirror was replaced by TV camera.

springs in combination with a De Dion system. The LeSabre name was given to a Buick series in 1959.

The following Buick dream cars had little new in engineering as they were GM Styling prototypes with no new engineering content. The experimental Wildcat of 1953 used a practically standard Buick chassis, shortened to provide the right proportions for a two-passenger convertible. It featured the panorama windshield in nearly the shape as it appeared on the 1954 production models, and its grille design foreshadowed the 1955 models.

Wildcat II, built in 1954, was a smaller and lighter unit built on a one hundred-inch wheelbase. Its overall lines resembled those of the Chevrolet Corvette, and like the Corvette, it used a fiberglass body, with a length of 170 inches. Buick's 1956 'dream car' was called Centurion. It was a two-door closed model with a fully transparent roof, and seating for four. It had a long, sloping hood that descended all the way to a small, horizontal grille. Front fenders rose above hood level and contained recessed head

lamps. Rear fenders incorporated a low canted wing design that spread into the deck lid. The least significant but most talked-about detail was a TV camera imbedded in the deck lid to present the rear view on a TV screen built into the center of the instrument panel, replacing the mirror.

Wildcat III did not appear until 1959, and looked older than the production cars. It had a wide Thunderbird grille and headlights set in the fender tops, almost like the 1952-model production Buicks. It was a four-passenger convertible built on a 110-inch wheelbase, low and sporty, its silhouette recalling the Wildcat II. The most notable feature in its interior was the use of a floor-mounted lever, on the transmission tunnel, to control the Dynaflow.

Judged in retrospect or by the trends of the time, Buick's 1959 styling was nothing if not dramatic. It represented a break with the past and presented visions of the jet age with its strong aerodynamic emphasis. Exterior styling highlights in the 1959 Buick included canted tailfins and fluted rear fenders; front fender lines that swept up from the grille in a wing-like design; compound-curve windshields extending into the roof panels; dual head lamps in stepped 'slant-eye' formation; and a new 'flat-roof' four-door hardtop with wraparound rear window. The new models were significantly lower, with height reductions from 3.1 to 4.8 inches, in comparison with the 1958 models. This was achieved without departing from the use of fifteen-inch wheels.

Above all, the 1959 bodies were clean. Ned Nickles had evolved a shape that could stand on its own, and looked its best when left alone. As a result, the old fear of leaving a large expanse of sheet metal, such as a fender skirt, undecorated, had vanished. From the 1951 LeSabre came the idea of stretching the grille frame into the fenders. Nickles did this by taking the top bar in the grille frame, bending it upwards at a thirty-degree angle on each side, and stretching it to the fender tips, bending it around to the sides, and continuing it in a straight line from the headlight brow to the taillight frame. The same theme was repeated at the rear, stretching a chrome molding along the tops of the tilted tailfins, sweeping down and inwards at the rear end to meet a chrome strip running across the rear edge of the deck lid. There was obvious influence from the 1956 Centurion here. In side view, the fender sculpturing said 'Buick' because of traditions stretching back to 1942. The tailfin line, emerging subtly from the belt line, substituted for the rear fender kickup.

The 1959 grille carried over the theme from the year before, with little chrome squares skewered on horizontal bars, but used far fewer squares, which gave the grille a more open, less elaborate appearance. The 1959 front bumper had a straight, horizontal bar along the top of the face, which supported chrome frames for wide turn signal and parking light lenses. Two vertical bars, recessed and tilted back toward the bottom, held the mounting bracket for the license plate in the center. The lower, recessed bumper face had two openings, shallow but very wide, serving as supplementary air intakes.

Not only had the cars undergone a major redesign, with the most striking styling change in ten years, but a complete set of new model names had been adopted. ''These cars are so new that we *had* to change the names,'' Ragsdale had said when he introduced the 1959 models. The 1959 lineup included seventeen models. LeSabre, the lowest priced series, had five models. It replaced the Special. The Century disappeared again. The Electra, the luxury series, had three models, supplemented by three companion

Buick Wildcat III show car of 1959 failed to attract the same attention that was lavished on the spectacularly new production models, and has been largely forgotten. Nor did it have any bearing on the future trends in Buick product planning.

models in the Electra 225 series. Where did the 225 come from? It was the overall length of the car in inches. It was pronounced two-twenty-five. 'Deuce-and-two-bits' is how it became known in Detroit's black slang a few years later. The Invicta, the middle line, replacing the Super, had five models. All three series included four-door sedans, four-door hardtops and two-door hardtops. Convertibles were two-door models, available in LeSabre, Invicta and Electra 225 series. A four-door Riviera sedan was included in the Electra 225 series, and a two-door sedan was available only as a LeSabre. Both LeSabre and Invicta series included four-door station wagons. The Invicta shared the LeSabre chassis and body but had its own grille and other identification marks. Internally, the LeSabre was known as Series 4400, the Invicta as Series 4600, the Electra as Series 4700, and the Electra 225 as Series 4800.

Despite full knowledge of the structural weakness in the design, the 1959 models continued with the panorama windshield, but the A-post was redesigned so that it curved into the roof from its reverse slant, and the windshield was extended upwards into the roof. All models had vent windows in the front doors. Four-door sedans had one-piece rear door glass,

Styling mockup for the 1959 'Special,' left, was completed in March 1957, and shows the styling concept in its formative stage. Triple taillights were to be replaced by single units and the fender line sharpened. Suggested bumper design was thrown out completely. Frontal aspect of styling mockup for 1959 'Limited,' right, completed in March 1957, came fairly close to actual Electra. The little bombs on the bumper were removed and the motif above the grille simplified and integrated, but the basic theme survived.

and rear quarter windows in the body. On four-door hardtops the rear window wrapped around far enough to meet the door glass at the thin C-post. Two-door sedans and hardtops had one-piece rear side windows. Wide one-piece rear windows for four-door hardtops had round corners and also extended into the roof panel to repeat the windshield design theme. On sedans and two-door hardtops the rear window ended at the C-posts, sweeping down from the rear edge of the roof. On four-door hardtops the C-post was placed at the edge of the rear door. Hardtop station wagons were discontinued at the end of the 1958 model year. The 1959-model Estate Wagon was based on the four-door sedan, with a slanting C-post and fixed rear side windows, plus rear quarter windows ahead of the C-posts. A roll-down tailgate window replaced the former lift-up glass. A third seat, facing forward, was available as an option. Called a 'junior seat' it was unsuitable for persons other than small children due to lack of width, height and legroom.

Increased interior dimensions, compared with the 1958 models, were greatest in the two lower-priced series. The overall lengths of the LeSabre and Invicta were extended by 5.6 inches, with a one-inch increase in wheelbase. At the same time, the Electra was 1.5 inches longer than the Roadmaster, while the Electra 225 was 1.7 inches shorter than the previous

year's Limited. All models had gained about one inch in front and rear seat legroom. This was necessary to cope with the lowered seats and rooflines. Still, differences in headroom showed that much had been sacrificed to styling. On the four-door hardtops, there was a loss of 2.8 inches of headroom from the 1958 models. The LeSabre and Invicta had gained more than three inches in hiproom (over the Special and Super) though the Electra had no noticeable gain in seat width over the Roadmaster. Front seats were lowered about an inch, while rear seats were raised between 1.2 and 2.1 inches. The increase in rear seat height was achieved by using a new depressed floor pan, approximately four inches lower than the door sill.

Lowering the floor was made possible by discarding the old cruciform frame and adopting a new K-type frame. The new frame for the 1959 models was a semi-perimeter type, reaching nearly the full body width in the area ahead of the rear wheels. From a point nearly in the middle of the wheelbase, the side members tapered inwards to a narrower frame section running between the front wheels. Cross members were fitted at front and rear edges, at the front suspension, at the transmission, under the front seat and at the rear suspension. K-type frame construction permitted the engine to be moved forward. This increased the weight on the front wheels, which Buick seized on to claim improvements in handling.

What really improved steering response, ride and roadholding was increased coil spring travel in the front and rear suspension systems, coupled with raised front and rear roll centers. The full four-corner air suspension system had been discontinued at the end of 1958, but a new rear-axle air suspension was offered as an option for all models. A new, improved Saginaw power steering system was lighter and more compact than the unit

Buick LeSabre for 1959 has 'slant-eye' look due to stepped head lamp formation. Front fenders repeat tailfin theme. Dogleg-shaped windshield posts did not do much for vision, but made entry difficult and robbed structure of strength.

K-type frame replaced former straight-girder frame with cross-bracing on the 1959 models. Buick still continued its torque tube drive and all-coil suspension, basically unchanged from 1957. Power unit was called Wildcat 445 and transmission Turbine Drive.

Buick Invicta for 1959 has unique tailfin treatment but taillights look as if they belong on a Ford, not a Buick. Wide rear window with curved glass was a laudable innovation. Invicta shared LeSabre's 123-inch wheelbase.

it replaced. The new design was co-axial, as before, with a positive-displacement vane-type pump employing a rotary valve actuated via a torsion bar. Steering effort was reduced, and so was feedback from the road wheels. With the 1958-type system, a force of two to 3½ pounds was required for small deviations from a straight course, 3½ to four pounds for street corners, four to 4½ pounds for parking. The new system required only one to two pounds of effort for small deviations, two to 2.375 pounds for corners, and no more than 2½ pounds for parking. This was accomplished by increasing fluid flow capacity by seventeen percent at idle, so that delivery was actually lower at higher engine speeds (which usually corresponds to higher vehicle speeds). At the same time, self-centering action was strengthened to improve down-the-road stability. The reliability was improved by reducing the number of hydraulic seals from eighteen to nine, cutting the number of possible leaks in half.

Torque tube drive was continued in 1959, with the driving thrust being taken up by a hefty bracket at the central cross member, right behind the transmission extension. In the 1959 models, Buick offered limited-slip differentials as an option on all models for the first time. Modifications for

1960 included lowering the transmission hump and floor in the front, and raising the seats to chair-height level. A reinforced front stabilizer bar was used to reduce body roll on curves, and rear track bars were reinforced for greater strength. Redesigned shock absorbers were fitted both front and rear. New wheel covers with slots and pressed-steel wheels with vent holes accelerated the air flow over the brake drums, adding to heat dissipation capacity. Power brakes were standard on the 1960 Electra and Electra 225, and optional for the LeSabre and Invicta. A new single transversely mounted muffler served for both single and dual exhaust systems. It was designed to minimize gas flow resistance as well as to silence the exhaust system.

The 1960 Buick had independent heater controls for front and rear seats, and the air conditioner had five outlets, of which three were directionally adjustable. The instrument panel had an adjustable mirror that

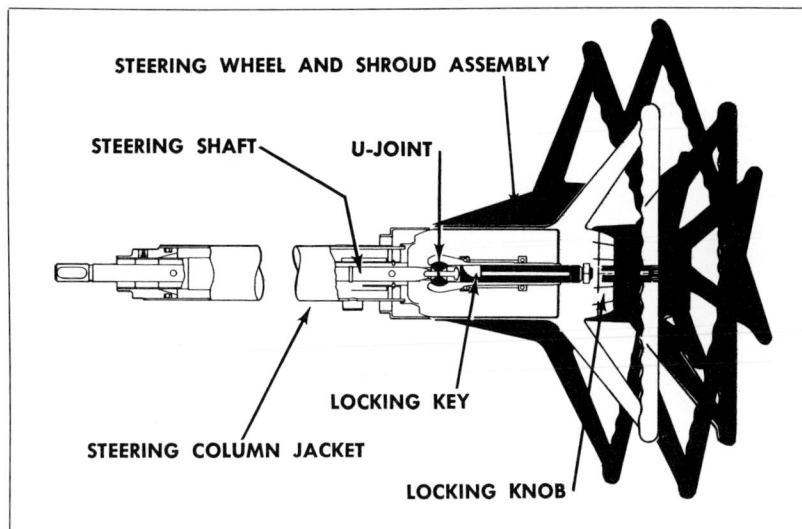

STEERING WHEEL AND SHROUD ASSEMBLY

STEERING SHAFT   U-JOINT

LOCKING KEY

STEERING COLUMN JACKET

LOCKING KNOB

Saginaw steering columns were made to both tilt and telescope. The telescoping motion was assured by a jacket around the steering shaft, and the tilt mechanism was built around a tiny universal joint below the steering wheel hub.

could be tilted for drivers of different height. A new option was the twilight sentinel, a device that automatically turned on the head lamps when dusk set in, and turned them off when daylight increased. "These 1960 models are the most reliable Buicks ever built," said Rollert, "quality in manufacture, plus our sculptured styling and fresh new features, make these the most outstanding cars we have ever produced."

Perhaps the most striking thing in the frontal aspect of the 1960 models was that the vertical panel surmounting the grille had been eliminated. Instead, the hood swept right down to the grille, which was a very low design with concavely curved vertical bars, reminiscent of the XP-300. Here, however, the grille was not a central ellipse, but a split rectangular design, carrying a large ringed Buick emblem in the center and ending at the side-by-side dual headlights. The fender panels rose from the hood at the front, blending into a congruous shape at cowl level after starting the fender with a wing-like extension, inherited from the 1959 models but toned down somewhat. It was said of the 1960 models that the front was cleaned up, and that's possibly true. But it's also true that the clean sides from the year

before were treated with several styling gimmicks that only destroyed the coherence of the overall shape.

For 1960 the side sheet metal was a strange mixture of curves and creases. The front fender line crossed the belt line at the A-post and continued in linear fashion to a circular pod containing a large-diameter tail-light lens. This line was a crease in the door and fender panels, and not highlighted by chrome. Below the front fender line was a torpedo sculpture in line with the head lamps, tapering off to a point in the front door panel. Further down was a horizontal accent line, with a chrome molding running from the front wheel opening to the rear bumper. It was uninterrupted by the rear wheel opening because the sheet metal covered the top part of the hub cap. As on the 1959 models, the slanting tailfin emerged from the belt line, starting at the A-post and growing in section as the fender line crease swept lower and lower. The fin line did not rise but was strictly horizontal. The Buick ventiports, missing from the 1958 and the 1959 models, were brought back in 1960, taking the form of stylized louvers. They were nonfunctional and no more than skin deep.

Buick's 1961 models had new skin again. Gone was the wild side sculpturing from the year before, and gone were the tailfins. This was a return to sobriety, but some earlier styling ideas were used to underline the Buick identification. The grille was a reasonably discreet type of mouth-organ design, with side-by-side dual head lamps on either side. The bumper was a throwback to 1959, with overriders on either side of the license plate, and even to 1958, with turbojet engine pod symbols in the upper corners, stretching back to the wheel openings. The belt line was straight and unbroken, from the front fender to the deck lid. The front fender tips came to a point, taking the rocket theme from the 1958-model rear fenders and stretching it out over the whole length of the body. Oval ventiports were mounted inside the 'rocket' sculpture at cowl level. A third horizontal line was marked by a chrome molding, running from the rear door panel to the top of the rear bumper. The tail end had a Z-profile, due to a concave profile in the vertical panel at the rear end of the deck lid. The taillights were moved inboard from the fenders. The 1961 station wagon bodies were revised, eliminating the sedan-type slanting C-post and stretching the rear side glass in one piece from rear door to tailgate frame. Buick continued the horizontal speedometer, but introduced a new and very elegant two-spoke steering wheel with a full horn ring.

Without doubt the most significant engineering news for 1961 was that a new true cruciform frame had been adopted for the 1961 Electra 225 series. Going from front to rear, the side members ran close in to provide engine mounts, and then tapered further in to link up around the propeller shaft, and separate again on the approach to the rear axle. The splaying continued until the frame reached full width aft of the rear wheels. There

Buick Electra four-door hardtop from 1960 received a cleaner front end, with side-by-side head lamps, while side sculpturing became increasingly complicated. All series had 'dogleg' A-posts and panorama windshields.

were cross members at the extreme front and rear, at the front and rear suspension points, and under the transmission. With the adoption of this frame, the Electra 225 abandoned torque tube drive and received an open propeller shaft. This broke with Buick traditions going back more than fifty years. That entailed a completely new rear suspension system, with radius arms to take up the driving thrust and torque arms to control torque reactions. This was achieved with an efficient three-link design that gave the axle freedom to move up and down during wheel deflections, but prevented it from moving in other planes. The same coil springs and track rod were retained. As a major step forward in electrical engineering, Buick adopted alternators on both major-line cars and compacts for the 1963 model year.

Rollert's management was beginning to pay off in 1961, when Buick registrations in the U.S. climbed to 290,623 and the market share came within an ace of five percent (4.96 to be exact). In the years of general prosperity that followed, the national car market expanded from 5.85 million units in 1961 to 6.9 million in 1962, 7.6 million in 1963, 8.1 million in 1964, and 9.3 million in 1965. Buick's sales recovered, slowly but surely, and the division again secured what must be called a 'fair' share of the market. The ranking list for 1961 shows Buick in seventh place, with Mercury sixth, Oldsmobile fifth, Pontiac fourth and Rambler third. Buick built its ten-millionth car on February 8, 1960, and its eleven-millionth on December 28, 1962. Buick's market share went up to 5.76 percent in 1962, with 400,267 cars registered, moving it one place up on the ranking list,

which was completely upset, and now reading, from the top: Chevrolet-Ford-Pontiac-Rambler-Oldsmobile-Buick. Buick moved into fifth place in 1963, as American Motors failed to increase production enough to maintain its penetration in an expanding market. Buick secured a 6.01-percent market share, with registrations of 454,237 cars, just over 20,000 units behind Oldsmobile, and 25,000 units ahead of Rambler.

A slight reverse hit Buick's recovery in 1964, when Plymouth took fifth place behind Oldsmobile by a margin of less than 12,000 cars over Buick. Buick's 481,043 registrations were equivalent to a 5.96-percent market share that year, which means that despite a sales increase of 26,806 cars, Buick lost 1/20 of a percent in market penetration. Key factors in the recovery were Buick's entry in the compact car field, with the revived Special as a 1961 model, and the launching of a personal-luxury car, the Riviera, as a 1963 model. The American industry had watched imported automobiles carve out a disturbingly generous slice of the market for themselves, from a modest one-half of a percent as late as 1953 to over ten percent in 1959. The compacts were designed specifically to recapture that segment of the market, and the first wave of compacts went on sale in the fall of 1959 as 1960 models. They were the Chevrolet Corvair, Ford Falcon and Plymouth Valiant. Imported car penetration sank to 7.5 percent in 1960. Then came

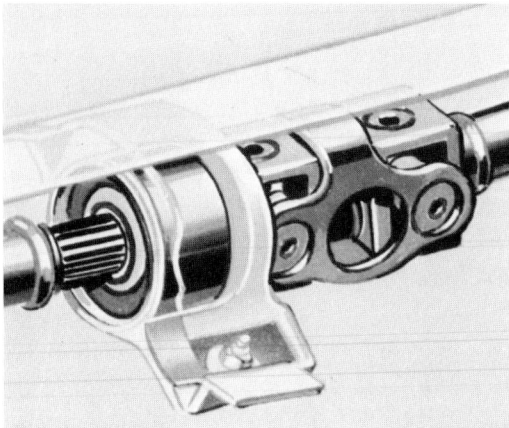

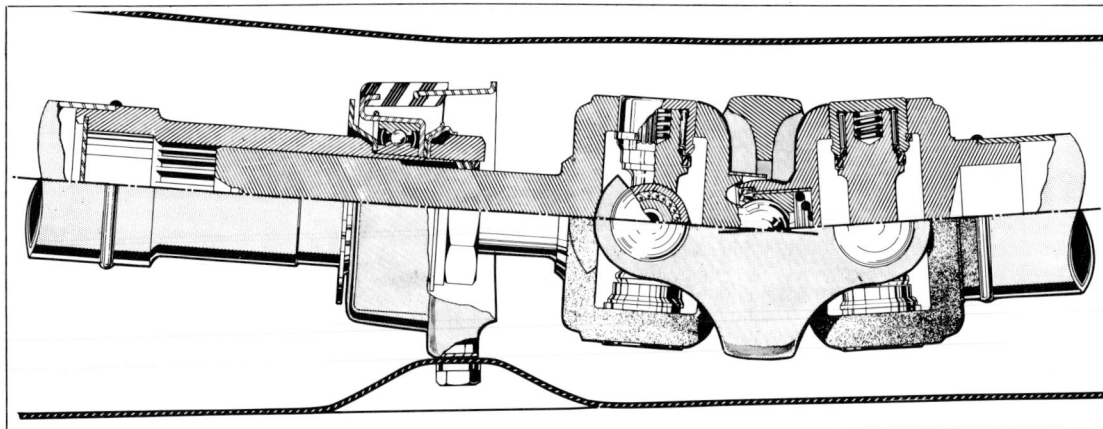

Left, when the Electra 225 changed from torque tube drive to the open propeller shaft, the constant-velocity universal joint was retained. Ahead of the joint is a center-bearing anchored in the frame. On the 1961 models, right, Buick adopted constant-velocity universal joints for the propeller shaft (still enclosed in torque tube). This design, with back-to-back universal joints, effectively canceled the speed variations as the shaft revolved.

the second wave of domestic compacts, including the Buick Special, and the foreign-car market share was depressed to the five-percent level in 1962 and 1963. The Riviera had only an indirect role to play in the market place. It was intended as a prestige-builder only and was outside the sales race. It was not conceived as a direct competitor to Ford's Thunderbird, whose annual sales were about 70,000 cars. Buick restricted Riviera production to 40,000 cars a year. This was a conscious effort to cultivate a certain exclusivity, arising from the sensible reasoning of Buick's national sales director, Roland S. Withers. His idea was to make people want it, but to keep it in short supply. Customers would have to wait in line for the Riviera, but while they were doing that, the Riviera provided a lot of showroom floor traffic, and helped sell other Buicks. The stories of the origin and evolution, engineering and styling, production and marketing, of the Special and Riviera will be told in separate chapters. At the moment we are concerned with the total picture of Buick Motor Division.

Buick had thirty models in 1963, up from twenty in 1960, twenty-one in 1961 and twenty-six in 1962. Ned Nickles had been transferred from the Buick studio to the corporate advanced styling office under the new vice president in charge of GM Styling, William L. Mitchell, who succeeded Harley J. Earl on his retirement in 1958. Mitchell had been chief designer of the

Cadillac studio from 1937 to 1953, when he was named assistant director of GM Styling and groomed for taking over Earl's position. Born on July 2, 1912, in Cleveland, Ohio, Mitchell had attended the Carnegie Institute of Technology and taken further studies at the Art Students League. He came to GM Styling in 1935 as a designer. He is personally credited with the styling of the 1938 Cadillac 60 Special, which was a trendsetting model. Later, Mitchell has been identified with the shapes that went into production as the Chevrolet Corvair, Buick Riviera and Corvette Sting Ray. William Lange became head of the Buick studio in 1958, to replace Nickles. But within a year he had been replaced by Stanley Parker as chief designer, and the youthful Henry Haga as senior designer. Mitchell kept moving his personnel around, and in 1961 transferred Parker to Cadillac and Haga to Chevrolet. Then Bernard M. Smith served as chief designer of the Buick studio for a two-year period starting in the middle of 1961. He was succeeded by David R. Holls whose influence first showed up in the strikingly new 1965 models. The creations of the teams headed by Lange, Parker and Smith had largely failed to present a strong Buick identity. The senior-series Buicks had adopted a 'corporate' look, as if these designers had no clear idea of what constituted a true Buick grille, Buick fender lines or Buick rear end appearance.

Even if the Buick silhouette showed little change from 1961 through 1964, several important changes were made in body engineering and design. For the 1961 models, GM retreated from the panorama windshield and adopted an A-post that lined up with the windshield slant except for a slight arc backwards into the base at the cowl. On the 1962 models, Buick returned to a sail-panel type of C-post, and lengthened the rear deck area. All Electra models were now labeled Electra 225. Four-door hardtops had

no window behind the one-piece rear door glass, except for a six-window model in the Electra series masquerading under the name of the Riviera sedan. Regular sedans had a rear quarter window also. Side sculpturing on the 1962 models was strictly horizontal. The real belt line was a sheet metal crease emerging from the front fenders and marking the top of the door panels, to blend into the rear fenders aft of the C-post. Below the belt line was a chrome molding running the full length of the body, bending into the head lamp housings in front and descending into the bumper at the rear. An accent line ran straight back from the lip over the front wheel opening, partnered by a second accent line about five inches lower. The lower accent line was a sheet metal crease, marked by a chrome strip on some models for all or part of its length, and unmarked on others.

Typically, the 1962 grille was low and wide, with wide frame bars top and bottom and a heavier accent bar in the middle. Horizontal bars filled the rest, separated by a large circular Buick emblem in the middle. The grille face was not straight, but came to a point in the middle, so that the grille-work had two sides receding toward the head lamps which were arranged side by side, each pair having a narrow separation panel between the two lenses. Taillights were removed from the rear fenders and contained in the panel below the deck lid. This was a major change, made in search of a new Buick rear end theme, as the 1960 models had used circular tail lamps, and the 1961 design prepared for the transition by introducing a rectangular frame and lens, arranged horizontally, and extending inwards from the fender tails. In the 1962 design the lenses were still lower and much wider, being separated only by the BUICK lettering on the deck lid.

Descended from three styling prototypes, the Wildcat name was introduced as a sports coupe in the Invicta series for the 1963 model year. The following year, Buick discontinued the Invicta, and the whole mid-level se-ries was renamed Wildcat. On the 1963 models the A-post was straight, and the break between windshield and roof was sharpened. Body sides were cleaned up, with a straight horizontal crease in the sheet metal from the front wheel opening to the tail of the rear fender. Another accent line ran horizontally from the head lamp brow to the middle of the front door, where it dipped and blended into the flat surface just above the mid-level crease. There was also a lower crease, just above wheel hub level, to emphasize the lowness of the design. The grille pattern was reinforced with a mouth-organ arrangement of horizontal bars sectioned at intervals by recessed vertical bars, and the grille theme was extended to the small panels separating the head lamps within each pair. At the rear end, the taillights returned to the fender tips, and a polished aluminum panel served to underline the edge of the deck lid.

Grilles on the 1964 models were full-width designs incorporating the head lamps, with six horizontal bars in the foreground, interspersed with recessed vertical bars. The grille was slightly pointed, as before, and Buick's three-shield emblem was positioned in a chrome ring at the center. On the body sides, the top accent line disappeared and the belt line was emphasized, running as a straight, horizontal line for the full length of the car. The front fender tips were more firmly defined, with a vertical line outside the head lamp clusters, tilting back forty-five degrees at the top. Below, the bumper profile bent backwards to create an impression of symmetry. Front wheel openings were dominated by a horizontal lip. This theme was repeated at a lower level for the rear wheel openings on the LeSabre and Wildcat, while the Electra 225 was fitted with spats in the rear fenders, and a straight unbroken chrome molding running at door sill level from the front wheel opening to the rear bumper. Taillight lenses remained in the rear fender tips, heavily accented units with a strong vertical theme. The rear panel below the deck lid continued the brushed aluminum strip, which now carried a Buick emblem in the middle. A new instrument panel was adopted for 1964, with a welcome return to a circular speedometer, set in the upper left area of the instrument cluster, matched by an equally large dial on the right containing the fuel gauge and warning lights. The radio was set in the center, with a big glovebox on the right. The steering wheel continued the two-spoke design, but the horn ring was abandoned in favor of a push-bar imbedded in the steering wheel spokes.

Drastic changes were in preparation for 1965, in both engineering and styling. Since the last big change, with the 1959 models, Buick had a new engineering team. The chief engineer who shepherded the 1959 models from the drawing board to the production stage was Oliver K. Kelley, none other than the man who was behind the original Dynaflow. Kelley was an engineer's engineer, but his bent was not the administrative type of work that a divisional chief engineer so easily gets bogged down in. He was not happy when he was separated from the actual hardware or from the drawing board. He had no experience in manufacturing, and could not get used to the Buick timetable, where all the engineering must be finished at the start of the year if production is to begin in August. He was used to working five years or more away from an actual production schedule, and that was his main problem at Buick. He made it his most important task at Buick to find a man for his own office, so he could return to the Engineering Staff. Still, it took him two years to pick an experienced engineer that he thought competent enough to handle the day-to-day technical business at Buick. And he stole him from Oldsmobile. The man was Lowell A. Kintigh, a career man who had then been with General Motors for thirty years. Kintigh came to Buick in December 1959, as chief engineer. Kelley then left Buick, worked at the Engineering Staff for six years, and served for one year as executive assistant to the vice president of engineering before retiring in 1967.

Kintigh was a tall, quiet-spoken engineer, and known inside GM as a man who knew every facet of the business. Born in Goshen, Indiana, in 1906 and an engineering graduate from Purdue University, Kintigh had joined the GM Research Laboratories in 1929 as a junior dynamics engineer. After a year's time he was transferred to Oldsmobile as a dynamometer operator. Rising through the ranks of Oldsmobile's engineering staff, he was promoted to staff engineer in 1940. Kintigh was assigned as a project engineer in ordnance at Oldsmobile in 1941 and worked on military projects until 1945, when he was given a title as experimental engineer and returned to automobile development. Oldsmobile's technical boss, Jack Wolfram, made Kintigh his assistant chief engineer in May 1949, and he served in that capacity for ten years.

One of the first things Kintigh did after arriving at Buick was to make McFarland executive assistant chief engineer. Joe Turlay had retired, and Cliff Studaker became top engine designer. Phil Bowser retained his title as director of research and development but was also given the rank of assistant chief engineer. Rollert had placed James R. Gretzinger in charge of reliability and quality control, and made Robert L. Kessler general manufacturing manager in 1961. As soon as Buick could finance improvement and further expansion of the production facilities out of its own profits, Rollert channeled all available funds into tooling and manufacturing equipment. When the first compact Special went on sale, it was produced only by the B-O-P Assembly Division, and not at all by Buick. But Buick started a new assembly line in its own Flint plant in 1962, to build compact cars on the same line where the large Buicks were made. Two years later the plant was expanded again, adding a second assembly line for the senior series which was to be used for the Wildcat and Riviera.

Fisher B- and C-bodies for 1965 introduced a new style, with increased front overhang, a spectacular rear fender kickup, and a very fast roofline on the two-door models. The new bodies were engineered for extra torsional rigidity, incorporating a number of strategically located reinforcements. These techniques had been developed through Fisher Body Division's experience with unit-construction bodies. The new body structures allowed the frames to be highly flexible, relying on the body for torsional strength rather than the other way around. The idea was to allow the frame to flex and to isolate it from the body by using fewer body mounts. The Buick had ten major weight-carrying body mounts, all concentrated within the wheelbase. Other body mounts were simply steady-rests for the body and did not carry load. A full perimeter type of frame was adopted, with straight side members right under the door sills. It was in this section that the main body mounts were located. The side members were thinner and ran closer together between the rear wheels, and in the forward section of the frame, they closed in on the cross member carrying the engine and front suspension system. There was only one other cross member, located ahead of the rear axle, tying together the spring housings for the rear suspension system. All models adopted the open propeller shaft drive line from the Electra and Riviera, combined with a four-link rear suspension system.

The 1965 Buick lineup consisted of thirty-nine models including twenty-four in the senior size, fourteen intermediates and one specialty car. LeSabre and Wildcat shared the B-body and a 123-inch wheelbase, while the Electra 225 used the C-body and a 126-inch wheelbase. The LeSabre line was split in two levels, LeSabre plain and LeSabre Custom. The Wildcat series was split into three levels: baseline Wildcat, Wildcat Deluxe and Wildcat Custom. The Deluxe, however, was dropped before the start of the 1966 model year. The plain Electra had been discontinued at the end of the 1962 model year; after which all Electras were Electra 225's. This series still had two levels for 1965, Electra 225 and Electra 225 Custom.

However, there was no station wagon in Buick's senior series in the 1965 model year. In 1964 Buick dealers had sold only 7,500 of the big wagons, compared with over 30,000 intermediate wagons. As a result, the big Buick accounted for less than one percent of America's wagon market, while the Special took about 3.5 percent. The new strategy must have worked, for Buick's share of the wagon market increased from 4.34 to 4.62 percent in 1965, after the demise of the big wagon.

The 1965 senior series styling featured a sober side treatment. The belt line was straight except for a rear fender kickup, which started aft of the door on the two-door models, and in the middle of the rear door on four-door models. The kickup, of course, was inspired by the Riviera. There were two accent lines, a crease in the sheet metal from the head lamp brow to the taillights, and an indentation all along the door sill, blending with the lips on the front and rear wheel openings. Bumpers went to a W-design, meaning that they came to a front point in the center, retracted to a point inboard of the side-by-side head lamps, and jutted forward again to the fender edges, where their side extensions faired into body panel cutouts and ended at the front wheel openings. Rear bumpers carried the same W-theme, where taillights were split into two horizontal lenses on each side filling the outer wing areas of the W-shape. Grilles were prominently horizontal, with a W-line on top, to provide unity with the bumper. A vertical center post was used in all three series, with two horizontal center bars to form a low and wide cross. Thin horizontal bars, recessed and subdued, filled the areas around the cross. On the Wildcat, a chrome circle carried the three-shield Buick emblem. LeSabre and Electra 225 had ventiports along the cowl, just below the body crease, but they were missing from the Wildcat, which instead had a 'waste-gate' louver design in the front fender skirt. All models had vent windows in the front doors, and none had rear-quarter windows. Four-door models had one-piece rear door glass, and two-door models had rear side windows that rolled down into the body panels. Windshields had a very slight curvature, almost a uniform arc all the way across, and the rear windows were one-piece curved glass, full-width but with no hint of a wraparound.

The 1965 Buicks were a sensation in the showroom and set a very hot sales pace. Deliveries were seriously delayed due to a sixty-day strike at the

Edward D. Rollert, left, must get the main credit for Buick's recovery in the 1960's. Buick people describe him as a 'straight guy' to work for, and the corporation took notice of his accomplishments and promoted him away from Buick. Lowell A. Kintigh, right, was a thorough engineer who put together a fine team of technical people in Flint but had little direct influence on the product. On leaving Buick, he went into one of the corporation's top engineering posts.

start of the model year, which was made up for by a lot of two-shift work during the winter. It was to be a very good year for Buick in the market place, but the year also brought another event that was much regretted by Buick's entire staff. Buick lost Rollert in July 1965, when he was made group vice president in charge of the Car & Truck Group. The corporation gave him the additional responsibility of the Body & Assembly Group in 1966; and then promoted him to head of the Operations Staff in November 1967 (succeeding Edward N. Cole). When Semon E. Knudsen resigned from the corporation in January 1968, Rollert took over his post as vice president in charge of the Overseas Operations, Non-Automotive, and Defense Group. While on a hunting trip in South Dakota in November 1969, he had a heart attack and died. The dynamo from Crete, Illinois, was burned out at the age of fifty-seven.

CHAPTER 8

From Aluminum V-8 to Cast Iron V-6

WEIGHT SAVING BECAME a primary consideration when Buick was developing its first compact car. It was natural, therefore, that the engineers should be attracted to the possibility of using an aluminum engine in the 1961 Special. Aluminum weighs about one-third as much as cast iron. But aluminum does not have the same strength, so thicker walls are needed. Therefore the aluminum block would weigh half of an iron block and not one-third, and alumunum cylinder heads would not be lighter than half the weight of iron heads. Since many other parts and ancillary equipment would remain unchanged, all one can realistically hope to achieve by going to aluminum engine construction is a weight-saving of one-third, but that's still very impressive.

Aluminum has other advantages, too. Its thermal conductivity is three times greater than that of iron. That holds a promise for better engine cooling. Aluminum is more easily formed by casting or forging than iron. Machining aluminum is faster than boring, drilling, honing, milling or turning iron. Those facts indicate some potential for savings in manufacturing costs.

However, aluminum as an engine material also has some problems. It has a higher coefficient of thermal expansion than iron, which can lead to mechanical disintegration if the aluminim parts are mismatched with other components in the same unit. Aluminum has less resistance to wear by friction, and is incompatible with itself in the sense that one can't run alumi-

num pistons up and down in an aluminum cylinder for very long. That means treating the aluminum surface in some way would be necessary, either by chrome-plating the cylinder bore, or inserting steel or iron cylinder liners. Corrosion becomes a problem any time water and aluminum get together, and because of the dynamic character of coolant flow in an auto engine, there is a risk of metal damage by cavitation.

Finally, there is cost. Aluminum is a far more expensive raw material than iron, on a pound-per-pound basis. Since fewer pounds of aluminum are needed, the disadvantage is somewhat diminished. One could hope to offset the remaining cost disadvantage by developing new casting techniques and speeding up the machining processes, but no one at the time had any proof of its being possible.

It is perfectly true that Buick had a lot of experience with aluminum. During World War II Buick operated an aluminum foundry in Flint, producing vast numbers of cylinder heads for aircraft engines. Buick also machined the cylinder heads and assembled the engines. But these were air-cooled engines, and Buick had no bank of knowledge concerning what happens to aluminum when its surfaces are exposed to water. Still, Buick decided on aluminum for its new small V-8, and committed itself to mass production of aluminum engines.

The origins of Buick's aluminum V-8 go back to 1950, when Charles A. Chayne decided to produce two show cars with advanced engineering as well as styling: XP-300 and LeSabre. His reasons for choosing a small aluminum V-8 become clear when one considers the styling requirements. With a short hood and a low hood line, there just wasn't enough room in the engine compartment for a conventional unit with enough horsepower to meet the performance targets. The solution was arrived at step by step. First the block had to be small, which meant small displacement (215 cubic inches). Secondly, lightweight materials had to be used wherever possible. That meant aluminum for the cylinder block and crankcase. To raise power output, the only possible answer was advanced technology. To Chayne, that meant hemispherical combustion chambers with splayed valves and high compression. It also meant supercharging and a special carburetor designed to mix gasoline and methanol in varying proportions according to speed and load. It was Joseph D. Turlay, head of the engine design group at Buick, who was given the task of translating Chayne's rough sketches into an actual design.

Turlay made an initial design which progressed into the mockup stage. But it turned out to be about six inches too tall to fit under the hood of the silhouette the stylists were projecting. What could be done? There are only three possible approaches to making a lower engine. The first is to redesign the basic unit, such as going to a 120-degree or a 180-degree V-angle. This approach was rejected as it would have meant a wider engine, resulting in installation difficulties due to wheel housing and steering gear interference. The second approach is to drop the engine closer to ground level, which tends to expose the crankcase and flywheel to greater risk of damage. The third approach is to remove all auxiliary equipment that adds to engine height, and space it out on the side, below or behind.

Turlay chose a combination of the second and third approaches. His solutions are worthy of attention, for first he reduced the size of the flywheel without giving up much weight. Knowing that bronze was heavier than iron or steel, he went to bronze for the flywheel material. Its cost made it an unacceptable proposition for a production car, but for a 'dream car' there was no objection to the use of high-priced materials. The high tensile strength of bronze, together with its high specific gravity, makes it an ideal flywheel material for high-speed engines.

At one stage Turlay considered dry-sump lubrication, which was common on racing cars, to eliminate the oil pan and reduce engine height. But this would have necessitated a separate oil reservoir, and the underhood area was going to be too crowded for that. So he came up with a compromise. He used a very shallow oil pan, with a tray to collect the oil, placed with just enough clearance from the crank throws to avoid metal-to-metal contact. The combination of this windage-tray sump and the bronze flywheel contributed about three inches towards the desired lowering. The

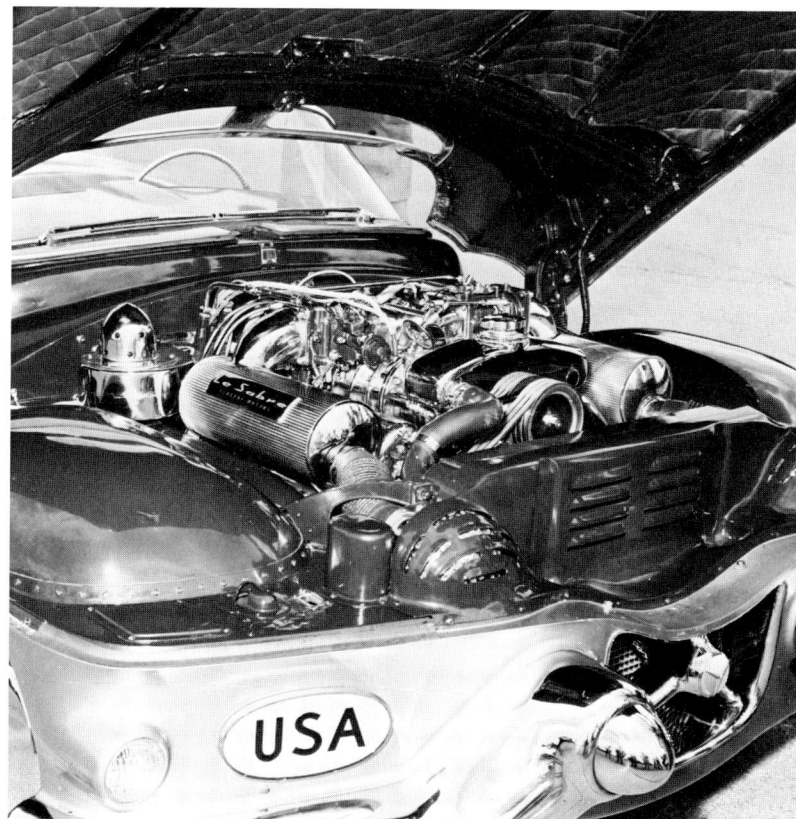

Supercharged aluminum V-8 engine installation in 1951 experimental car called LeSabre. Mechanically the car is a pure Buick project. The engine did not act as a forerunner for the production-type aluminum engine, which had corporate roots.

rest was done by rethinking the whole cylinder block head and manifold combination in terms of height reduction and rearranging the supercharger and carburetor mounting. Next, Turlay integrated the intake manifold with the top of the engine block, which resulted in a two-piece engine construction method. The upper unit, containing the manifold, also held the camshaft and valve lifters. The lower unit was the basic cylinder block and

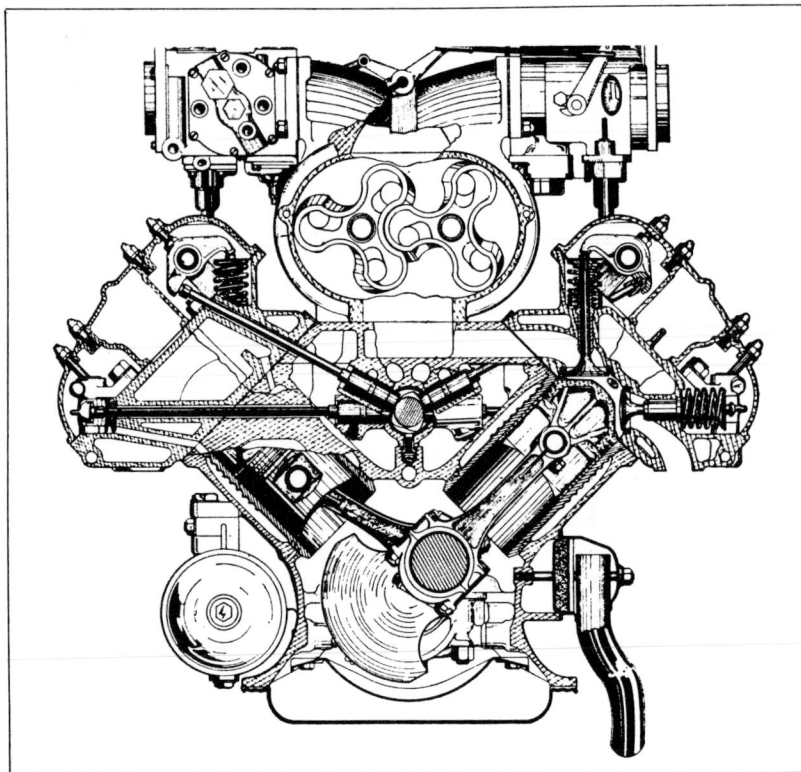

Cross section of XP-300 engine shows unusual valve gear layout with pushrods in four planes, intake manifold depressed into block valley to make room for supercharger and carburetors, and windage tray below crankshaft.

exhaust valves were opened by rocker arms mounted on eight separate stub shafts running at ninety-degree angles to the camshaft. The intake valve rocker arm shaft ran lengthwise on top of the cylinder head in the normal manner. The camshaft was driven by chain from the front of the crankshaft and had cam profiles designed for crankshaft speeds up to 6500 rpm. Regardless of the high-performance image for this engine, it was designed for speeds considerably below those of modern racing engines, and valve size, port configuration and cam-profiles were conservatively set. It was even able to use self-adjusting zero-lash hydraulic valve lifters.

The carburetors were pressurized, aircraft-type instruments made by Bendix-Eclipse, replacing the usual float-chamber type. One carburetor supplied a gasoline mixture and the other a methanol-saturated gas. The gasoline carburetor did all normal work alone up to about 2500 rpm, after which the methanol carburetor would come in and supply the needed fuel-supply boost for acceleration or very high-speed operation. The supercharger was placed on top of the manifold, receiving the mixture from the carburetors. The supercharger was a three-lobe Roots-type blower, as used for Detroit Diesel engines, driven by triple belts. The engine had a 10:1 compression ratio, and the supercharger boost raised manifold pressure at 5000 rpm to 18.2 psi.

With equal bore and stroke of 3.25 x 3.25 inches the engine had 215.7-cubic-inch displacement. Wet cylinder liners were used, which means they were inserted directly into the coolant space and not into outer cylinder bores. The liners were made of Ni-resist iron with an unusually high expansion coefficient. The forged-steel crankshaft ran in five main bearings. The upper halves of the main bearings were backed up by steel inserts, and the lower halves had forged steel caps, cross-bolted in place. Pistons were internally ribbed for extra strength and the connecting rods were made of forged steel.

Each cylinder head was an aluminum casting incorporating fully machined hemispherical combustion chambers, with the spark plugs located at the top, facing the center of the piston crown. Aluminum-bronze valve guides and steel valve seat inserts were used, and exhaust valves had hollow stems filled with sodium for better cooling. Special laminated steel cylinder head gaskets were used to withstand the very high combustion pressures. Rocker covers and spark plug covers were made of aluminum, but the collector-type exhaust manifolds were fabricated from stainless steel. The engine weighed 550 pounds, or nearly 250 pounds less than the contemporary Roadmaster engine. The engine was named XP-300 because of its target output, 300 hp at 5000 rpm. Actually it was found to give as much as 335 hp in dynamometer tests.

In a parallel but unconnected effort, the GM Engineering Staff began a

crankcase, containing main bearings and cylinder liners. In the final design, engine height was brought down to twenty-seven inches overall.

Valve gear design was planned around a single central camshaft, with four rows of pushrods to overhead valves laid out in four different planes. The valves were positioned at an included angle of ninety degrees to each other, so that intake valves were vertical to the ground and the exhaust valves horizontal. This layout necessitated routing the exhaust valve pushrods through holes drilled in the block in the spaces between the cylinders. The research and development program on aluminum engines in 1951, and Buick became involved at an early date by serving as a prime supplier of parts. First, the GM Engineering Staff designed a 253-cubic-inch aluminum V-8 and built several test engines that were installed in Chevrolet cars, beginning in 1952. Another series of test engines relied mainly on Buick-made aluminum parts, but used the crankshaft and connecting rods of the 283-cubic-inch Chevrolet V-8. After a late start Buick was soon leading the industry in applying aluminum parts to mass-production engines. The first use of aluminum die castings for engine parts at Buick goes back to the date when aluminum pistons were adopted in the 1936-model straight-eight engine. The 1953-model V-8 had aluminum rocker arm shaft brackets and oil filter base. By 1955 it had an aluminum water outlet, and two years later an aluminum water pump cover. On the 1958 models, an aluminum timing chain cover was used. On the 1961-model cast-iron V-8, aluminum was used for rocker arms, water pump impeller, generator end frames, generator bracket, fan spacer, fuel pump dome and body. Design studies for a production-type aluminum V-8 had begun at the GM Engineering Staff in 1956. This program was led by Darl F. Caris. When we say 'production-type' that means manufacturing methods and cost considerations are taken into account. It also means that the operating conditions in the field must be kept in mind. The opposite is often true of experimental engines. For instance, the XP-300 engine became a highly sophisticated piece of machinery, simply because of what it was designed for. The aluminum-block Buick V-8 developed into a design of clever simplicity, because of the design goals for it. One was for a dream car; the other for a mass-produced American passenger car.

Caris and his designers first laid out a small V-8 with 183-cubic-inch displacement, but engineering vice president Charles A. Chayne thought that would not be enough. So the engine was enlarged to 215 cubic inches, with 3.50-inch bore and 2.80-inch stroke, and those are the dimensions that were used for the production engine. These cylinder dimensions gave the same stroke/bore ratio of 0.80 as the original Buick 322-cubic-inch V-8, and the cylinder displacement came within 0.7 cubic inches of equaling that of the first aluminum engine, the XP-300. Naturally, O. K. Kelley was fully informed of everything that went on inside GM Engineering Staff, and wanted Buick to produce the aluminum engine. His friends at the GM Engineering Staff happily lent their support to get corporate approval for going into production with it. The project was handed over to Buick in the spring of 1958, and a period of intensive experimentation and testing followed. The production design for the aluminum V-8 began in December 1958. Joe Turlay was in charge of the overall project, assisted by Cliff Studaker. Ed Holtzkemper was the production specialist on the team.

Several fundamental changes were made from the prototype design from GM Engineering Staff, which had flat-face cylinder heads, pistons with a circular depression, and valves in line with the cylinder center lines. The intake manifold was separated from the block by about $1\frac{1}{2}$ inches of air, and did not have the benefit of hot-spot heating of the fresh mixture for warmup. It also stood out for not using cylinder liners at all. Even at this early date, GM Engineering was experimenting with sprayed-on metal coatings and other ideas to protect aluminum surfaces. The first production-model application was to be the 1971 Chevrolet Vega. It had never been a consideration for the senior-series Buick V-8 to run on anything but premium gasoline. When Buick was caught up in the horsepower race, with higher and higher (nominal) compression ratios, that automatically excluded the use of regular gasoline. For the new compact, the situation was reversed. Here it was considered essential to have an engine that could run smoothly and pull strongly on the lowest-priced regular fuel.

As a result of the need for using regular gas, the combustion chamber shape could not be adapted from the big V-8, but had to be developed from scratch. The key elements were taken from the Caris design, but the shape that finally resulted was a slanted, elongated saucer indented in the cylinder head, accompanied by a shallow circular depression in the piston crown. A narrow annular topland encircled this depression. It was 0.35 inches wide and accounted for no more than fifteen percent of total piston crown surface. This ring-shaped land was designed to promote turbulence during compression and make for a more compact combustion chamber at the moment of firing. The spark plug was positioned as nearly in the middle as possible, and its center electrode was actually no more than 0.4 inches from the cylinder center line. A swirl pattern in the gas flow was induced by a slight offset in the intake port. Tests proved that this combustion chamber, even with deposits after a certain mileage, could run on 92-octane (Research method) fuel with a compression ratio of 8.8:1 without a trace of abnormal combustion.

Camshaft drive was by chain from the crankshaft. The valve gear was not substantially different from that used on the big Buick V-8's, with a single central camshaft, hydraulic valve lifters, reasonably short pushrods, a single rocker arm shaft per bank, and all valves in one line. Die-cast aluminum rocker arms were used, with a 1.6:1 rocker arm ratio. To keep internal stress levels low, the breathing was restricted by small valves and conservative timing. Intake valve head diameter was 1.50 inches, with exhaust valves correspondingly smaller at 1.3125 inches. That meant the intake valve head diameter was less than forty-three percent of the cylinder bore. Valve lift was the same for both intake and exhaust valves, at 0.383 inches. The cam profiles gave a duration of 280 degrees for all valves, and an overlap of sixty-two degrees. The intake valves opened sixty-seven degrees before top dead center and closed seventy-one degrees after bottom dead center, while the exhaust valves opened sixty-seven degrees before bottom dead center and closed thirty-three degrees after top dead center.

For this engine, Buick changed the firing order to 1-8-4-3-6-5-7-2, departing from previous practice with the big V-8's, and moving into line with the small-block Chevrolet. The intake manifold was sand-cast aluminum, with maximum body size and minimum branch size consistent with proper breathing characteristics. Manifold heat was provided by a water jacket that all the coolant traveled through on the way to the outlet, which gave rapid warmup. Valve covers were steel stampings, zinc-plated for corrosion resistance.

While Turlay had happily used wet liners on the XP-300, there was no way Buick's manufacturing engineers would accept that principle for a production engine. The designers were fully aware of the risk of coolant loss from a poorly sealed liner. Any leak would lead to a presence of water in the crankcase, where it would be mixed with the lubricating oil and circulate all through the engine, ruining the oil film in critical areas and giving rise to other problems as well. The engine was therefore designed with dry liners, made of iron, centrifugally cast. A method of casting the block around the liners was chosen rather than press-fitting the liners into a fully cast block. The outside diameter of the liner was machined with a multitude of circumferential grooves, which served to lock the liners to the block during the casting process. The block was cast by the semi-permanent mold process, which means that the molten metal flowed by gravity into external molds (of steel) with sand cores forming the internal passages.

Taking the advice of John Lapin and other experts from GM's Central Foundry at Bedford, Indiana, where the aluminum parts were to be cast, Buick had rejected the more expensive die-casting method (which was used by Chrysler and American Motors for their aluminum-block in-line sixes at the time). Die-casting means forcing the molten aluminum into the steel molds under very high pressure (8,000 to 10,000 psi).

The integral block and crankcase extended 2.25 inches below the crankshaft center line. Water jackets were 4.06 inches long, compared with a full cylinder length of 5.56 inches. The jackets were kept short to reduce heat rejection to the coolant in the interest of faster warmup, counting on radiator size and water pump capacity to provide an adequate cooling effect.

Pistons were one-piece aluminum castings, with full skirts, two compression rings and one oil-control ring. Forged steel connecting rods were used, having a center-to-center distance of 5.66 inches. This gave a conservative rod length to stroke ratio of 2.02:1, at a time when the industry average was about 1.80:1. It was a retrograde step compared with earlier Buick engines, for it had been 1.91:1 in the straight-eight and 1.875:1 in the orig-

inal cast-iron V-8. The aluminum V-8 was the first Buick engine that used a cast-iron crankshaft. The finished crankshaft weighed only 38.4 pounds. It was a five-bearing design, counterweighted, with counterweights formed to provide adequate clearance from the piston skirts. With a main journal diameter of 2.30 inches and a crankpin diameter of 2.00 inches, coupled with a crank throw of 1.40 inches, the shaft had a 0.75-inch overlap. Cylinder heads were semi-permanent mold castings, using dry sand cores for water jackets and ports. Valve seat inserts of cast iron were shrink-fitted into the cylinder head, while valve guides were press-fitted. The exhaust port and channel were kept short to minimize the heat-rejection from the combustion gases to the coolant.

The aluminum V-8 weighed 324 pounds. That's 1.5 pounds per cubic inch, whereas the industry average was about 2.5, and no other engine then in production had a weight to displacement ratio lower than two pounds per cubic inch. The Buick V-8 weighed 2.09 pounds per hp, in standard form, and the next best in the industry at the time was 3.5 pounds per hp. The standard engine with two-barrel carburetor delivered 155 SAE gross hp at 4600 rpm, and had a maximum torque of 220 pounds-feet at 2400 rpm. An optional high-performance version (for premium gasoline) differed in having high-compression (10.25:1) cylinder heads and a four-barrel carburetor. It delivered 185 SAE gross hp at 4800 rpm, with a peak torque of 230 pounds-feet at 2800 rpm.

In service the aluminum V-8 did run into corrosion and reliability problems despite everything that had been done to assure freedom from these troubles. Incomplete cleaning out of the blocks could lead to serious problems. Though it was a rare occurrence, it was difficult to guard against aluminum machining chips remaining inside the engine castings after assembly. They would eventually flush out into the radiator and enter into an electrolytic action with the copper in the radiator core. As a result of the partial clogging which ensued, the engine would suffer cooling problems. But what really sealed its fate was the high production cost. Buick's calculations had always shown the aluminum V-8 to be somewhat more expensive to make than an equivalent unit of cast iron. But the actual production costs far exceeded the estimates. The semi-permanent mold casting process was slower and more expensive than the permanent mold process used to cast the gray-iron cylinder blocks and heads. The cylinder liners were machined on both inside and outside surfaces, preheated, and placed on retractable mandrels in the mold. The six sand cores for the block were set by hand, the mold closed by hydraulic means, and the metal was poured into the mold with ladles. After cleaning, the finished parts passed through a furnace to undergo structural stabilization by heat treatment consisting of five hours at 400 degrees Fahrenheit.

Any lightweight production engine attracts the attention of makers of speed equipment and racing car builders. The Buick aluminum V-8 was no exception. Mickey Thompson, holder of a long list of speed records and owner of a speed shop in Long Beach, California, actually decided to use the Buick engine in a team of cars he was planning for the 1962 Indianapolis 500.

The engine underwent a number of modifications, starting with boring out the block to 3.625 inches to raise the displacement to 255 cubic inches, with a new crankshaft giving a longer 3.1-inch stroke. The crankshafts were steel forgings and carried special vibration dampers designed for maximum smoothness in the 5000- to 7000-rpm region. The blocks were equipped with heavy-duty main bearing bulkheads, and the standard oil pan was replaced by a cast-aluminum dry sump. A gear train accessory drive replaced the standard timing chain.

High-compression cylinder heads with larger valves (1.625 inches for the intake valve-head diameter and 1.4375 inches for the exhaust valve-head diameter) were designed. Ports and gas passages were enlarged and straightened. The carburetor and intake manifold was replaced by a Hilborn fuel-injection system. Power output was 330 hp at 6500 rpm, on a fifteen-to-one compression ratio.

Four cars were built, with special transaxles to permit midships engine installation. Only two forward speeds were judged necessary for Indy, with a final drive ratio of 3.78:1. The cars were fast—Dan Gurney qualified one with a four-lap average speed of 147.8 mph, and fuel consumption was lower than for the Offenhauser-powered cars. The Buick-powered cars gave nearly 4 mpg, against 2½ mpg for its rivals. In the race, the engine held up well, but the car was eliminated due to a broken transmission gear. The following year, Mickey Thompson went to Chevrolet for power units for his Indy entries. No Buick-based engine was ever again to appear at the 'brickyard.'

Back in Flint, the Buick executives were also having second thoughts about the aluminum V-8, mainly because of what it did to the price of the Special.

Buick desperately needed a cheaper engine. The division was losing money on the aluminum V-8, and losing sales because the Special used a V-8 as its baseline engine. Making a V-8 engine standard in a compact did not make commercial sense. What it needed was a six, or possibly a big four. Pontiac had made a slant-four by cutting its V-8 down the middle. Buick rejected that idea. And the existing compact body did not have room for the in-line sixes then in production at GM. What could Buick do? A short lightweight V-6 would be an ideal solution. But there was none available within the corporation. Buick would have to make one. But there was

no time to start an all-new engine program, which would take about five years. The V-6 was needed, as they said, "like yesterday." But perhaps Buick could build a V-6 from a V-8 by cutting off one cylinder on each bank? This concept came from Joe Turlay. He made some V-6 design proposals based on the aluminum V-8 design, and developed a 198-cubic-inch aluminum V-6 for evaluation. It was unusual for a V-6 in that it had the banks disposed in a ninety-degree V-formation, and this was done strictly in order to share the tooling for the V-8. It resulted in some rather odd solutions, such as the crankshaft layout, but it was a soundly engineered design. When the time came for Rollert to make a decision about producing the V-6 he was hesitant about building another engine at all, for it was essentially a stopgap measure, to help sell the compact for the short period that remained until the Special and Skylark went to intermediate size for the 1964 model year, and for them a small V-8 would be a reasonable engine.

Rollert calmly handed out three momentous commands: First, make the V-6, but make it of cast iron and make it available in the 1962 Special. Second, prepare a small-block cast-iron V-8 for the 1964 Special. Third, drop the aluminum V-8 at the end of the 1963 model year. From the time Ed Rollert gave the green light for putting the V-6 in production, only six months were available to design and tool up for it. That effectively locked the V-6 into the same ninety-degree layout as the V-8, instead of the sixty-degree configuration more common in V-6's, in order to use existing tooling and equipment to the fullest possible extent. Consequently, the V-6 used the same 4.24-inch cylinder center spacing as the V-8, for instance. The urgency also led Turlay and Studaker to use a maximum of components from the aluminum V-8. As a result, the V-6 had the same timing chain cover, water pump, oil pump, valve gear, bearings, flywheel and most of the accessories.

Balancing a V-6 engine is something of a problem no matter what angle is chosen. And Buick calculated rotating and rocking couples for a number of hypothetical engines with sixty-, ninety-, and 120-degree V-formations. With these imaginary engines running at 4000 rpm, it was calculated that the sixty-degree V-6 would have a secondary rotating couple of 219 pounds-feet, while the ninety-degree V-6 would have a rocking couple of 304 pounds-feet acting in the horizontal plane. The 120-degree V-6 showed a variable rotating couple, cycling from 107 pounds-feet vertically to 322 pounds-feet in the horizontal plane, and back again. Despite the forty percent higher values of the horizontal rocking couple in the ninety-degree V-6, the Buick engineers thought its vibrations could be isolated through the motor mount design. It also had the advantage of avoiding vibrations caused by the twisting torque in the sixty-degree and 120-degree V-6's.

To get evenly spaced firing impulses in a ninety-degree V-6, it would be necessary to make a crankshaft with six individual crankpins, spaced 120

Cast-iron Buick V-6 engine became standard in the 1962 Special. It started with 198-cubic-inch displacement and grew to 225. Buick sold its V-6 engine line in 1967, only to buy it back in 1975.

By 1966 the 300-cubic-inch Buick V-8 had cast-iron cylinder heads as well as a cast-iron block. Derived from the V-6, it bears no resemblance to the 'nailhead' V-8 then used in the senior series. It was soon to be further enlarged.

degrees apart. But this would cost more than mounting connecting rods from opposite cylinders side by side on a common crankpin (as in the aluminum V-8), so Buick was forced to design a crankshaft with two deviating intervals, one of ninety degrees and one of 150 degrees, with the four remaining intervals at 120 degrees. This compromise gave the following sequence of firing intervals: 90°—120°—120°—150°—120°—120°. But this could only be obtained by a firing order that involved successively firing all the plugs on one bank, followed by a similar process on the other bank. That produced excessive variations in the torque impulses on the crankshaft

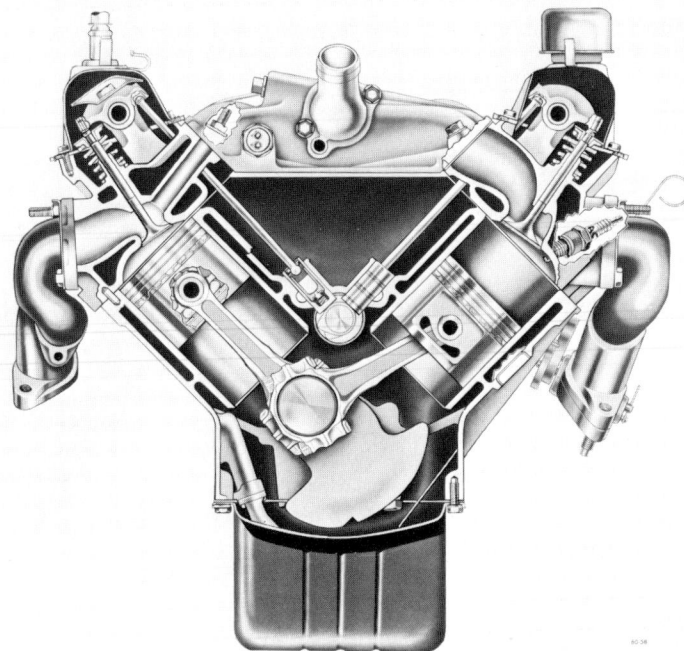

and led to a roughness in low-speed operation. While this roughness was small in magnitude, it corresponded to the natural frequency of the engine on its mounts, and the disturbance was magnified and transmitted to the passenger compartment. The solution that was adopted is surprising in that it consisted not of trying to rectify one wrong, but in adding another wrong. In fact, by phasing two more cylinders to fire at ninety- and 150-degree intervals, it became possible to alter the firing order so as to fire across the block and back again in alternation and avoid successive firing of any two plugs on the same bank. This arrangement gave a 1-6-5-4-3-2 firing order, with a numbering system that puts cylinder number 1 at the front of the left bank and cylinder number 2 at the front of the right bank. Looking at the engine from the back (as from the driver's seat), you have cylinders 6-4-2 in line straight ahead, and cylinders 5-3-1 in line on the right side. By accepting larger disorders in balance, the frequency was reduced, and could therefore be isolated more easily. To overcome the vibration problem on cars with synchromesh transmission, a new flywheel with nearly twice the inertia was adopted. On cars equipped with Dual-Path drive, the standard flywheel proved adequate, due to the inertia effect of the torque converter.

The crankshaft was cast from pearlitic malleable iron, with counter-weights disposed on both sides of each crankpin, in the opposite direction from the crankshaft center. The shaft was carried in four 0.864-inch-wide main bearings of 2.3-inch diameter. End thrust was taken by number two bearing, which was widened to 1.057 inches. Crankpin journals were 2.00 inches in diameter and 0.737 inches wide, with aluminum-surfaced steel-backed bearing shells. With a crank throw of 1.60 inches, that provided an overlap of only 0.45 inches. All bearing shells were identical with those used in the aluminum V-8 engine. Connecting rods were malleable iron castings, each with a weight of 20.8 ounces. Compared with the aluminum V-8, rod length was increased from 5.66 to 5.86 inches, center to center. The cam-ground piston weighed 17.34 ounces and carried two compression rings and one oil control ring. The depression in the crown was modified to adjust the compression ratio.

The V-6 block was a thin-wall precision casting. Cylinder bore was 3.625 inches, and the stroke 3.20 inches, giving a displacement of 198 cubic inches. Stroke/bore ratio had evened out to a value of 0.88, compared with 0.8 in the aluminum V-8. The cylinder heads, inheriting the same combustion chamber design that was used on the aluminum V-8, were also made of malleable cast iron. The valve gear design was essentially unchanged, except for longer pushrods, shorter camshaft and a hardened camshaft sprocket. The V-6 inherited the valves from the aluminum V-8, with a head diameter of 1.50 inches for the intake and 1.3125 inches for the exhaust valves. With the bigger bore, the valve head diameter-to-bore ratio dropped below 41.5, which restricted breathing and assured low internal stress levels. Cam profiles were designed with the same 0.385-inch lift for all valves. To compensate for the small valve size, the timing was changed to give longer duration. Intake valves opened eighteen degrees before top dead center and closed eighty-two degrees after bottom dead center, and the exhaust valves opened sixty-two degrees before bottom dead center and closed thirty-eight degrees after top dead center. This gave the same 280-degree duration for all valves, and an overlap of fifty-six degrees. In addition to giving the best balance, it turned out that firing alternately across the banks also gave the best breathing characteristics. The intake manifold was designed as a simple log-type with a separate header section for each bank. Exhaust gas pulses were spaced out at a uniform 240 degrees in the manifold.

Buick's original V-6 weighed 414.06 pounds, complete with accessories, which was 50.2 pounds more than the aluminum V-8 loaded with corresponding equipment. While the V-8 block weighed only 68.84 pounds, the V-6 block weighed 105.6 pounds. Cylinder head weight, despite the nearly twenty-five-percent reduction in length, increased from 31.25 to 59.3 pounds. Turlay and Studaker shared the credit for the en-gine's development with N. W. Kunz and W. B. Hoffman. As with the aluminum V-8, it was Ed Holtzkemper who carried it into production. The Buick V-6 was first offered as standard equipment on the 1962 Special. It delivered 135 SAE gross hp at 4600 rpm, with a peak torque of 205 pounds-feet at 2400 rpm, breathing through a two-barrel carburetor and running with a compression ratio of 8.8:1. These specifications remained unchanged in 1963 and 1964. As scheduled, Buick discontinued its aluminum V-8 in 1963. Rights to manufacture the aluminum V-8 design were sold to the Rover Motor Company, of Solihull, Birmingham, England in 1967. Rover is still making the engine, practically without modifications. It is standard equipment in the Rover 3500 and Range-Rover.

The V-6 was kept in Buick's production program for five consecutive years. For the 1965 models, displacement was increased to 225 cubic inches, with a 3.75-inch bore and a 3.40-inch stroke. In this version, the stroke/bore ratio went to 0.906. Compression ratio was raised to 9.0:1, and power output went up to 155 SAE gross hp at 4400 rpm, with a maximum torque of 225 pounds-feet at 2400 rpm. Cam profiles were redesigned to give the same 0.401-inch lift for both intake and exhaust valves, with 285-degree duration for the intake valves and 295-degree duration for the exhaust valves. Valve-head diameter was increased to 1.63 inches for the intake valves and 1.38 inches for the exhaust valves. That improved the breathing capacity of the engine, for the valve-head diameter to cylinder bore ratio rose to fractionally above forty-four percent. A new crankshaft was produced, with main bearing diameter increased to 2.50 inches. This engine had a weight-to-horsepower ratio of 2.75 pounds per hp, and its specific power output was 0.71 hp per cubic inch displacement. Its installation weight, including all accessories, was about 440 pounds.

At the end of the 1967 model run the V-6 disappeared from the Buick lineup, and the whole engine manufacturing line was sold to Kaiser Jeep Corporation in Toledo, Ohio. In short order the Jeep CJ-5 and the new Jeepster became available with V-6 power. Towards the end of 1969, American Motors acquired control of Kaiser Jeep. The former Buick engine was a serious rival to the AMC engines, and the parent corporation gradually curtailed V-6 production until it ceased altogether at the beginning of 1972.

But that was not the end of the road for the Buick V-6. When the fuel crisis hit America in 1973, all manufacturers had to scramble to increase production of their smallest-displacement engines. Buick was in a bind. There was just nothing smaller than a 350-cubic-inch V-8 being built at Buick.

Fortunately, Phil Bowser, who had been named chief engineer in 1968, remembered the V-6. He was on vacation in Florida when it hit him, and he immediately walked back from the golf course to the club house and

FIRING ORDER
1 6 5 4 3 2

ODD FIRING DESIGN

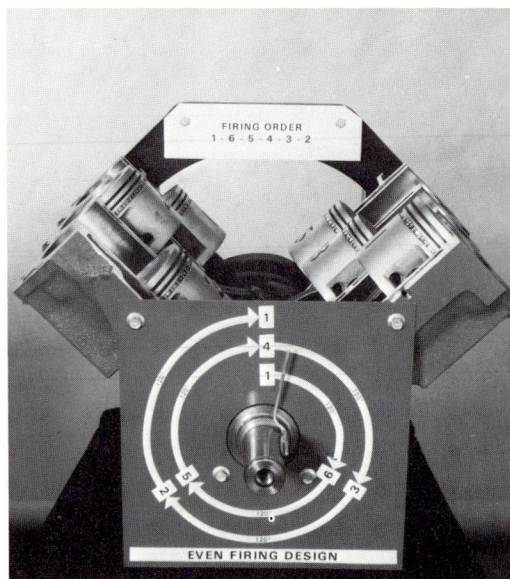

FIRING ORDER
1 6 5 4 3 2

EVEN FIRING DESIGN

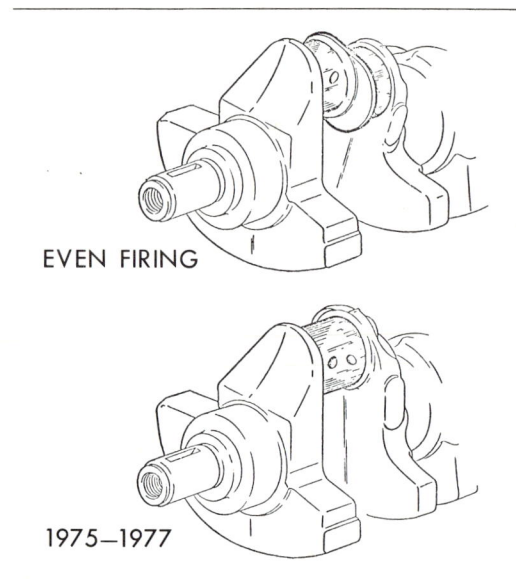

EVEN FIRING

1975–1977

Left, in the odd-firing V-6, with intervals of 90 degrees alternating with intervals of 150 degrees, the engine built up a big rocking couple due to uneven torque impulses. Cylinders 1-3-5 are on the right, with 2-4-6 on the left. No change in firing order was needed to obtain even firing intervals with the new crankshaft, middle. Some crankpins were moved 30 degrees ahead, and others 30 degrees back, until all were spaced at 120 degrees from their predecessors and followers. Right, V-6 crankshaft ran with paired connecting rods from 1975 to 1977, firing at odd intervals. The new version has separate journals on each crankpin, as shown above. To maintain strength, bearing diameter was increased from 2.0 to 2.25 inches.

called Studaker. Buick quickly bought some old V-6's from junkyards and installed them in Skylarks for evaluation. A special car was prepared for GM President Ed Cole to test, and he came up to Flint, picked up Studaker one afternoon, and they drove together to Toledo to look at the V-6 engine line in the American Motors plant there. They decided it was complete and in fairly good shape, and arranged to have the financial people talk to AMC about putting the line back to work and supplying V-6 engines to General Motors until the fuel situation resolved itself. These negotiations broke off near the end of 1973. But in the spring of 1974 Buick purchased the V-6 engine line back from American Motors. In the summer of 1974 the entire engine line was shipped back to Flint, and reinstalled exactly where it had been originally, without a snag.

At the start of the 1975 model year, Buick had capacity for 700 V-6 engines daily. The bore was increased to match that of the 350-cubic-inch V-8 Buick was then building (3.80 inches) while keeping the stroke at 3.40 inches, which raised displacement to 231 cubic inches, and enabled Buick to use pistons that were already in production. This version of the Buick V-6 was to be used in Buick's own new compacts (X-body Apollo/Skylark) and the intermediate (A-body Century). Beyond that, it was to be supplied to Pontiac and Oldsmobile for installation in their cars in the same categories. This engine is now helping General Motors speed its transition to smaller, lighter cars with better fuel economy for all divisions. The 231-cubic-inch V-6 was standard in the 1977 Skyhawk, Skylark, Century and LeSabre. For 1978 the 231-cubic-inch V-6 will get a new crankshaft with even firing intervals. By offsetting adjacent crankpin journals by thirty degrees, it became possible to fire one cylinder every thirty degrees of crankshaft rotation. The result will be that the V-6 can idle and run with nearly the same steadiness and lack of vibration as a V-8. In addition to this V-6, Buick will also produce a smaller, 196-cubic-inch version of the same engine for its 1978 models, and for sale to other GM divisions. The smaller displacement was obtained by reducing the bore from 3.80 to 3.50 inches.

A turbocharged version of the 231-cubic-inch V-6 is under development

for use in the 1978 Buick Century. The Turbo V-6 with two-barrel carburetor will be standard equipment on the 1978 Regal Sport Coupe and
LeSabre Sport Coupe. A four-barrel version of the Turbo V-6 will be added
as an option later in the year. A turbocharger is an exhaust-driven compressor, using the energy of the hot exhaust gases to drive a turbine whose shaft
turns a compressor wheel that pumps air under pressure into the engine.
General Motors had considerable experience with turbocharged cars, starting with Oldsmobile's 1963 Jetfire and a special version of the Chevrolet
Corvair in 1964. Without adding more than a little weight or bulk to the
engine, the turbocharger can provide a fifty-percent (or greater) power
boost. It's also regarded as a fuel saving unit, because it's an 'on-demand'
device that only comes into effect when extra power is needed, and does
not cause increased energy consumption under light-load conditions. Depending on the installation and adjustment details, it can also be helpful in
controlling emission levels. Buick's V-6 may turn out to be the prevailing
powerplant within General Motors, and the V-6 layout may come to domi-
nation throughout the American auto industry in the future. And it is when

The small-block cast-iron V-8 developed
from the aluminum V-8 design grew from
300 to 350 cubic inches and is still in
production. This is the 1974 version with
four-barrel carburetor and full
emission-control equipment.

Buick V-6 for 1978 has even firing impulses due to redesigned crankshaft.
Each crankpin is split into two journals,
spaced at 30 degrees, which gives firing
at 120-degree intervals. Counterweighting was reduced by 20 pounds in the
process!

viewing its prospects that we should remind ourselves it was only developed and put into production as a stopgap measure, and then disposed
of to a buyer who did not realize its value and let production lapse. In the
fairy tales from Flint, the V-6 engine story is a modern parallel to Ander-
sen's Ugly Duckling which grew up into a beautiful swan.

CHAPTER 9

Buick Builds a Compact

COMPACT CARS WERE not new when Buick introduced its entry in this market segment, but it was a new way to describe American cars that provided fairly average seating accommodation and luggage capacity within a smaller and lighter package than the stylized pace-setting full-size cars. Not only had Buick consistently stayed out of this market, but General Motors as a whole had shunned it. So did Ford and Chrysler. But they were forced into it by the success of two models during the fifties: the domestic Rambler and the imported Volkswagen. Sales of the compact Rambler went from 91,000 in 1957 and 186,227 in 1958 to 368,464 in 1959. By 1960, Rambler was number four in the U. S. sales race. Volkswagen sales in the U.S. were less than 1,000 cars in 1953, but soared to 80,000 in 1958, 120,000 in 1959 and 160,000 in 1960. On its coattails were hordes of other small European cars.

Detroit launched its counterattack in the fall of 1959: Chevrolet with its Corvair, Ford with its Falcon and Chrysler with its Valiant. All were eminently successful, and GM decided to build Pontiac, Oldsmobile and Buick compacts as well. The development program had actually started as early as 1957, when the compact car share of the market was still relatively minor. Independently, Chevrolet was well ahead of the game, having started work on a compact car project in 1955. It was conceived as an American type of Volkswagen, with a six-cylinder air-cooled engine installed in the rear end of the chassis. Engineered under the direction of Edward N. Cole and styled by Ned Nickles, it went into production as the Corvair.

For the compacts to be built by Buick, Oldsmobile and Pontiac, it was decided to develop a new version of the unit-construction body Fisher was making for the Chevrolet Corvair. General Motors had been building unit-construction bodies in Europe since 1937, for its Opel and Vauxhall subsidiaries, but the Corvair was the first U.S.-built GM car with a combined body and frame. Much of the engineering on this body was carried out by a group under the direction of James Wernig, who was Fisher Body Division's engineering director at the time.

At the corporate level, the B-O-P compact was known as project X-100. But Buick took an early lead in developing a merchandising philosophy for the compact car, and consequently came to count heavily in the product planning process. The name of the car was an obvious choice: Special (since that name had been dropped at the end of the 1958 model year). Since the reasons why Buick wanted a compact car were based on market phenomena, the planning of the new Special began with establishing the marketing strategy and pricing policy. This approach predetermined certain physical aspects of the end product. For instance, it had to be a family car, matching Buick's background and image. It must be capable of attracting new buyers to Buick without offending the traditional Buick owner. It must

1961 Buick Special two-door sedan was built on a 112-inch wheelbase and had a lightweight aluminum V-8 as the standard power unit. The styling followed the overall theme of the senior series, right down to the ventiports.

be the kind of car that could be handled by Buick's dealer organization alongside the senior car lines. The question of selling the car on the strength of pure price competition was answered by an emphatic "no." Although the new Special was created to meet a specific price target, that price was set high enough to allow Buick to endow the product with high-grade trim, finish and equipment. But the overall questions of vehicle configuration and architecture had first to be solved. And in the usual Buick fashion, the program started at square one, with the basic concept.

Since the Corvair was a rear-engine car, it was natural for Buick to start by evaluating this type of chassis layout. It was discarded for several reasons. First, Buick determined that an engine capable of meeting Buick's performance targets for the car would be too big for retention of stable handling characteristics if installed in the tail. Secondly, a rear engine installation would leave insufficient luggage space to satisfy Buick's product planners, because the width was largely lost to make room for the front wheels to turn. Front-wheel drive was considered but dismissed after a brief study of the extra cost, the changes needed in Buick's manufacturing setup, and GM's lack of experience with front-wheel drive. In the final analysis, it was

decided to go the obvious route of scaling down the standard Buick to the point where Fisher could build the body using the same tooling that was installed for Corvair body production. Price was part of this decision, but it was not the overriding cause. What really tipped the balance in favor of the traditional Buick layout was the corporation's insistence on keeping the way open for successive upgrading, which in the thinking of that time meant up-scaling the product. With a bigger, heavier car, Buick's engineers agreed that only the front-engine, rear-axle drive chassis layout could be realistically contemplated, especially in the short term. This line of thought tended to confirm that Buick was right in planning a V-8 as the only engine for the new Special.

As early as 1958, prototype V-8 engines were installed in Opel Rekord test cars. This was a smaller and lighter vehicle than the Special was to be, but it served to develop the drive train. The body package was developed

99

Front suspension on the 1961 Buick Special shows a near-vertical coil spring standing on the lower A-arm. A stabilizer bar was also linked to the lower A-arm. Cast-iron brake drums had no cooling fins.

around a seating buck, which consists of a platform where the front and rear bench seats are set in their real in-car configuration. From this formation the floor length is determined. It also fixes the dashboard and cowl location and the wheelbase. Seating dimensions ended up being close to those of the LeSabre, especially for leg room and head room. Hip room and shoulder room were reduced, for the car was not visualized as a full-time six-seater, but as a comfortable four-seater with ability to carry six when necessary. The Special four-door sedan (Model 4019) had 43.5 inches of front leg room and thirty-four inches of front head room. Shoulder room in front was 55.2 inches. The rear seat had 38.7 inches of leg room, 33.9 inches of head room and a shoulder-to-shoulder width of 54.6 inches. It was

found that the Corvair 108-inch wheelbase was unacceptable for a compact car as projected by Buick—their minimum was 112 inches. Overall length was kept down to 188.4 inches, primarily by making cuts in the overhang areas, front and rear.

Major structural modifications were needed in the body. Apart from the greater length, the stress distribution was completely different, mainly due to the redisposition of the masses, with the engine in front instead of in the rear. Two strong rails were welded into the floor, running the full length from the front bumper-mounting cross member to the tail end, aft of the fuel tank. These rails carried torque-boxes connecting them to the rocker sections and door sills, with the cowl section acting as a stabilizing bulkhead for the entire structure. The entire rear end was part of the body shell, including fender skirts and the rear panel below the deck. At the front end, only the inner wheel housings were part of the shell. The fenders and front end sheet metal were bolted to the main structure.

Chassis engineering followed the same pattern as laid down for the senior-series Buicks, with coil springs for all four wheels. The front suspension had upper and lower A-arms, with the spring standing on the lower A-arm. A stabilizer bar was standard. At the rear end, the axle was located by a four-link system. Track, both front and rear, was set at fifty-six inches. A three-speed synchromesh transmission supplied by Chevrolet was standard, and the new Dual-Path Turbine Drive was optional. Column shifts were used for both types of transmissions. The propeller shaft had a set of double universal joints at the center bearing, and single joints at both ends. It was the center joint that worked at the widest angles, and it was here that it was most important to assure constant velocity regardless of angularity. Hypoid bevel final drive, with semi-floating axles, was used, just as on the larger Buicks. Final drive ratio was 3.36:1 with the synchromesh transmission and 3.08:1 with automatic drive. The brake system had 9.5-inch-diameter drums on all four wheels. They were cast iron drums without fins, and the shoes were attached in the duo-servo arrangement, by which the primary shoe pivots on a moveable bearing and transfers part of its load to the secondary shoe. Primary shoes had extrusion-molded linings, and secondary shoes dry-mix molded linings. Wider shoes and drums were used in the front wheels, with a lining width of two inches compared with 1.75 inches in the rear. There was no power assist for the brakes. Standard steering was a Saginaw gear with recirculating balls and a parallelogram linkage. Power steering was optional.

Buick introduced its compact Special in the dealer showrooms on October 5, 1960, as a 1961 model. Production had actually started (in the B-O-P assembly plants) on August 1, 1960. At the start of the model year, only two body styles were offered: four-door sedan and four-door station wagon. A two-door coupe went into production on April 17, 1961. A deluxe version of this coupe revived the Skylark name.

The 1961 Special styling mirrored the appearance of the senior series. The silhouette was like a smaller version of the same shape, with a greenhouse placed between hood and deck; the hood only slightly longer than the deck. The body side treatment was overdone, to say the least. First, it carried the full-length rocket theme from the major series, with a nose cone up the front fender tip, flaring towards the end. Secondly, it had the falling accent line. It took the form of a crease in the sheet metal, starting near the point of the rocket nose, sloping through the door panels, topping both front and rear wheel openings, and ending at the rear bumper. This accent line came to mark the lower edge of the rocket sculpture, and the crease led to a hollow (concave) in the surface between the upper and lower rocket lines. This hollow held the three ventiports at cowl level, provided a panel for the door handles and gave a starting point for a long flare leading to the taillights.

The 1961 Special's front bumper was a nearly straight bar, with the license plate held between low-level relieved overriders in the middle, and a slightly stylized protrusion to mark the corner. The grille was a mouthorgan type of design, flanked by dual head lamps in a side-by-side arrangement. Parking lights and turn signals were recessed in the bumper face, below the main bar, near the ends. The station wagon had the same overall length as the sedan, and the tailgate was hinged in the roof, swinging up from bumper level. A rear-facing third seat was optional. The Skylark had the same basic body but featured its own specific grille and pioneered a vinyl roof. The Skylark grille had horizontal bars only, with thicker members top and bottom to form a frame, and was split at the center by a vertical Buick emblem. Skylark taillight lenses were wrapped around the corners, and the rear panel was different.

Driving the 1961 Buick Special for the first time, one tended to concentrate on engine performance. And it's true that the Special set new standards for compact cars. Going from standstill to 60 mph was a matter of a mere fifteen seconds (with Dual-Path automatic transmission). It covered the standing-start quarter-mile in 20.5 seconds with a terminal speed of 70 mph. Top speed was a little shy of 100 mph. Fuel economy was excellent. Cruising at 70 mph on Michigan highways, one could count on at least 20 mpg. In city and suburban driving, the gasoline mileage ranged from 16 to 21 mpg, according to conditions.

In a way, the car was overpowered, for the chassis was not quite up to the performance levels of the engine. The tires seemed undersized, and the springs too soft. Body roll on curves was not excessive, but the car was ill at ease when thrown into a curve at sports-car speeds. At the limit, it went

Rear axle on the 1961 Buick Special was attached to the body shell via two parallel radius arms that carried the coil springs, and widely splayed control rods to help locate the axle laterally and counteract torque reactions.

into an attitude of extreme understeer, front tires scrubbing sideways, and one rear wheel lifting off the pavement. The ride was almost like a big Buick on good roads, but bouncier on bad surfaces, and pitch motions could set in at certain speeds. Shock damping was not truly adequate. With power steering, response was reasonably quick, but the steering wheel had a 'dead' feel which discouraged fast driving on winding roads.

Because the car was quite light, the standard drum brakes were generally satisfactory. On hard stops, the rear wheels tended to lock prematurely, pulling the rear end to one side. But in normal use, complaints were few.

The unit-construction body was tight and rattle-free, but road shocks were both heard and felt throughout the interior. The drive train, on the other hand, was remarkably quiet, and the exhaust note was well muffled. It was a civilized little car, and its compact size was to win many Americans

Buick Special went to intermediate size in 1964, with bodies nearly a foot longer, and wheelbase increased to 115 inches. Exterior appearance is devoid of traditional Buick trademarks, such as sweepspears and ventiports, and has weak Buick identification.

over to the idea of smaller cars, for it was also a very practical design, suitable for most one-car families.

During its first year on the market, Buick's Special ran seventh in the compact car market, behind the Ford Falcon, Rambler, Corvair, Mercury Comet, Plymouth Valiant and Pontiac Tempest. The Special beat off the Oldsmobile F-85 by 11,000 units, the Dodge Lancer by 13,000 and the Studebaker Lark by 26,000. But the Special made important gains the next year, nearly doubling its output and ranking sixth, dropping the Valiant to seventh position among compacts (because a newcomer, the Chevy II, had been launched, which immediately jumped into third place). One reason for the pickup in the Special's popularity was the new V-6 engine, which became standard, relegating the V-8 to optional use. This lowered the Special's basic price. The lowest-priced two-door sedan was listed at $2,304, compared with $3,227 for the four-door LeSabre. No important styling changes were made in the 1962 models, but it is noteworthy that a convertible was added. This called for further strengthening of the body floor, so that the two-door convertible weighed about 2,820 pounds, or 200 pounds more than the four-door sedan.

A major restyling job was done for the 1963 Special. Retaining the same basic body shell, but using all-new skin, it really looked like a totally new car. It was not quite as compact as before, overall length increasing to 192.1 inches, mainly by added rear overhang. Body sides were cleaned up, presenting a slab-type look, broken up only by two accent lines. The top one extended backwards from the headlight brow and ran horizontally through the doors, sweeping down slightly from the C-post to the taillight lens. The lower one started in the rear door panel on four-door models, aft of the door on two-door models, and ran horizontally to the top of the rear bumper. Three rectangular ventiports sat on the fender panel at the side of the cowl. Taillights were changed from the Ford-like round lenses to more Buick-like horizontal rectangles, filling the sides of the rear panel between the deck lid and the bumper. There were no major changes in the front end aspect. A convertible was added to the Skylark series, which now had the aluminum V-8 engine as standard. During the 1963 model year, the Special accounted for one in three of all Buicks sold. And the Special station wagon outsold the big station wagon at a rate of three to two. The 1963 Special ranked sixth among compacts—behind the Chevy II, Falcon, Corvair, Valiant and Dart, with a small lead over its sister cars, the Oldsmobile F-85 and Pontiac Tempest.

An undeniable roughness in the V-6 engine was apparent mainly when idling and under low-speed acceleration. But at speeds of 80 to 85 mph it was both quiet and vibrationless, and on top of that it had a surprising power reserve near the top end of its speed range. Fuel economy did not differ substantially from the aluminum V-8's, but the V-6 tended to have the edge under most conditions. It did not have the same sparkling acceleration; however, it was still capable of holding its own against the in-line six-cylinder compacts from Ford and Chrysler (Falcon and Valiant). The Special V-6 of 1963 could go from standstill to 60 mph in eighteen seconds, and reached 65 mph at the end of the standing-start quarter-mile, with an elapsed time of twenty-three seconds.

With the start of the 1964 model year, the Buick Special and Skylark went to intermediate size. Incidentally, through 1963 the Skylark had officially been designated Special Skylark, but from 1964 on the Skylark name stood alone. As for the term intermediate size, it meant between compact and full size. GM made the move because Chevrolet wanted a car to fill the gap between the Chevy II and the Impala, and Buick, Oldsmobile and Pontiac were given their own versions of this new car, which Chevrolet called the Chevelle. The unit-body 'Bopettes,' as the compacts made by the B-O-P assembly plants were nicknamed, were phased out. Only the Corvair continued. The new Special, F-85 and Tempest went to separate frame and body construction. A completely new chassis was developed for the 1964

Special, with a torque-box perimeter frame, new front suspension with pressed-steel control arms, new rear suspension with a four-link set of control arms and a one-piece propeller shaft.

The Bopettes were charming cars, but not as quiet as the senior series from their respective manufacturers. Behind the move away from unit-construction bodies was a costly, dedicated effort to reduce noise and vibration. Work done by Chevrolet and Pontiac proved that separate frame construction gave better results in cars of intermediate size. The type of frame that was chosen was a very flexible type, whose real task was to absorb twisting and bending loads. Its job was not to stiffen the body, for the body actually had higher torsional stiffness than the frame. Indeed, the body structure had a lot in common with a unit-body shell, but instead of frame-members welded into it as reinforcements, it was separated by large body mounts from a separate and flexible frame. The frame served, in other words, as an additional insulating stage between the road and the passengers. The frame had two side members, running the full width of the floor pan in the door area. They converged at a slight angle to pass between the rear wheels. At the front, they turned into transverse torque boxes to link up with a narrow frame section serving as an engine cradle, spreading out at the extreme front to provide bumper mounts. Only three main cross members connected the frame side members—one to carry the front suspension, one above the rear axle and one ahead of the rear axle. There was a fourth cross member at the extreme rear end and a fifth at the transmission extension, but these were only supporting members built of very light steel sections to twist easily but not stretch.

Coil springs were retained in both front and rear suspension systems. At the front end, the lower A-arm served as a platform for the coil spring, which enclosed a telescopic shock absorber. The frame provided an upper abutment for the coil spring, and the upper control arm served as a locating member only. The control arms were specifically designed and positioned to allow the steering knuckles to move up and down during wheel deflections in a vertical arc. This was intended to keep the front wheel spindle horizontal at all times. Side roll in the front suspension was controlled by a spring-steel stabilizer bar anchored in the frame, with its two ends linked to each lower A-arm. At the rear end, a new type of four-link suspension system had been developed. Radius arms running straight fore-and-aft linked the axle housing to the frame. These arms were spaced as far apart as possible. Diagonal torque arms connected the top of the differential housing with a frame cross-member, ahead of the axle. All these arms were anchored in large natural-rubber pivot bushings. The coil springs were mounted on bases carried on the axle housing itself, thereby reducing the load on the control arm bushings and permitting the use of softer bushings

for better vibration isolation. At the top end the springs were kept from direct contact with the frame seat by a tubular insulator.

The 1964 Special and Skylark were built on a 115-inch wheelbase, except for the 'skyroof' wagon which had a 120-inch wheelbase. Other body styles included the four-door sedan, two-door coupe, two-door hardtop and convertible. Interior dimensions increased considerably; trunk capacity was raised by fifty percent, overall length went up by five percent, and the weight increase was in the order of fifteen percent. Styling themes were developed to give the new Special and Skylark a big-car look. Much progress was also made in body engineering. The use of curved side glass was not just a styling gimmick, for it also enabled the body engineers to make thinner doors. Windshields had reduced curvature to minimize corner distortion and provide a better surface for wiping action. On station wagons, the tailgate was of the usual type used on big cars, with a roll down window and hinges at floor level, tipping out above the bumper to form a platform extension. The standard engine was the V-6, with the small-block cast-iron V-8 as an option. Power brakes and power steering were optional on all models.

The 1964 Buick Special and Skylark had a clean, balanced look, with a deck just about as long as the hood. A discreet grille flanked by dual-headlight clusters gave a wide, horizontal theme to the front end. The belt line ran straight throughout, uniting the front and rear fenders via the door panels into a single styling element. A horizontal accent line ran from head lamps to taillights, just above wheel opening height, and served to underline the three ventiports on the front fenders. Wheel openings revived the wide-open look of the 1955-model senior series, with an abrupt rise at the front end, a flattish top and a sweeping fall into the fender skirt. The whole opening was emphasized by a lip, tapering into the panels at their lower ends. A crease in the sheet metal, also horizontal, just above the door sills, contributed to making the cars look lower. Taillights were horizontal and set in the rear panel areas that swept out and back to the fender tips, an idea that was to be adopted for the senior series the following year. This shows how two separate car lines in the same stable can feed off each other for ideas, with benefit to both. Normally, features flow from the higher-priced cars to the lower levels, as the junior members undergo the usual upgrading process, but at Buick there are several examples of styling elements originating in the lower-line models and being adopted by the senior series a year or two later.

The 1964 Special and Skylark had a plain two-spoke steering wheel, with the horn activated by pressing down on a bar running straight across the hub from one spoke to the other. Instrumentation was simple in the extreme, with a wide, horizontal speedometer below a padding that extended

Buick Skylark coupe for 1970 was built on a 112-inch wheelbase and was available with a Chevrolet six or Buick V-8 engine. It was a bargain at $2,796 and sales picked up considerably. Drum brakes were still used on all Skylarks.

Sport Wagons belonged in the Special/Skylark series despite long wheelbase of 121.5 inches. Own frame was used, but sheet metal and grille came from the Skylark. Domed roof was an Oldsmobile idea that Fisher Body sold to Buick.

towards the wheel to prevent reflections from the instruments on the windshield at night. Small controls were grouped around the panel below the instrument cluster. A radio occupied the center space, and a glove box was located outside the padded framework on the extreme right.

On the road, the 1964 Buick Special seemed the ideal family car. It was every bit as roomy as the big Buicks of ten years earlier. It had a superior combination of ride comfort and stability. With the base V-6 it gave excellent fuel economy with acceptable performance levels. The optional 300-cubic-inch V-8 was available with a two-barrel carburetor for ordinary driving with high loads, and with a four-barrel carburetor for the performance enthusiast. The V-8's gave higher levels of refinement and driving pleasure, and gasoline mileage remained reasonable.

Few people bought the standard three-speed synchromesh gearbox but opted for the new Super Turbine 300, which proved to be smooth, quiet and trouble-free. Power steering was another popular option, much improved from earlier versions available on the Special. Remaining light, it now gave more feedback from the wheels, without transmitting road shocks and vibration. Steering response was improved, too, and the car's handling characteristic remained a firm, stable understeer. Despite tighter shock-absorber calibration and higher spring rates, the ride was soft and pleasant, while handling precision and cornering stability now approached Wildcat levels. For customers who wanted extra sportiness, Buick introduced the Gran Sport concept.

The GS addition to model designations was first used on a 1964½ model. Apart from unique ornamentation, the difference between a Skylark

and a Skylark GS lay in engine modifications to get more power (or a larger engine altogether); and chassis with higher spring rates, reinforced stabilizer bars and recalibrated shock absorbers. Wide-rim wheels and wide-tread tires, often blackwalls, became part of the GS package. Heavy-duty brakes were also included, and special instrumentation became optional (tachometer for instance). The Skylark GS was available with the 401-cubic-inch engine from the Wildcat. Cars with that engine were usually equipped with the Super Turbine 400 transmission, but Buick, in line with all other divisions offering high-powered intermediates, or 'muscle cars' as they were called in the car buff magazines at the time, also offered a four-speed manual floor shift transmission (a unit built by Chevrolet's gearbox factory in Muncie, Indiana, and therefore known among enthusiasts as 'the Muncie box'). The 1965 Skylark GS was equipped with the 401-cubic-inch V-8 engine as standard. The GS package was extended from the previous year, with a different instrument panel and steering wheel, and greater choice of exterior trim. The GS option was available for all two-door Skylarks (hardtop and convertible) but not for four-door cars and not for the base-line Special.

No sheet metal changes appeared on the 1965-model Special and Skylark, but some of the brightwork was given greater emphasis. A new horizontal-bar grille made the front end look heavier and the car more distinctive. A considerable facelift gave a completely new look to the 1966 models. Instead of a straight grille, the new design came to a point, with a vertical center bar. The bumper design was a mild copy of the W-front bumper used on the senior series Buicks at the time. Dual head lamps, set side by side at grille level, helped give the car a sleek, low look. In profile, the most obvious change was the belt line, with a marked rear-fender kick-up. The front fender tips adopted the sharply defined lines of the bigger cars. A full-length accent line ran from the headlight brow to the taillights, emphasizing the rear fender kickup, and the ventiports were mounted right

Skylark GS for 1966 has dummy air scoops in the hood, and a front fender decoration intended as ventiports. Power unit was a 400-cubic-inch V-8, combined with either automatic transmission or a four-speed all-synchromesh gearbox.

on this line. The sill-height crease was eliminated, and the door panels blended right into the sills. This style was retained practically without change for 1967.

The 1966 Special and Skylark were available with engines from 160 to 260 SAE gross hp. The standard power plant was the 225-cubic-inch V-6, with the 300- and 340-cubic-inch V-8's as optional. The 220-hp version of the new 340-cubic-inch V-8 was standard in the Sportwagon, and the 401-cubic-inch V-8 continued as standard in the Skylark GS. There were two Skylark GS power trains for 1967, the GS-340 and the GS-400. The numbers indicated the cubic-inch displacement of the engines. But they were not the regular 340- and 400-cubic-inch V-8's. They were high-compression versions, with bigger-bodied carburetors with higher air flow capacity, high-overlap camshafts and dual exhaust systems.

How did the intermediate Buicks do in the market place? To start at the beginning, model-year output rose by twenty-four percent from 1963 to 1964. The Special/Skylark line finished eighth in its field, behind the Chevelle, Fairlane, Valiant, Tempest, Rambler Classic, Dodge Dart and Mercury Comet. Looking at calendar-year registrations, we find that the Special went from 150,000 sales in 1964 to 183,000 the following year. At the same time Special wagon sales went up by nearly fifty percent! Among

intermediate cars, only the Chevelle and the Tempest were produced in greater quantity during 1965. There was a decline in 1966 (while the senior series maintained their sales pace) which continued throughout 1967. Buick was last among the GM intermediates that year, with only 198,000 units against the F-85's 260,000, the Tempest's 297,000, and the Chevelle's 375,000. But the Special/Skylark line did better than all Ford Motor Company, Chrysler Corporation and American Motors intermediates, placing fourth in its class, and accounting for a reasonable proportion of Buick sales (thirty-five percent), compared with its sister divisions (nineteen percent intermediates at Chevrolet, 35.5 at Pontiac and forty-seven at Oldsmobile).

For 1968, General Motors changed all its intermediates, and introduced the dual-wheelbase principle. The two-door models were built on a four-inch shorter wheelbase than the four-door models, so that the two-door Buick Special could compete better against compact cars, and the four-door Special could compete better against full-size cars of low-priced makes. Buick built its sixteen-millionth car in 1969. It was a 1970-model Skylark coupe.

CHAPTER 10
The Riviera

A 'PERSONAL CAR' is what Ford called its Thunderbird after making the 1958 model a four-seater coupe. Until Buick launched the 1963-model Riviera, Ford had this market almost exclusively to itself. This type of car differed from the standard coupe or two-door sedan in having its own unique styling and competing in a higher price bracket. This category has been called 'specialty cars' and 'personal-luxury cars.' Ford started it, but it was the Riviera that made it fashionable. It was the Riviera that put some *class* into this market segment.

The Buick Riviera became the car to copy. The car to beat. It gave rise to several imitators, inside and outside GM, like the Pontiac Grand Prix, Chevrolet Monte Carlo and, eventually, the Chrysler Cordoba. The Riviera was also a thoroughly good car. When it appeared, it was certainly one of the best cars ever built in America. It was not out of place anywhere, from Park Avenue in New York to Mulholland Drive in California, from the Kansas Turnpike to the Skyline Drive in Virginia. It had urban elegance, streamlining and a performance image combined into one package. It had the power and speed to back it up, and the steering, handling, and brakes to permit full use of its performance. It was safe, stable, quiet and comfortable. It was thoroughly civilized, yet endowed with a savage streak in its personality. It was like a full-blooded Arabian horse. Next to it, the Thunderbird looked like Ferdinand the Bull.

Actually, the Riviera name had been around Buick a long time. The first Roadmaster Riviera coupe marked the creation of a new production body style in 1949. The 'hardtop' was an idea from GM Styling, which was made possible by Fisher Body Division, and Buick put it on the market. The Riviera name was extended to Super and Roadmaster four-door sedans in 1950, but only the coupes were hardtops. A Special Riviera followed in 1951. The Riviera name was applied to hardtop coupes only in 1955, but in 1956, when four-door hardtops were introduced, they were also called Riviera.

The Riviera name was almost forgotten in the big renaming festival of 1959, but finally it was applied to one model, a four-door hardtop with a different roofline, in the Electra 225 series. This Riviera continued from 1959 through the 1962 model year. Then that model was renamed the Electra 225 six-window hardtop, liberating the Riviera label for a project that was then known only as XP-715. The XP-715 did not originate at Buick, however. It was a GM Styling project, instituted because Cadillac was considering introducing a junior car line at the time. Around General Motors the XP-715 was generally referred to as the La Salle project. When the XP-715 was shown to the Cadillac bosses, however, they turned it down. Not because they did not like it, but because the market conditions had changed, and they had their hands full just filling the orders coming in for the cars already in production. So, when Ed Rollert found out that the La

First production Riviera came remarkably close to the original styling concept in every way. The original body was replaced after only three model years, making it an instant classic. The simulated scoops in the rear fenders disappeared in 1965.

Salle mockup was just sitting at GM Styling gathering dust, he decided to get the board's approval for Buick to take it over. He would have to compete against the general managers of Pontiac and Oldsmobile, and possibly even Chevrolet.

Buick wanted the Riviera because its market research indicated that an increasing share of sales were going to a new segment made up of high-priced imports and domestic sports/luxury cars. Buick's studies also showed that this market was growing at the expense of the division's traditional market. The obvious conclusion was for Buick to develop a car specifically for this market. Among the criteria laid down before Rollert's market researchers and product planners knew about the XP-715 were several basic design objectives. The styling must be a *lot different,* not just a little different, from other Buicks. Roomy and comfortable seating for four was essential. Brisk performance was desirable, but only to the extent it could be combined with low exhaust noise, smooth idle, etc. The car must have good roadholding and precise steering, without compromising the luxury ride associated with a Buick product.

Two of Buick's brightest young engineers became involved with this research project: Phil Bowser and Shirrell Richey. They felt it was possible to

meet all these objectives by making use of Buick's regular parts bin for chassis and power train, but to get a totally new body. And the body, Rollert told them, was sitting in Bill Mitchell's advanced design studio at GM Styling in Warren, Michigan. The Buick team overwhelmed the top corporate management with its presentation. Buick convinced the brass that they alone had valid reasons why they wanted to build the XP-715 and that they alone understood how to market it.

Inspiration for the Riviera is reported to have struck Bill Mitchell while looking at a custom-bodied, knife-edge Rolls-Royce one foggy evening on a busy London street, with the car illuminated by myriad lights, none of which could penetrate the mist and make the car show up in sharp focus. This vaguely conceived shape of crisp lines intrigued Mitchell so much he could not let go of the impression. Back at the Styling Center, he explained his vision to none other than Buick's former chief designer, Ned Nickles,

Left, Riviera mockup came into being as a proposal for La Salle II but Cadillac refused it. Buick seized it eagerly as being just the right clothing for the planned sports/luxury model. By April 1961, it was given Buick identity marks. Phil Bowser, right, and his team engineered the 1963 Riviera as a research-and-development project, separate from normal product-planning routine. It was Bowser who set the performance targets for the Riviera and made sure it was closer to a Corvette than to a Thunderbird.

who was then working in the advanced-projects studio. It was Nickles who made the first sketches, and Mitchell liked them so much that he ordered a full-size clay model to be made. That was the start of project XP-715.

The styling concept was a low-silhouette coupe with a long hood and short deck. It had an aggressive, forward-thrusting front edge, and bulging rear fenders to hint at the power in the driving wheels. Fender lines were smooth and almost free of decor. Only two dummy NACA ducts were placed in the front part of the rear fenders to hint at air scoops for brake cooling. The hood was an enormous panel, nearly flat, with a thin tapered central divider line, and shallow NACA ducts on each side to serve as air scoops for the heating and ventilation system. Front fender lines ran higher than the hood level, which sloped to a lip above the grille. The Riviera introduced a novel idea for protecting the turn signals and parking lights,

which were enclosed behind die-cast aluminum grilles positioned vertically in the front fender tips. The dual headlights were at opposite sides of the wide mouth-organ pattern grille.

Wheel openings followed the theme of the senior-series Buicks of the time, with a horizontal lip on top, blending into a pyramid-base, which rested on a full-length crease in the body sheet metal. There were no ventiports, no chrome strips. One other accent line was used, and was very effective, running horizontally backwards from the top of the parking-light grille through the door panel, after which it swept upwards to emphasize the rear fender kickup, and ran parallel with the rear fender slope to a point near the end, where it plunged down to bumper level, in perfect harmony with the rear fender tip. Taillight lenses were horizontally set in the rear panel below the deck lid. The windshield had an almost uniform curve on top, but the base ran nearly straight in the center section, only to turn more sharply into the A-posts. The rear window glass was almost straight, and did not extend all the way up to the roof panel, nor all the way to the C-post edges on the sides. The doors had vent windows, and rear side windows rolled down into the body panels. Not only was the new Riviera a hardtop, but it introduced frameless door glass on an American car for the first time. That looked like a real headache for the body engineers, and they hoped to

Grilles in fender tips were intended as miniature reproductions of the 1939/40 La Salle front. Main air intake was given low emphasis, and headlight arrangements were reworked several times. The R-in-oval hood ornament came later on.

By May 1961, the rear end of the Riviera was approaching its final shape. The bumper was cleaned up, and it became a design where every line had a statement to make in the overall shape. It remained uncluttered when it went into production, too.

get framed windows for the production model. The solution was found at Fisher Body, not at Buick, and consisted in a new type of door assembly with a detachable outer panel. That would enable the glass to be adjusted against the door seals, with enough pressure to prevent water leaks and eliminate wind noise, after the doors had been mounted on their hinges.

The XP-715 had individual bucket seats both front and rear, and the first production-model Rivieras had a split back seat, but in view of the Riviera's width Buick decided to make seating for three in the back, and went to a rear bench about four months into the model year. Front bucket seats were separated by a console with a slanted panel at the head to hold the ashtray and the radio. The console held the Turbine-Drive selector lever, which looked like a manual floorshift, but worked in a quadrant with its usual P-R-N-D-S-L pattern, reading front to back. The top of the knob had a latch button to prevent overshoot or accidental engagement of reverse. An illuminated bezel on the console indicated the selected position. The instrument panel was designed as a cluster with two main elements. The large circular dial on the left was the speedometer, and a dial of the same size on the right contained a fuel gauge and a number of warning lights. A small dash clock was positioned between them. The Saginaw tilt-wheel became optional in 1964. Fitted with a universal joint near the top of the steering column, the wheel could be adjusted to any one of seven different positions.

It was discussed whether to base the Riviera on the unit-construction Skylark body, but this idea was rejected because there was greater design flexibility with separate frame and body. Any modifications in a unit-construction body would be quite expensive. Bowser and Richey also felt that the best combination of structural strength and noise insulation for a car of the Riviera's size could be obtained with separate frame and body. They chose a 117-inch wheelbase, which was five inches more than the Special and nine inches less than the Electra 225. Front and rear track were set at sixty and fifty-nine inches respectively, to maintain the same proportions as in the Electra (which had a front track of sixty-two inches and a rear track of sixty-one inches). To give the Riviera the low look that was sought, it was judged wise to keep nearly to the Electra's width of seventy-eight inches. Actually, the Riviera body's full width came to 76.6 inches. Its height, however, was only 53.2 inches compared with the Electra's fifty-seven inches. With its generous front overhang and aggressive front end, the Riviera still did not exceed an overall length of 208 inches. Its curb weight

Four bucket seats of 1963 Riviera were unique in Buick history, but the following year, a rear bench seat was adopted. Console with transmission lever carries headboard blending into dashboard below the radio.

Instrument panel on 1963 Riviera had large circular speedometer, small dash clock and warning lights only for oil pressure and coolant temperature. Note the chrome moldings on accelerator pedal.

came to 4,140 pounds. That's 285 pounds less than the Electra 225. The Riviera had a stronger forward bias in weight distribution, carrying 54.8 percent on the front wheels and 45.2 percent on the rear wheels (static and unladen).

A cruciform frame for the Riviera was developed from the Electra frame, and the front and rear suspension systems were basically the same. The Riviera frame was designed with higher torsional stiffness, and the suspension geometry for the Riviera was tailored for higher-speed cornering, although certain suspension components remained interchangeable with standard Electra parts. The Riviera rear axle was located by a three-link and track rod combination that was known to minimize brake lift and have quite restricted roll steer effect. Two main radius arms ran diagonally from mounts on the axle, as near the wheels as possible, parallel with the frame members to strong mounting brackets well ahead of the axle. These arms

took up the driving thrust. They also provided mounts for the rear coil springs, ahead of the axle, leaning slightly forward and inward, abutting into brackets on a frame cross-member. Torque reactions in the axle were taken up by the third link, a short rod mounted on the right side of the axle, and running forward to a mounting bracket on the inside of the frame. This link was effective in preventing axle tramp and wheelspin. Lateral location of the axle was assured by a track rod, running across the car behind the rear axle, and attached to an axle-mounted bracket on the right and to the frame side-member on the left. Telescopic shock absorbers leaned forward and inward from their mounts at the rear end of the radius arms, with their upper ends secured to brackets on the frame kickup.

Since the Riviera was a four-passenger car with front bucket seats separated by a console, the engineers saw no harm in a high rear floor tunnel. They used this to straighten out the propeller shaft, limiting the angularity of the three universal joints. This saved some money, too, for it meant that the center joint need not be the constant-velocity type used on the Electra 225, but a simple universal joint like those at the transmission output shaft and the head of the pinion shaft. The senior-series Buicks of that time had a front suspension composed of a lower cross-arm with a drag strut, and an upper A-arm, with a coil spring mounted near the middle of the cross-arm and rising almost vertically into a spring housing in the front frame cross-member. A hefty stabilizer bar linked the two cross-arms via anchor points on the frame side-members near the front end. This suspension design was one of the best in the industry for keeping the front wheels vertical during all deflections, and was judged acceptable for the Riviera. Saginaw was asked to supply a faster-response steering gear, and came up with a unit that had a ratio of 17.5:1. Combined with a parellelogram type of linkage with a 1.18:1 ratio, this gave an overall steering ratio of 20.7:1, which meant 3½ turns of the wheel from full left to full right, with a 43.2-foot turning diameter.

Due to its low center of gravity, less than twenty inches above ground level, the Riviera was able to give a flat ride on curves despite its soft springs. In the way of ride and handling, the Riviera was unquestionably a new and unique combination. Chevrolet has an all-out sports car in the Corvette, but the Corvette's lack of ride comfort would not be acceptable in a Buick product. The credit for giving the Riviera its road behavior goes above all to Phil Bowser. He had worked at Chevrolet, and had been associated with Maurice Olley who had first developed independent front suspension (knee-action) for Cadillac and introduced the concept of vehicle dynamics as a science all of its own. Bowser insisted on very high cornering power for the Riviera. It would be intolerable to him that a Riviera could come second best to a regular car driven by somebody in a hurry, and he did all he could to provide it with handling characteristics that would make it a safe and predictable car at extraordinarily high speeds. His insistence on stability in cornering led the tire companies to come up with a new tire design especially for the Riviera. The tires had a rounder shoulder and wider tread giving extra sidebite to cope with higher cornering speeds and higher lateral forces. As a result of the difference in package size and weight, the Riviera did not need the huge 8.00-15 four-ply tires that were standard for the Electra 225, but would run on two-ply 7.10-15 tires without suffering in ride comfort or handling characteristics.

Power train for the Riviera comprised the biggest engine Buick was making at the time, mated with the most advanced automatic transmission. That was, of course, the 401-cubic-inch V-8, and the Turbine Drive. On the 1963 Riviera, the rear axle had a final drive ratio of 3.23:1. The axle was similar to that used on the Electra 225, but two inches narrower. The housing was a banjo type, and the shafts were semi-floating. The brake system of the Electra needed little modification for the Riviera. The main difference lay in the use of specially developed organic brake linings.

Public introduction date for the Riviera was October 4, 1962, when its list price of $4,333 was announced. Buick built 14,830 Riviera coupes by year-end, 1962. Due to the Riviera's great weight, it was felt necessary to

Front view of the 1963 Riviera shows the La Salle-inspired grilles covering the parking lights and turn signals. Head lamps were set in fixed position. Oval hood ornament carried stylized letter 'R.'

offer extra performance for those customers who wanted it. That was the reason why Buick decided to bore out the engine to 425 cubic inches. The extra cubes gave enough additional horsepower to place the Riviera closer to the Corvette than to the Thunderbird in acceleration and speed as well as in steering response and handling precision.

For its second model year, the Riviera continued with the same standard 325-hp V-8 but was offered with two more powerful versions, 340 and 360 SAE gross hp, depending on choice of carburetion. Equipped with the 340 SAE gross hp version of the 425-cubic-inch V-8, Super Turbine 400 transmission, and a 3.07:1 final drive ratio, the 1964 Riviera could go from standstill to 60 mph in 8.3 seconds and reach 100 mph in 25.5 seconds! The standing-start quarter-mile took 16.6 seconds, with a terminal speed of 83 mph. Top speed was 120 mph, and the car would cruise comfortably at 90 mph. Overall gasoline mileage was about fifteen miles per gallon. For the driver, the main difference between the Super Turbine 400 transmission and the Turbine Drive of the 1963 model, was the fact that now, in Drive range, the car would start off in Low whereas the Turbine Drive gearing was programmed to start off in intermediate range (mainly to prevent wheelspin on wet and slippery roads). This gave a more positive feeling when moving off the line on a dry surface. Power-operated front seats were a new option introduced for the 1964-model Riviera. The following year the body remained essentially the same, but overall length was stretched to 209 inches. The Riviera reverted to the 401-cubic-inch V-8 as the standard power unit, making the 425 optional. The standard axle ratio was 3.23:1 which gave the car a top speed of 125 mph. Cruising at 100 mph, the engine was relatively unstressed at just over 4000 rpm. Tire size was increased to 8.45-15. At the same time the simulated air scoops at the front of the rear fender panels were removed. The 1965-model Riviera also had concealed headlights, tipping out from hinged grille sections where the fixed head lamps had been mounted on earlier versions.

The Riviera GS (for Gran Sport) was announced in 1965. The package included a Super Wildcat engine rated at 360 SAE gross hp, a rear axle with 3.42:1 final drive ratio, and different interior decor. An even higher 3.58:1 final drive ratio was offered as an option for the GS. But the first Riviera GS did not have heavy-duty suspension. Buick felt that the basic Riviera suspension system had the proper spring rates to handle the extra power and performance. Saginaw power steering was standard on all Rivieras, but the GS came with a faster ratio, giving three turns lock to lock, compared with 3.4 turns for the regular setup. Top speed for the GS was slightly lower, about 112 mph, but the car had even more brutal acceleration, being capable of covering the standing-start quarter-mile in less than sixteen seconds, and going from zero to sixty in under eight seconds.

During 1963-64, Fisher Body and Oldsmobile were preparing a brand-new body for a planned front-wheel-drive car to be built by Oldsmobile. Since this project (which became the 1966 Toronado) was the same size car as the Riviera, addressed to the same market segment, the corporation decided that the 1966 Riviera was to share the new E-body. Seldom have two cars sharing the same basic body looked more different. Working inside the same envelope, with a number of identical key dimensions, Dave Holls in the Buick studio created a car with a completely different stance, from the shape Stanley Wilen developed in the Oldsmobile studio. The new Riviera remained lithe in appearance, and looked smaller and lighter than its actual size and weight gave it any right to. Wheelbase was increased from 117 to 119 inches, and the curb weight went up to 4,316 pounds.

Some essential quality of the XP-715 may have been preserved, but when you look at the whole car you see that the 1966 Riviera was quite different in character from the original. The aggressive nose had been replaced by a soft-lined design of great simplicity. The grille was a very low and wide air intake, with subtle horizontal bars recessed into the frame, whose corners were rounded off. The center was marked by edging the bars forward to a point. The sloping hood descended to the top of the grille, with a smooth slope from the cowl to the nose, where a lip came down to meet the grille frame. The W-form of the bumper was repeated in the fenders, which jutted forward from the grille ends, containing parking lights and turn signals. The headlights were concealed behind pivoted grille sections at either end. No sheet metal appeared below bumper level. The bumper contained a wide slot running the full width of the grille to serve as an air intake. The front fender line repeated the semi-hexagonal forward edge from the senior series, rose to the top of the cowl and then separated from the belt line in an easy downward sweep to blend into the door panels toward their rear edge. The rear fender line of the 1966 Riviera began at the door opening, with a bulging kickup into the sail panel, which intruded on the rear quarter windows and resulted in the window sill being curved upward and meeting the C-post at a higher level. The profile was cleverly accented by creases in the sheet metal. The upper crease was taken from the original Riviera, a series of subtle curves. The lower crease ran horizontally at wheel hub level, from fender opening to fender opening, right through the door, continuing in the rear fender skirt, and matching the bumper line in the front fender. On the 1966 Riviera, the vent windows in the doors were eliminated but the wiper arms were still cowl-mounted.

The 425-cubic-inch V-8 had now been made standard, rated at 340 SAE gross hp, and there was no higher-powered option. The variable-pitch Super Turbine 400 continued, and the axle ratio was lowered to 3.07 in order to reduce noise levels during high-speed cruising. Top speed was about 130 mph, and average fuel economy remained unchanged at about fifteen miles per gallon. Riviera buyers were given a choice of bench or bucket front seats for the first time, and cars equipped with bench seats also had column shift instead of console shift. The longer wheelbase may have had a slight benefit on the ride comfort, and heightened the stability of the car without damaging its steering response. The Riviera remained a superb road car, continuing its unique combination of soft ride with sporty handling.

In the meantime, the Electra and other senior-series Buicks had switched to a perimeter frame, so that the Riviera was now the only model in the Buick lineup to use the cruciform frame. It was also a frame that no other division wanted to share. This exclusivity meant that Buick had to pay a premium price for the Riviera frame, and this forced the division to raise the price of the car. That had no effect on the demand, however. Customers were still putting their names on waiting lists for the Riviera. Buick continued the Gran Sport option for the Riviera in 1966, and now heavy-duty suspension was added to the package. It included higher-rate front and rear coil springs, reinforced stabilizer bar and recalibrated shock absorbers. It

made for a tauter chassis, kept the car from heaving on undulating roadways and reduced body roll on curves. The 1967 Riviera received the new 430-cubic-inch V-8, but there were no major changes in either chassis or body. Despite the 20-hp increase, top speed remained the same, about 130 mph, but acceleration times were cut somewhat.

The 1968 Riviera received new refinements in the rear suspension, while retaining the three-link design. The track rod was lowered on both sides, which resulted in a lowering of the roll center, and a reduction in rear-end roll understeer. The torque arm was lengthened and its pivot point raised for improved isolation of road shocks. The cruciform frame remained practically unchanged. On the 1968 Riviera, front disc brakes became an option. It was the same Delco-Moraine system that had been made optional on the senior-series Buicks the year before, with ventilated discs and two-cylinder calipers. Steering gear modifications added 4½ feet to the turn diameter, and the lock-to-lock steering wheel movement increased to 3.6 turns. Handling response was becoming less sporty, though the car still held the road remarkably well for a vehicle in its weight class. At the same time, the Riviera body received a major facelift. A radical new bumper enveloped the split grille, rising to meet the hood, and containing the turn signals and parking lights, while the head lamps were concealed in the grille as before. The new front bumper added about four inches to the length of the car, and its overall length was now 215.2 inches. A new windshield was used, in combination with concealed wipers, mounted under the rear lip of the hood.

For the 1969 model, the grille was provided with three widely spaced horizontal bars, but no changes were made in the sheet metal. On the engineering side, the 1969 Riviera received an electric fuel pump as standard. The pump was integrated with the sensor unit for the gas tank gauge inside the tank, immersed in the fuel, and had a motor-driven impeller. The pump pushed fuel under pressure through the fuel line to the carburetor. The electric pump effectively eliminated vapor lock, and enabled the engine to run at a steady idle in a traffic jam, even with the air conditioner in use. New front suspension geometry increased directional stability but added understeer, which was the last thing the Riviera needed more of. Its overall characteristic was now changing into a highway cruiser, whereas earlier Rivieras had been quite at home on winding country roads, too.

The following year the Riviera engine was enlarged to 455 cubic inches. Power output increased to 370 SAE gross hp, and the Turbo-HydraMatic replaced the Super Turbine 400. With the standard axle ratio of 2.78:1 top speed was an even 120 mph. Cruising at 75 mph, the engine was 'loafing' just above 2500 rpm. And a 3.07:1 final drive was optional, as well as a 3.42:1 final drive for faster acceleration. Other engineering changes included adoption of a semi-closed cooling system, with a sealed radiator and

1968
MECHANICAL
FUEL PUMP

1969
ELECTRIC PUMP

Electric fuel pump was made standard on the 1969 Riviera, replacing the mechanical pump which had been in use since 1926. The electric pump weighed only five ounces and supplied a continuous fuel flow under steady pressure.

Styling changes for 1970 included a new grille, still integral with the bumper, but not including the head lamps. Fixed, open head lamps were adopted, placed side by side on either side of the grille. The grille was slightly pointed at the center and carried a number of thin vertical bars. No sheet metal changes were made, but spats were fitted in the rear wheel openings making the tail end look heavier. A new E-body had been created for the 1971 Riviera. It was mainly created by Donald C. Lasky who had replaced David R. Holls as chief designer of the Buick studio in 1968. It had a new front end with a narrow grille, the usual long hood, and a generally aggressive look. It also had a dramatic fastback roofline, with a rear window that came around the rear quarters on both sides, something in the manner of the 1963 Corvette Sting Ray coupe. This roofline had been kicked around GM Styling for twenty years or more. Most proposals that featured this roof never got further than the drawing board. Once it got as far as a dream car, the Oldsmobile Cutlass, back in 1956. Styling Director Bill Mitchell liked it, and kept it alive. It was because of his encouragement that it was adopted for the Corvette (though it was dropped again within five years). And it was Mitchell who pushed it through for the 1971 Riviera. The grille reverted to horizontal bars, but was tall and narrow rather than wide and low. This was disguised by running the bumper bar across the grille about one third of the way up, shaping the cast chrome grille with a slight V-angle at its center, and tilting it slightly forward at the top. Bumper overriders on the 1971 Riviera were carried in front of the grille and spaced only far enough apart to carry the license plate between their lower extensions. The rest of the front was very simple, with dual side-by-side head lamps set in squared-off bezels on both sides, immediately above bumper level, and turn signals and parking lights in wide horizontal lenses immediately below the bumper.

a separate overflow tank. When the coolant expanded beyond the capacity of the basic system, the overflow would be collected in the reservoir, and when the engine cooled off, the fluid in the reservoir would be syphoned back into the radiator. The power steering pump was revised to reduce oil temperature. This was achieved by replacing the former sharp-edged orifice in the flow control valve with a new venturi-type of orifice. In addition, the input shaft to the pump was equipped with a helix seal. A tandem power brake booster was adopted, and Riviera buyers who chose disc brakes for the front wheels would get a floating type of caliper with a single piston. The caliper was called 'floating' because it would automatically adjust its lateral position retative to the disc to straddle it evenly and apply equal pressure on both sides. Variable-ratio power steering was standardized, giving fairly slow change in steering angle at the wheels when first turning the wheel away from the straight-ahead position, but progressively advancing the steering angle when the driver continued to turn the wheel. Steering wheel turns, lock to lock, on the 1970 Riviera were only 2.9, compared with 3.3 on the LeSabre. Standard tire size was H78-15, with 8.55-15 and wide-tread H70-15 tires optional.

The front fender blended smoothly into the door, and the rear fender emerged from the body side without its exact starting point being obvious. As an accent line, the 1971 Riviera carried a chrome molding from the brow over the headlights, sweeping down in a gentle arc to a sharp point ahead of the rear wheel opening, where it went up in an arc above the wheel and then straight back to coincide with the rear deck profile. This was a line closely identified with Buick, having originated on the 1953 Skylark. The curved body crease tracing the fender lines at the widest point along the whole body side was lowered in relation to the belt line, but served to retain a strong Riviera flavor in the body. The roofline ended in a taper, giving rise to a boattail theme at the rear end. The rear fenders widened in a corresponding taper from the sail panels to the taillights, which were horizontal lenses inserted in the body panel below the deck lid. Both front and rear bumpers came to a sharp point in the middle.

Boat tail theme of the 1971 Riviera was wildly controversial, but its defenders say it's an old tradition at Buick, traceable back through the experimental LeSabre of 1951 to the Y-Job of 1939. It was practical enough, but looked wrong for its time.

For 1973 the Riviera GS had revised front and rear end styling, radial tires and a new suspension-tuning package. The short vinyl top was another innovation. But the Riviera kept losing popularity, and a change was going to become necessary soon.

Inside the car, the Riviera had to share the standard instrument panel from the other senior series. It was redesigned for greater service accessibility, so that the entire panel could be loosened and pulled off to bare the backs of the instruments and their wiring in a matter of minutes. The speedometer was a rectangular design, flanked by side panels tilted toward the driver, with heater controls, switches for lights and wipers/washers on the left and a dash clock at right. The radio was placed above the huge ashtray at the head of the console. The 1971 Riviera was built on a shortened Electra chassis. The cruciform frame had been taken out of production, and Riviera chassis engineering was brought fully in line with the senior series Buicks. Size and weight increased again. The 1971 Riviera was built on a 122-inch wheelbase and was 217.4 inches long overall. Curb weight was 4,464 pounds. The frame was a perimeter type, wide side members coming out almost to the full body width between the front and rear wheels, narrowing slightly before being kicked up over the rear axle, and coming in to embrace the engine between the front wheels. Sharing this type of frame with the Electra series permitted the Riviera to share the Electra's four-link rear axle suspension system as well.

Self-leveling rear suspension became optional at the same time. Available on the Electra since 1967, it was a Delco system with pneumatic bellows mounted on top of the shock absorbers, connected to an engine-driven compressor. It would go into action automatically when carrying heavy loads in the trunk, or rear seat passengers, to keep the static load from compressing the springs, using up the deflection reserve, and giving the whole car a squat-tail attitude.

Horsepower fell to 315 SAE gross as the compression ratio had been reduced to 8.5:1, and acceleration times were stretched. About 10 mph of top speed were lost, too. An optional version of the same engine, with special carburetion and a different camshaft, was rated at 335 SAE gross hp.

Front disc brakes were standardized, and a new anti-wheelspin device was made optional. It was a joint development between AC and Buick, with Robert A. Grimm of AC handling the electronics and production side and James H. Moran of Buick taking charge of vehicle installation. Called the Max-Trac system, it consisted of a small electronic computer with two sensors. One sensor was mounted at the transmission output line and measured driving-wheel speed. The other sensor was mounted on the left front wheel hub and registered front wheel speed. The transistorized computer continuously compared the input from the two sensors, and went into action when the difference exceeded a certain value—ten percent faster rotation in the rear wheels. The 12-volt feed wire to the ignition coil was routed through the computer, and when the computer signaled to ease off on the power, an oscillator would actuate a power switch hooked into the coil-feed wire and break the ignition circuit for ten milliseconds at a time. The cycle could be repeated up to fifty times a second, depending on the severity of the wheelspin. The computer signals would continue until the speed difference had subsided to eight percent. Max-Trac was made available on all the senior-series Buicks during 1971 and 1972, but then it was killed because in 1973

Built on a 122-inch wheelbase, the 1975 Riviera was almost fully integrated with the B- and C-body cars in the Buick range. It had its own grille and ornamentation, but the old distinction was gone. Buick decided to make it smaller for 1977.

new emission-control standards came into effect, and engines with intermittent firing could not meet them.

The 1970 Riviera had a long 2.78:1 final drive ratio. This was changed to 2.93:1 for 1971 as a result of the additional weight. The Riviera GS, however, came with a 3.42:1 final drive ratio in both years. For 1972 the Riviera went to a mouth-organ grille pattern, inside the same vertical frame. At the same time, the taillight design was revised, and an electrically operated sunroof became optional. The following year, the whole front end was facelifted. The grille was lowered and its heavy frame toned down. The parking lights and turn signals were moved up to the fender corners outside of the head lamps, and a less aggressive bumper was fitted. At the rear end, the taillights were integrated with the bumper. There were no sheet metal changes. This design continued practically without change through 1974.

Performance levels were maintained in the 1972 models, for the actual power had not changed much, only the methods of testing and measuring (from SAE gross to SAE net hp). The net hp of the 1971 baseline engine was 259, while it was 253 the following year (and advertised as 250). For the optional higher-powered engine, 1971 net output was 269 hp and for 1972 it was 264 (advertised as 260). The Riviera still had a top speed of 112 mph. Turbo-HydraMatic remained standard, with column shift for all seating options. It was for the 1973 model that Buick finally cleared steel-belted radial-ply tires for the Riviera. The tread was a GM design, which five major tire makers agreed to supply (Goodyear, Firestone, B.F. Goodrich, Uniroyal and General). In 1972 the only option was the wide-tread low-profile H70-15, but on 1973 models, one could specify HR70-15 radials, though

the standard Riviera tire remained a bias-ply H78-15 on six-inch-wide rims. The following year Buick decided to increase tire sizes in order to keep up with the load increase. The Riviera had gained over 200 pounds in three years—mainly due to bumper standards. While J78-15's on six-inch rims became standard, customers could order JR78-15 radials on seven-inch rims. Speed capacity remained almost the same, despite successive cuts in power output. While the 1974 engine delivered its maximum output of 230 SAE net hp at only 3800 rpm, the car was still capable of exceeding 100 mph by a clear margin. But fuel consumption had increased dramatically, due to the effect of the emission-control systems adopted, along with the weight increase. It was not uncommon for Riviera owners to get eight to eleven miles per gallon in 1973-74.

But 1974 was to be the last year of the Riviera's distinctively individual styling. With the 1975 model, the Riviera lost its main distinction from the rest of the Buick line. It was using more and more of the B-body sheet metal, and no longer had a clear styling theme of its own. The 1975-model Riviera had a long hood and a fast roofline with a short sloping deck. But it was a notchback, not a fastback anymore. The fender line was unbroken, running horizontally from the front and melting into the belt line in the front door, then sweeping down to the rear bumper. The traditional Riviera accent line had been obliterated, and the rear fender kickup erased. The 1975 Riviera had a rectangular grille, fairly narrow, but with a horizontal outline, though the bars were vertical. A mouth-organ pattern was adopted for the 1976 model. On both sides of the grille were rectangular headlights, now permitted by the Department of Transportation, inserted in the fender panels, with rectangular turn signals and parking lights in the fender edges.

The 1975 Riviera continued on a 122-inch wheelbase, and overall length grew to 233 inches. Its curb weight now reached 4,700 pounds. Engine displacement remained unchanged, but compression was lowered to 7.9:1, which further reduced power output to 205 SAE net hp, without boosting gasoline mileage at all. For 1976, the final drive ratio was lowered from 2.93:1 to 2.56:1 in an effort to save fuel by turning the engine more slowly. But the results in actual consumer use did not give the same benefits as were promised by proving-ground tests. At the same time, the Riviera's performance fell to levels reached by many ordinary cars, and part of the Riviera appeal had been lost. This was hardly the kind of car that could enhance Buick's image in the new era with its emphasis on fuel economy. Sales fell abruptly to about 20,000 in 1974, and did not even come to 15,000 the following year. Far from being an asset, the Riviera had become a colossal liability. The answer, obviously, was a new and smaller Riviera. It appeared as a 1977 model.

The 1977 Riviera was more than 700 pounds lighter and about five in-

Compare this profile with the 1963-model Riviera, and you'll see that the actual proportions are very similar, but the 1977 car lacks the individual styling; the dramatic elegance that set its ancestor apart from all other cars.

ches shorter than the 1976 model. Built on a 115.9-inch wheelbase, the new Riviera was powered by Buick's 350-cubic-inch V-8 as the standard engine, while a 403-cubic-inch V-8 made by Oldsmobile was optional. With the standard engine, top speed was only about 90 mph, while the optional power unit could barely reach 100 mph. The 1977 Riviera was built with its own edition of the new Fisher B-body. No longer a hardtop, it had a pillared roof, and doors with full frames around the glass.

Its major engineering change was the adoption of four-wheel disc brakes as standard equipment. Using discs on all four wheels brings important benefits. Most important is better front/rear balance or compatibility, because rear-wheel disc brakes will give the same basic performance throughout their full range of operating temperature as the front-wheel discs—something that drum brakes cannot achieve. Secondly, the use of rear-wheel discs reduces the risk of premature locking of the rear wheels, because disc brakes are fully dependent on line pressure for brake force and not subject to self-energizing effects (as drums are). Brake pad life for a four-wheel disc brake system can be up to fifty percent greater than in disc/drum combinations. Because of lower sensitivity to water, disc brakes on the rear wheels will make sure the rear wheels perform a fuller share of the braking duties.

While sharing the Electra frame and body, suspension and steering units, the Riviera still has some essential differences, such as spring rates and shock absorber calibration. "The Riviera has been moving toward the Electra," admits Buick's chief engineer, Lloyd Reuss, "but the 1977 model has different ride and handling than the Electra. We worked toward getting a crisp feel." The point isn't what the Riviera has in common with the Electra or how it differs. The point is that it's no longer the same type of car that Buick launched in 1963 and that did so much to enhance Buick's reputation. The name Riviera had become just another merchandising label. It's a great name, and the current model probably sells better because of it than if it had been named Electra GS or Electra S/R. New E-body cars are under development for the 1979 model year (though the program may be delayed until 1980). The E-body car family will then again include the Riviera, Toronado and Eldorado. All will be front-wheel-drive cars, as pioneered by Oldsmobile, but on a smaller scale. All three cars are expected to adopt a 116-inch wheelbase, and the new E-body to follow European design trends, with considerable emphasis on improved aerodynamics. Perhaps the Riviera will then regain its lost glory.

CHAPTER 11

Buick's Modern V-8 Engines

No TIME! That was the situation when Joe Turlay and Cliff Studaker were told to come up with a small cast-iron V-8 for the new intermediate-size Special due to go into production in September 1963. They had hardly got the V-6 off the drawing board before they were called upon to meet a seemingly impossible schedule for getting a new V-8 ready for production. As a matter of fact, there was no time to tool up for a brand-new engine, even if they could design and develop one. The engine designers had to work under the obligation of using existing parts and building the engine on an existing line. As a result, it made maximum use of design elements from both the aluminum V-8 and the cast-iron V-6. In strict terms, it must be said that Buick's small cast-iron V-8 was developed from the V-6, which means that it was indirectly derived from the aluminum V-8. It had the same cylinder bore spacing and the same bore and stroke as the V-6, which gave it a displacement of 300 cubic inches. The 300-cubic-inch cast-iron V-8 was manufactured on the same machine line that had been used for the 215-cubic-inch aluminum V-8.

Taking over the aluminum cylinder heads from the light alloy V-8, it was reworked with larger valves, ports and intake manifold. But for 1965, new cast-iron cylinder heads were introduced. At the same time, a new cast-iron intake manifold was added, and the water-jacket was eliminated in favor of normal exhaust heating for warmup. In the process, the engine's net weight went from 405 to 467 pounds. In its initial, base form, with two-

barrel carburetor and a 9.0:1 compression ratio, the 300-cubic-inch V-8 was rated at 210 SAE gross hp at 4600 rpm, with a maximum torque of 310 pounds-feet at 2400 rpm. It was optional in both Specials and Skylarks, which used the V-6 as their standard power unit. The following year, Buick developed a Gran Sport version of this engine, with four-barrel carburetor and a nominal compression ratio of 11.0:1. For this high-performance version, Buick claimed 250 SAE gross hp at 4800 rpm, with a peak torque of 335 pounds-feet at 3000 rpm. In addition to serving in the junior series, the base version of the 300-cubic-inch V-8 was standard on the 1965 LeSabre, and the high-performance version was optional.

Both versions lacked the necessary torque to come up to Buick standards of smoothness and driveability in the LeSabre, even if they did a perfectly adequate job in the intermediates. Buick therefore decided to increase its displacement. The 340-cubic-inch V-8 was introduced for the 1966 model year. It was a stroked version of the existing 300-cubic-inch V-8, which continued in production, with the same cylinder bore of 3.75 inches, but a longer stroke of 3.85 inches instead of 3.40 inches. As far as stroke/bore ratios are concerned, this was a reversal of Buick policy since the commencement of V-8 production, in that all previous units were 'over-square' but here the stroke was longer, with a stroke/bore ratio of 1.026:1. The base version of the 340-cubic-inch V-8 was equipped with a two-barrel carburetor and had a compression ratio of 9:1. Its power output was 220

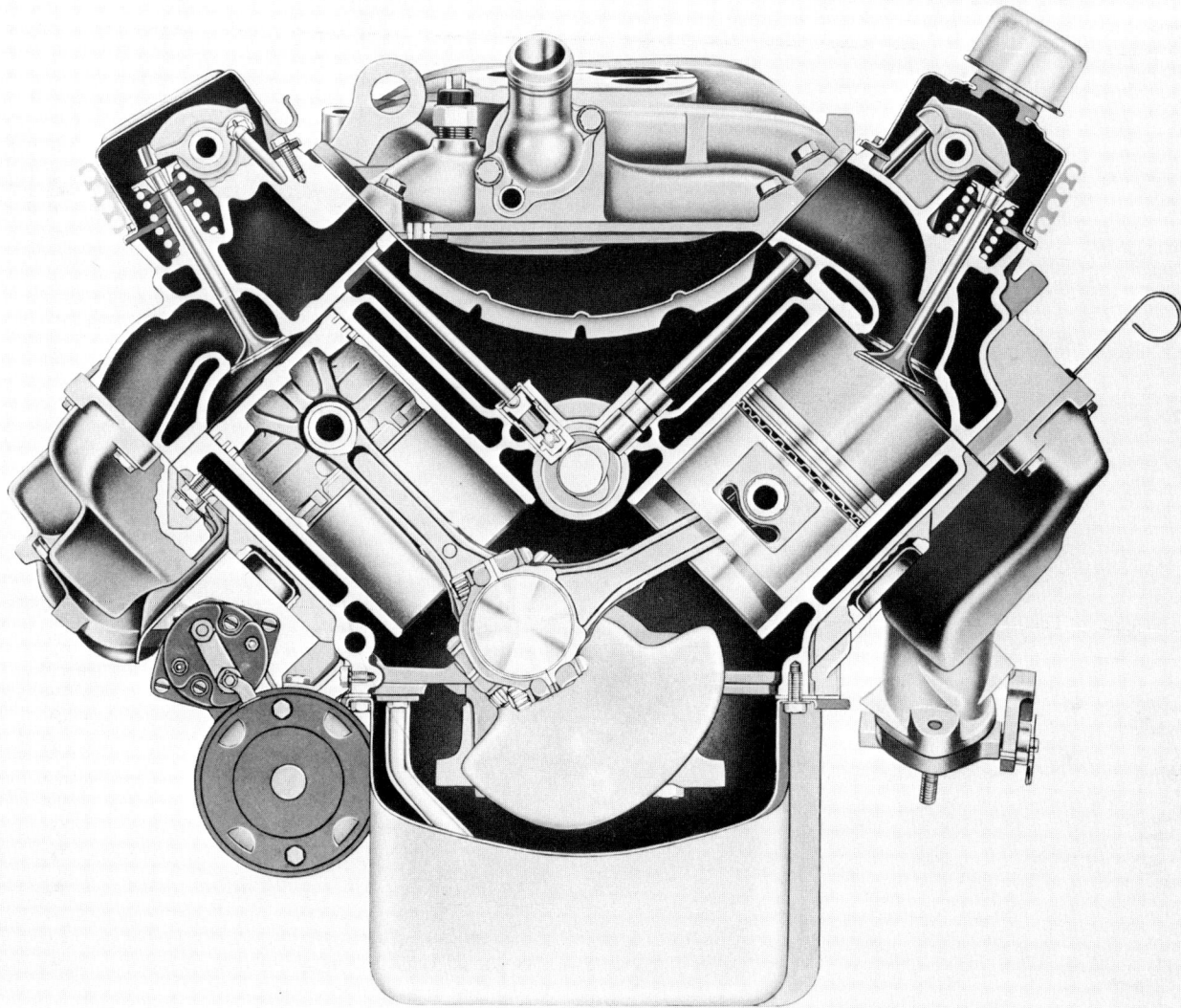

Cross section of the 1967-model 430-cubic-inch engine shows entirely new valve gear, pistons with slightly recessed crowns and compact wedge-shaped combustion chambers. Crankcase is shorter in depth than traditionally in Buick engines.

119

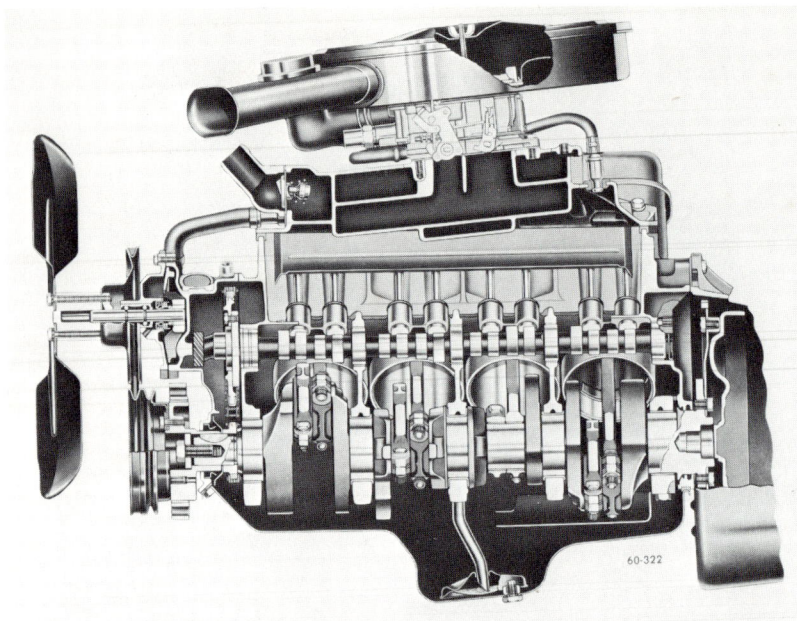

Sectioned side view of Buick's 455-cubic-inch V-8 shows rugged crankshaft with large bearings and full counter-weighting. A torsional vibration damper was attached at the front end, behind the belt drive pulley.

SAE gross hp at 4200 rpm, and its peak torque 340 pounds-feet, realized at a speed of 2400 rpm. The high-performance version came with a four-barrel carburetor and a 10.25:1 compression ratio, which raised the output to 260 SAE gross hp at 4000 rpm, and the maximum torque to 365 pounds-feet at 2800 rpm.

Buick test engineers found that the induction system of the 1967-model 340-cubic-inch V-8 did not control the air/fuel ratio sufficiently to meet the new emission control standards coming into effect in 1968. Consequently, cylinder heads and manifolds were redesigned to bring them in line with the components used for the 400- and 430-cubic-inch V-8's, which had gone into production for the 1967 model year. This was the start of a very successful crossbreeding of the 'small-block' and 'big-block' Buick V-8's, which was to go on for the greater part of a decade. These 'big-block' en-gines were a new generation of V-8 designs, incorporating the fruits of Cliff Studaker's entire experience, and were the concrete result of the advances made in Buick's engine technology over the course of fifteen years.

Preliminary studies for the new generation of V-8 engines began in 1962. At this stage, even the basic engine arrangement of the ninety-degree V-8 was questioned, but a thorough examination of all possible configurations with regard to the potential for reducing engine height and weight, and exploiting the newest foundry and machining techniques, showed that the ninety-degree V-8 did indeed provide the best layout with a minimum of compromise. The main reason for Buick's decision to bring out completely new V-8 engines at this time was technical. The old engines had reached the end of their development potential, and contained compromise solutions that were beginning to give rise to new problems. The older engines, expanded to their limit, were lacking in breathing capacity, because valve spacing and port configurations were not as easily altered as bore and stroke changes could be made. As a result, Buick was forced to make up for the deficiencies in porting and valve size by extending valve duration and overlap beyond normal limits. Excessive overlap and duration make for a rough idle and poor low-speed operation, wastes fuel under light-load conditions, and creates emission-control problems.

Cliff Studaker set the following objectives for the new engines: They must have increased breathing potential and operate with greater smoothness and lower noise levels under light load conditions; they must give greater durability; and wherever possible, the design must be simplified for easier manufacturing, assembly, service and repair. It is noteworthy that the design goals omitted any consideration of air pollution and emission controls. There was no Clean Air Act at the time the design was started, and no emission standards had been set by the date of production startup.

Actual design work started in June 1964. Since improved volumetric efficiency was the primary objective, Studaker started with the design elements that are connected with gas flow. He chose a Rochester Quadrajet four-barrel carburetor with 1.375-inch-diameter primaries and 2.25-inch-diameter secondaries, for the most suitable combination of unrestricted breathing under wide-open throttle acceleration and accurate control over air/fuel ratios under a wide variety of part-throttle conditions. The primary inlets were centered on the manifold, with the secondaries located further forward. There was no advantage in offsetting the secondaries, but it was important to center the primaries in order to minimize variations in fuel-mixture distribution between the cylinders when the engine was running only on the primaries. The manifold was designed for the lowest restriction to air flow from the carburetor flange to each intake port. As a result, it became quite voluminous, with a cross-sectional area of 3.42 square inches in the main fore-and-aft runners, and 2.59 square inches in the individual branches.

The intake ports in the cylinder heads were 2.65 square inches in cross-sectional area, and straight pipes led directly to the valves, where the ports were contoured to induce a swirl in the gas flow. The combustion chamber was more closely related to the design developed for the small-block V-8 than to the pentroof layout of the earlier big-block units. The type of pistons used was the same as in the 300- and 340-cubic-inch V-8's with a circular depression surrounded by an annular topland. Combustion chambers in the cylinder head were shallow, slanted saucer shapes, with the valves inclined no more than fifteen degrees from the cylinder center line. The topland corresponded to only 15.3 percent of piston area, so that the quench area was quite small. The compact combustion space also assured a low surface-to-volume ratio, which was a wonderful piece of serendipity, since that was to be regarded in later years as a basic condition for controlling hydrocarbon emissions.

The engine was built in two sizes, both with the same 3.90-inch stroke, and bores of 4.04 and 4.188 inches to give 400- and 430-cubic-inch displacement. Stroke/bore ratio was 0.965 in the smaller unit and 0.931 in the larger one. Intake valve heads were 2.00 inches in diameter, and exhaust valve heads 1.625 inches. In the smaller version, the valve head diameter was 49.5 percent of the bore, and in the larger one, 47.75 percent. The valve center line intersected the cylinder center line at 'deck' level, with the spark plug as close to the center as its 14-mm thread would permit. Valves were practically unshrouded, providing unhindered entry for the fresh charge and a ready exit for the exhaust gases. The exhaust port was curved quite sharply (due to the valve inclination towards the intake side) but port area was fifty-six percent greater than in the 425-cubic-inch engine, so the flow characteristics were dramatically improved. The intake port cross-sectional area on the 430 V-8 was eighteen percent greater than on the 425-cubic-inch V-8.

A clever arrangement was made for preheating the air and fuel in the intake manifold during warmup. The cylinder heads contained a drilled hole of 0.687-inch diameter at each of the two central exhaust ports, serving as a crossover to the intake manifold. A new air cleaner with less than half the restriction of the 1966 model used with the same carburetor aided materially towards good cylinder filling. The new engine had almost no interchangeable parts with the earlier unit. About the only thing that remained in the new block was the same bore spacing of 4.75 inches. But the bore staggering was reversed, and consequently the new engine could not be manufactured on the same line. New machinery was installed.

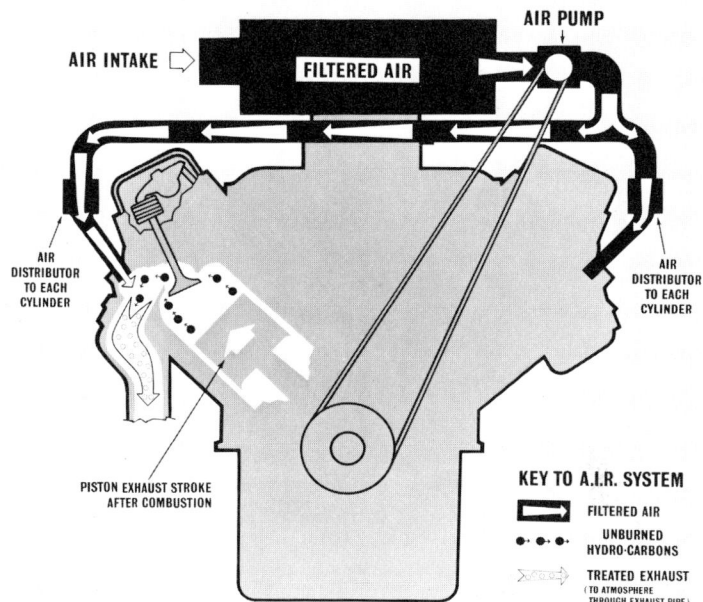

AIR PUMP
AIR INTAKE
FILTERED AIR
AIR DISTRIBUTOR TO EACH CYLINDER
AIR DISTRIBUTOR TO EACH CYLINDER
PISTON EXHAUST STROKE AFTER COMBUSTION

KEY TO A.I.R. SYSTEM
FILTERED AIR
UNBURNED HYDRO-CARBONS
TREATED EXHAUST (TO ATMOSPHERE THROUGH EXHAUST PIPE)

Air-Injection-Reactor system was mainly aimed at consuming unburned hydrocarbons escaping from the combustion process. A belt-driven air pump drew fresh air from the air cleaner and delivered it under pressure to the exhaust port areas.

The block and crankcase ended 0.25 of an inch below the crankshaft center line, in contrast with previous Buick engineering practice. The crankshaft was cast from nodular iron with five main bearings of 3.25-inch diameter. Crankpin journals had 2.25-inch diameter, which combined with a crank throw of 1.95 inches gave an overlap of 0.65 inches with an overlap cross section of 1.04 square inches.

A series of test engines had been made with crankshafts of three-inch main bearing diameter, and proved satisfactory in initial tests. But in durability testing, a number of broken crankshafts turned up. Typically they cracked and then fractured in the crank arm between the number-three crankpin and the number-four main bearing. As a result of these failures,

BUICK'S 455 ENGINE

NICKEL PLATED

INCREASED DEPRESSION

1971   1970

Left, new intake manifolds were designed for two-barrel (bottom) and four-barrel (top) carburetor versions of the 400- and 430-cubic-inch V-8's introduced for the 1967 models. They were made for better breathing, but with no regard for emission control. Right, for the 1971 models, Buick redesigned the 455-cubic-inch engine to run on unleaded gasoline and reduced the compression ratio from 10:1 to 8.5:1 by increasing the depression in the piston crown. Exhaust valves were nickel-plated to protect them against sticking to the seats.

crankshaft main bearing diameter was increased to 3.25 inches and the cylinder block bulkhead was made thicker to give better support. Counterweights were precision-cast to size and needed no machining. Final balancing was accomplished by drilling radial holes in counterweights that were too heavy. The crankshaft also carried twenty-six ounce-inches of external counterweighting in both the vibration-damper and flywheel. Connecting rods and caps were one-piece steel forgings, machined as a unit and then split for assembly. The full-skirted pistons carried two compression rings and an oil control ring. The oil pump was integral with the front cover. The pump drew in oil from the sump through an intake screen mounted on the center main bearing bulkhead. Drilled holes provided passages to the front of the cylinder block and the oil-pump cavity. Pressurized oil from the pump circulated in two galleries to the main and connecting rod bearings, camshaft bearings, valve lifters and overhead valve gear. The distributor shaft gears were lubricated by leakage oil from the front camshaft bearing. Spill oil thrown from the gears was used to lubricate the fuel pump eccentric and timing chain.

Cylinder head bolts were increased from 0.437 inch to 0.50 inch in order to provide the desired clamping load between the cylinder head, the steel-beaded head gasket and the cylinder block. Rocker arm shafts were cast integrally with the cylinder heads, and the saddles for the rocker arm shaft were broached during basic head machining. That assured accurate positioning of the rocker arms relative to the valves. The intake manifold was mounted above the V-area between the cylinder heads, with a single-piece gasket to seal the junction of the manifold with both heads. This gasket also served as a baffle and heat shield for the crossover section of the manifold. This arrangement provided a large open air space under the manifold in the valve-lifter gallery. To evacuate ventilation gases from this cavity, the PCV valve was located at the rear of the manifold.

Water pump cover, impeller, water outlet, engine front cover and oil pump cover were aluminum die-castings. Both new V-8's weighed 605 pounds including accessories, compared with 611 pounds for the ultimate 425-cubic-inch unit. That works out at a weight/power ratio of 1.68 pounds per hp in the larger unit and 1.78 in the smaller one. The 400-cubic-inch V-8 was advertised as delivering 340 SAE gross hp at 5000 rpm, with a maximum torque of 440 pounds-feet at 3200 rpm. Its specific power output was 0.85 hp per cubic inch. It was equipped with a four-barrel carburetor and had a 10.25:1 compression ratio. The 430-cubic-inch V-8 breathed through a four-barrel carburetor and had a compression ratio of 10.25:1. It delivered 360 SAE gross hp at 5000 rpm, and had a maximum torque of 475 pounds-feet at 3200 rpm. Its specific power output was 0.837 hp per cubic inch.

Buick's new 430-cubic-inch V-8 was standard equipment for the 1967 Wildcat, Electra 225 and Riviera. The 400-cubic-inch V-8 was standard in the Skylark GS-400 and optional in the Sportwagon. All engines destined for cars to be sold in California were equipped with a new device developed to meet that state's stricter emission controls. It was called AIR (Air Injection Reactor), and had been under development since August 1964. It was first applied to 1966 models (Buick 401- and 425-cubic-inch engines). AIR was developed by George W. Niepoth and Stanley H. Mick of the GM Engineering Staff and made available to all car divisions. The system was based on the idea of pumping fresh air into the exhaust manifold to dilute the pollutant concentrations in the exhaust gases. A Saginaw rotary pump compressed fresh air and delivered it through hoses, air distribution manifolds and injection tubes to the exhaust ports. The system included two check valves to prevent back flow of exhaust gases, an anti-backfiring valve to prevent spontaneous ignition in the exhaust manifold and a relief valve to prevent overcharging at high rpm.

Engines for all the 1968 models had a new Buick-developed set of emission controls called CCS for Controlled Combustion System. The CCS

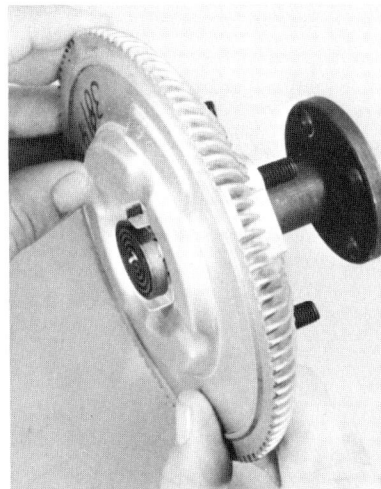

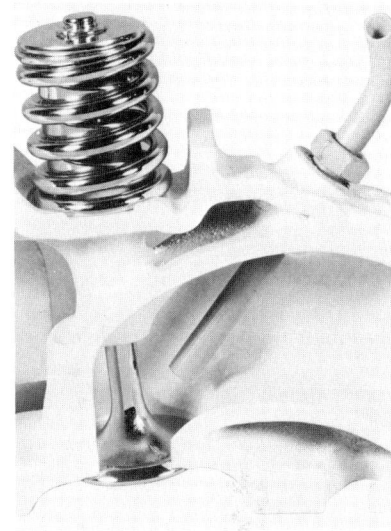

Left, Buick adopted the Delco viscous fan coupling on its 1968-model V-8 engines. The thermostat coil can be seen in the hub. The fan was allowed to run at lower speed when less cooling was required, thereby saving power losses in the fan drive. Right, air nozzle for A.I.R. system was inserted into the exhaust manifold and delivered a steady flow of fresh air with high oxygen content to ignite and consume unburned combustion products. Air quantity varied with engine speed.

package included preheated air, lean carburetion, modified spark advance curve and a closed crankcase ventilation system. The left bank exhaust manifold served as a heater for the intake air. When the engine was cold, air flowed over the exhaust manifold surface between the manifold casting and its sheet-metal shroud. This air was pulled through a pipe connected to the air cleaner, where a thermostat regulated hot-air admission according to temperature in the combined air flow. Other modifications included the adoption of an improved oil-wetted pleated-paper air filter for the 1968 engines. At the same time a wick oiler was added to the ignition distributor to minimize rubbing-block wear.

For the 1968 model year, the small-block V-8 was bored out to 3.80 inches, which raised the displacement from 340 to 350 cubic inches, and modified the stroke/bore ratio to 1.013:1. Among structural modifications for the 350-cubic-inch V-8 were rocker-arm-shaft mounting brackets cast integrally with the cylinder head, just as on the big-block engine. The 350-cubic-inch V-8 also received a new camshaft, with cam profiles reworked to give smoother idle and assist in emission control. Valves were enlarged, and the choke thermostat was relocated in the manifold for more accurate sensing. The fuel pump was provided with stronger springs to improve pressure control and a self-aligning wear pad on the pump arm to reduce wear. In its base form, the 350-cubic-inch V-8 delivered 230 SAE gross hp at 4400 rpm with a maximum torque of 350 pounds-feet at 2400 rpm. It was equipped with a two-barrel carburetor and had a compression ratio of 9.0:1. The high-performance version had a 10.25:1 compression ratio and a four-barrel carburetor, which raised the output to 280 SAE gross hp at 4600 rpm, with a maximum torque of 375 pounds-feet at 3200 rpm. The base version of the 350-cubic-inch V-8 was standard on the 1968 LeSabre, with the high-performance edition available as an option.

The smaller edition of the big-block engine was found to be superfluous as the small-block engine increased in displacement, and the 400-cubic-inch V-8 was dropped at the end of the 1969 model year. One year later, the 430-cubic-inch V-8 was replaced by the 455-cubic-inch V-8, for the 1970 models. The new engine was basically a bored-out version of the 430-cubic-inch units but it had a totally new cylinder block and valve gear. The 455-cubic-inch V-8 had a bore and stroke of 4.313×3.90 inches, which gave a stroke/bore ratio of 0.904. Intake valve head diameter remained at 2.00 inches, which now regressed to 46.4 percent of the cylinder bore. Exhaust valve head diameter, on the other hand, was increased to 1.75 inches.

Valve gear for the 455-cubic-inch V-8 represented a new departure in Buick's engineering practice. The design retained the central camshaft with pushrods to shaft-mounted rocker arms. The major new elements consisted of tubular pushrods which were supplied with oil under pressure from the hydraulic valve lifters, and delivered oil to the rocker arms. A new rocker arm shaft was produced by extrusion and had a carbonitrided surface for greater wear resistance. Rocker arms were die-cast aluminum, retained on the shaft by nylon buttons in place of the spacer springs used on the 430-cubic-inch V-8. The block had an enlarged main oil gallery designed to reduce the pressure drop at high flow rates. The oil passages had been redesigned to accommodate the new valve gear. Main bearing caps were provided with a deeper section and equipped with a different type of bolt.

The 1970-model 455-cubic-inch V-8 had a carburetor with a new time-modulated choke control, in which the 0.170-inch-thick cast wall which surrounded the thermostatic coil was replaced by a 0.042-inch-thick stainless steel pocket that gave better heat transfer. This resulted in easier starting and quicker disengagement of the choke, which helped reduce emission levels. The 1970 emission control system included transmission-controlled spark advance. Cars destined for California also were equipped with an evaporative control system, which consisted of a charcoal-filled canister intended to store gasoline vapors escaping from the fuel system when the car was parked. For the 1970 models the 350-cubic-inch V-8 was refined in several areas, being brought in line with the latest advances from the 455-cubic-inch big-block engine. It received a new valve train with tubular pushrods. They were filled with oil, bled from the hydraulic valve lifters, and lubricated the rocker arms when this oil was forced out at the top end.

For 1971 the 455-cubic-inch V-8 was redesigned to run on regular gasoline, and the compression ratio was lowered from 10:1 to 8.5:1. This was done by increasing the depression in the piston crown. Valve springs and camshafts were reworked. New exhaust cam profiles gave reduced valve acceleration rates for both opening and closing. Dampeners with higher load were used to prevent valve spring surge and to make valve movement conform more closely to the actual cam profile. Exhaust valves were nickel-plated to increase durability. Another modification in the 1971 455-cubic-inch engine was adding one-eighth inch to the primary throat's diameter in the four-barrel Rochester carburetor. The water pump shaft bearing was redesigned with greater load capacity, and the shaft itself was extended to carry the fan clutch. On earlier engines, the fan clutch was piloted on the hub. In order to maintain a certain performance superiority in the Gran Sport engine, the 1971 Riviera GS engine had larger intake valves (one-eighth inch larger valve head diameter) than the regular engine, and a camshaft with 0.032-inch higher lift and three degrees longer intake valve duration. But horsepower fell drastically due to the cut in compression ratio. The engine was offered in three versions: 315 hp for the LeSabre GS, 330 hp for the Riviera and Centurion, and 345 hp for the Riviera GS. At the start of the 1972 model year, the industry switched to SAE net horsepower. The term 'net' is to be understood as *installed* horsepower, reflecting the power actually delivered at the flywheel the way the engine is equipped in the car. Under this net formula, the engine is tested with its complete intake and exhaust systems, cooling system, generator, starter motor and full emission-control equipment. The accompanying table shows what happened to the horsepower ratings. These two V-8 engines (350 and 455 cubic inches) continued without noteworthy change in 1973 and 1974. But for 1975 they were equipped with catalytic converters in order to meet the new and stricter emission control standards. Compared with 1974, the maximum permitted levels of the regulated pollutants were cut in half. This table shows how we got there (all numbers are listed in grams per mile):

Year	Standard	Unburned hydrocarbons	Carbon monoxide	Oxides of nitrogen
1968	Uncontrolled	15.0	90	5.0
1974	Federal	3.0	28	3.1
1974	California	2.9	28	2.1
1975	Federal	1.5	15	3.1
1975	California	0.9	9.0	2.0

Since 1970, the GM Research Laboratories, GM Engineering Staff, the car divisions and AC Spark Plug Division had been developing a catalytic converter system that would enable existing engines to meet the 1975 standards. The catalyst in the AC system is an oxidizing catalyst. The converter must oxidize toxic carbon monoxide into harmless carbon dioxide and water vapor. The catalyst was needed to make this chemical reaction take place fast enough, and it had to be of a type that would repeatedly emerge unchanged after taking part in the process. GM chose two noble metals, platinum and palladium. They were applied to the surface of a supporting substrate pellet structure, containing a multitude of small alumina balls, about one-eighth inch in diameter. Alumina is known to chemists as Al_2O_3 and is a lightweight metallic substance that gives an enormous surface area in relation to unit volume. The catalyst bed was wrapped in a thin aluminum cover contained in a double-shelled stainless steel container that was incorporated in the exhaust system, ahead of the muffler. Buick used three sizes of catalytic converters, Model 135 (with 135-cubic-inch displacement) for the V-6; Model 175 for the 350-cubic-inch V-8; and Model 260 for the 455-cubic-inch V-8. Because the catalytic converters were able to handle greater pollutant volume than 1974-model engines emitted, they offered an opportunity to restore some efficiency and driveability. Buick, as one of many, went to a steeper spark advance curve. In addition, carburetors were set for a leaner mixture to give more economical running. Though in-car fuel economy was improved from 1974 to 1975, largely by gearing and other modifications, engine horsepower ratings continued to decline. Here is what happened to Buick's V-8's:

Cu. in.	Carb.	1974 Net hp @ rpm	1975 Net hp @ rpm
350	2-bbl.	150 @ 3600	145 @ 3200
350	4-bbl.	175 @ 3800	165 @ 3800
455	4-bbl.	210 @ 3600	205 @ 3800

By 1974 the 455-cubic-inch V-8 carried, in addition to the Air Injection Reactor, pre-heated intake air, retarded spark timing and exhaust gas recirculation. A small amount of exhaust gas was fed back into the engine to reduce nitrous oxide emissions.

At the end of the 1976 model year, the 455-cubic-inch V-8 was discontinued. The only V-8 now produced by Buick is the 350-cubic-inch cast-iron V-8 which can be traced back to the aluminum engine for the first compact Special. Buick now buys engines from the other divisions to round out its power train availability, such as a lightweight 301-cubic-inch V-8 made by Pontiac and a 403-cubic-inch V-8 made by Oldsmobile. General Motors is drifting towards a corporate engine plan, the same way all divisions share the same Fisher bodies, for instance. Buick, which was an engine producer before building complete cars, may eventually be left out of the corporate engine manufacturing program altogether.

CHAPTER 12

The Road to Proliferation

BACK IN 1965 cars carrying the Buick name came in only two sizes. Ten years later Buick was to be represented in four different size groups: subcompact, compact, intermediate and full-size. For those who think that the new small Buicks aren't real Buicks, and defy Buick's traditions, we can only say they are looking at the wrong time frame for their idea of tradition. Don't forget that it was a light car powered by a two-cylinder engine that put Buick on the map, and it was the four-cylinder Buick that made Flint the home of an auto industry giant. What is all too apparent, however, is a certain sameness throughout all GM car programs, within each class, so that all compacts look alike, all intermediates resemble each other, and all standard cars have great similarities, regardless of which division they belong to. All divisions now compete in all price classes, except for a thin wedge reserved for Cadillac at the top end, and a minuscule margin set aside for Chevrolet at the bottom end. The overlap among Buick, Oldsmobile and Pontiac is complete. But each division does offer a complete line of at least four basically different series, in various sizes, from subcompact to standard. In Buick's case the 1975 lineup stood like this:

Subcompact	Skyhawk	Standard	LeSabre
Compact	Skylark	Standard (luxury)	Electra 225
Intermediate	Century	Standard (specialty)	Riviera

This proliferation at the product end has come about simultaneously with the adoption of firm corporate coordination of all corporate engineering and manufacturing programs. Without that, Buick could not profitably compete in so many segments of the market. By accepting the advantages of lower cost that comes from sharing corporate components, however, Buick has had to give up a great deal of its independence in the product planning, development and production areas. This process has not been completed without upheaval. Many new outside factors came to dictate certain aspects of product policy throughout General Motors—the Motor Vehicle Safety Act of 1966, the Clean Air Act (Amendment) of 1970, the energy shortage and the erosion of the dollar—have all played a part in setting Buick's course in recent times.

To take charge of Buick after Rollert's departure in 1965 was, in Broadway terms, a tough act to follow. GM chose to promote his successor from the ranks of Buick executives rather than to look for outside talent. Since the corporation recognized the value of manufacturing experience in a general manager of Buick, the choice fell on Robert L. Kessler, who had been Buick's general manufacturing manager since 1961. A born Hoosier, Kessler came into the world at Indianapolis in 1914, as the son of a setup man at the Nicholson File Company. He went to Purdue University, where he was on the basketball team and could have turned to a career in professional

1965 Buick Wildcat introduced a new 'open' wheel design that was to become typical of Buick high-performance cars for nearly a decade. Roofline blends into decklid so smoothly it looks almost like a fastback.

sports, but he chose industry. Buick wanted him when he graduated in 1936—not for his engineering skills, but for Buick's basketball team—however, he went instead to Delco-Remy in Anderson, Indiana. He worked in a variety of positions at Delco-Remy, from chief process engineer, assistant master mechanic and master mechanic, to manufacturing manager. He became works manager in 1959.

When Kessler became general manager of Buick in June 1965, Kintigh continued as chief engineer. McFarland retired, and his place was filled by promoting Charles Chapman to assistant chief engineer. At the same time, Rudolf Gorsky was named executive transmission engineer. Buick also lost some good men, if not always completely. Frank Daley had left Buick in 1964 to become chief engineer of Delco-Moraine, and from there he was to make as great a contribution to all of GM as he had formerly made at Buick. He developed disc brakes for all GM cars, including Buick, where Charlie Holton remained in charge of brake engineering. When Edward N. Cole became president of General Motors he formalized the arrangement that had developed on an ad hoc basis for new products which were to be shared by several divisions. Up to the creation of the compact cars in the late 1950's, it had been a case of 'every man for himself' in the sense of letting each division go its own way. Naturally, some of them went off in opposite directions. Cole came down to see Frank Daley at Delco-Moraine

and gave him what Cole called 'systems responsibility' for brake systems for the entire corporation. This produced what Daley later called a "very interesting situation" because his division had to develop things that would be sold on its merit to the car divisions. In other words, Buick (as well as Pontiac, Oldsmobile or Cadillac) could refuse a Delco-Moraine proposal, but the divisions were also under an obligation to get their brakes from Delco-Moraine. "Hopefully," said Daley, "by reason of its merits, our system would be sufficiently uniform in its appeal to enable all divisions to coordinate their brake specifications on the basis of our designs. Of course, doing that, from a position of supplier division ain't easy."

Buick's role in terms of systems responsibility was slow in being defined. Buick's engineering department had many strong suits and no weaknesses. The division was self-contained to an extent that tended to slow down its integration. But as corporate planning began to take effect, big changes occurred at Buick. In 1967 Kintigh had as his assistant chief engineers Bowser, Chapman, Richey and George R. Ryder. Then Shirrell C. Richey, who had been in on the Riviera project from the start and played a part in making it the kind of car it was, left Buick in 1968 and went to

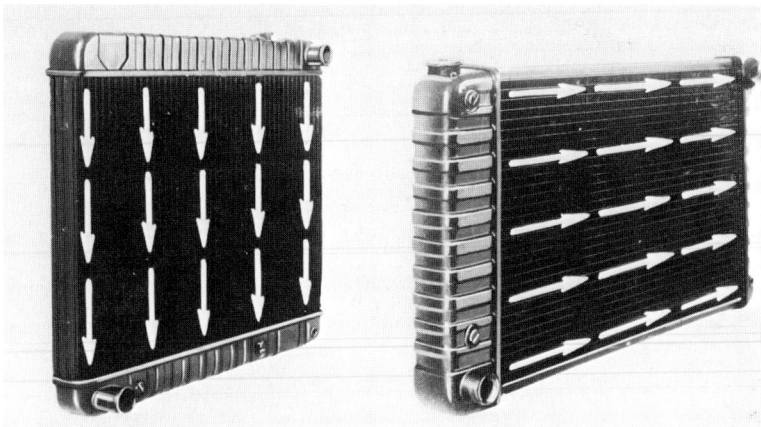

Buick went from vertical-flow to crossflow radiators on the senior-series models in 1965. This necessitated side tanks on both sides of the radiator, instead of top and bottom tanks. Claimed advantages were never proved.

Chassis for Buick's senior series in 1965 shows new four-link rear suspension, perimeter frame and two-piece open propeller shaft. The engine is the standard 401-cubic-inch V-8 with Super Turbine 400 automatic transmission.

GMC in Pontiac, Michigan, to work on truck engineering. Kintigh left Buick in May 1968, to take over a corporate office as director of forward planning and in August 1969, he was named executive in charge of the GM Engineering Staff. One month later he was elected a vice president of General Motors. Kintigh retired in May 1971. His place as chief engineer of Buick was filled by Phil Bowser. Bowser came from Columbus, Ohio, where he was born on April 14, 1927. He graduated from Ohio State University in 1950 with a bachelor's degree in mechanical engineering. He joined GM Research Laboratories in 1950 as a project engineer, and was transferred to Chevrolet in 1952. By 1955 he was assistant to Chevrolet's research and development director and two years later he went to Buick. After working as Buick's director of research and development since 1957 and assistant chief engineer since 1961, he was named chief engineer in May 1968. He immediately picked a new team of assistant chief engineers. Cliff Studaker was placed in charge of engine design, and Doug Remy was given responsibility for advanced design and planning. Douglas R. Remy had joined Chevrolet as a staff engineer in 1959 and was transferred to Buick in 1964. The posts vacated by Richey and Chapman (who had gone to Germany in 1967 as chief engineer of Opel) were filled by Charles Hagler and George W. Drew.

Kessler's tenure as general manager of Buick was not to be of long duration. We who saw him regularly at press conferences saw a marked change in the man after two years in office. No longer the smiling, outgoing, confident new boss, he had come to grips with Buick's problems, and the stress threatened his health. He looked tired, drawn, haggard and was probably developing an ulcer. He was not at ease with the responsibilities of running Buick and making thousands of decisions that would always go against somebody's wishes. But it took the corporation another two years to find him a suitable position without demoting him from vice presidential level. Kessler was taken away from Buick in April 1969, and named general manager of Fisher Body Division, a post which he held until his retirement at the end of 1976. Here he found his customers captive, and his principal duties relatively free of settling conflicting demands. To take over at Buick, GM President Edward N. Cole picked a salesman, a man who was at the same time a cool, determined bargainer, a first-rate administrator, and a smiling diplomat who could get along with the dealers. His name was Lee Mays, and he had been general sales manager of Chevrolet for two years when he came to Buick. He was born in Findlay, Ohio, in 1908, and graduated from Ohio State University with a degree in business administration. He joined the Chevrolet sales force in 1935, served in the U.S. Air Force from 1942 to 1945, and returned to Chevrolet. Rising steadily in the ranks, he was assistant general sales manager for the western states by 1959. Then he served as general sales manager of Cadillac from 1962 to 1967. He brought to Buick more than thirty-eight years experience of selling and distributing cars. A brief glance backwards over the Kessler years will illuminate the situation at Buick when Mays took over and provide some background for an assessment of Mays as a general manager.

The total U.S. car market expanded to 9.3 million cars in 1965, and Buick sales soared to 608,620 units, coming within 310 cars of catching Oldsmobile, but remaining in sixth position. Buick assembly points were, first and foremost, Flint, Michigan; and then the corporate plants at Atlanta; Kansas City, Kansas; Kansas City, Missouri; South Gate, California; Wilmington, Delaware; Baltimore; and Fremont, California. For 1966, Buick had a new body on the Riviera, and a heavily restyled Special/Skylark series, but practically no change in the LeSabre, Wildcat and Electra 225, which were all-new in 1965.

With 569,131 new-car registrations in 1966, Buick held on to sixth place, 11,000 units behind Oldsmobile but 25,000 units ahead of Dodge. Buick's market share slipped from 6.53 percent in 1965 to 6.32 percent in 1966. The following year the senior series had a new look. David R. Holls, chief designer of the Buick studio since 1964, had found an ingenious new way to revive the sweepspear. Holls drew the sweepspear as a curved link between horizontal lines in the front and rear fenders, high in front and low in the rear. It was most effective in giving the car a mark of Buick identity, as well as making the most of the length of the B- and C-bodies of 1967. The W-front was sharpened, to the great distress of people who could not shake the preconceived notion that only a straight bumper can be a safe bumper. Grilles remained horizontal, and the taillights were now so wide that they almost met in the middle. Buick passed Oldsmobile in new-car registrations in 1967, with 565,313 sales against 551,274, to retake fifth place, the ranking list now showing Chevrolet leading Ford, Pontiac and Plymouth ahead of Buick.

Buick managed to hold on to its fifth place in 1968, with 627,159 registrations in the U.S. market, but was seriously pressured by Oldsmobile which ended up less than 3,000 cars behind. The big Buicks remained strong, running second to Pontiac and ahead of Oldsmobile in their market segment, in 1967 and 1968. The Special/Skylark ran fifth among intermediate cars in 1967, behind the Chevelle, Tempest, F-85 and Ford Fairlane.

When the Special/Skylark received new bodies for 1966, they also changed personality to some extent. The 1964-65 models had been too much like the Chevelle to establish an identity of their own. They had Buick engines fitted into a corporate chassis with a corporate body shell. But they did not share the basic traits of the big Buicks. Too obviously, the Special/Skylark did not have the same roadholding or the same braking performance as the senior series. Starting with the 1966 models, this was partly remedied. Making these extensive changes after only two years entailed a

Buick Electra 225 for 1967 had a brand-new 430-cubic-inch V-8 rated at 360 hp, and front disc brakes were offered as an extra-cost option for the first time. Pointed grille and fenders earned the design the nickname W-front.

repetition of the process after only another two years, since the corporation was preparing a totally new range of intermediates for 1968 with features that were to be widely copied by other auto manufacturers. The introduction of the 1968 Special and Skylark gave Buick an important marketing advantage (except vis-a-vis its GM sister divisions, which had the same benefit), and production went up by 17.65 percent over year-earlier levels. But at the same time the intermediate car market expanded from 1.9 to 2.3 million cars, so Buick slipped to sixth place, being overtaken by the Plymouth Belvedere.

What was so great about the new intermediates that year was the dual wheelbase. It could almost be said that Buick had three separate car lines using the same Fisher A-body. The two-door models were built on a 112-inch wheelbase, while the four-door models had a longer 116-inch wheelbase. In addition, the Sportwagon was built on a 121-inch wheelbase. Engineering changes stemmed mainly from inter-divisional coordination. For instance, Buick had sold its V-6 engine line to Kaiser Jeep Corporation in Toledo, and the standard engine for the 1968 Special was an in-line six, manufactured by Chevrolet and supplied to the other divisions. Chassis engineering changes were evolutionary, consisting of minor improvements in suspension, steering and brakes. Styling, on the other hand, was dramatically new. The sweepspear appeared on the intermediates, ending at the front of the rear wheel opening. This gave the car a profile that said 'Buick' as clearly as if it had been spelled out on a billboard. The grille design was

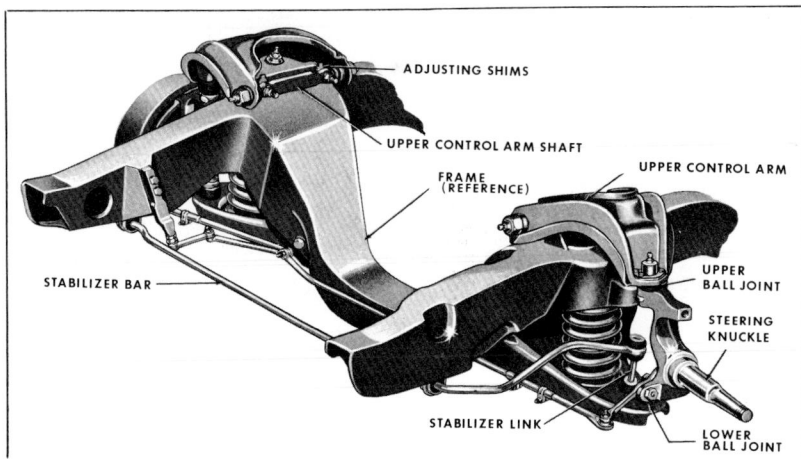

Front suspension for the intermediate Special was patterned on the design used on the senior-series Buicks, with coil springs standing on the lower A-arms and abutting in spring housings built into the frame side members.

New rear suspension adopted for the intermediate Special had four-link axle location and coil springs. Open propeller shaft ran straight and without a center bearing. The frame was a perimeter design with considerable flexibility.

inspired by the Riviera's, and taillights were mounted in the deep-face rear bumper. Two-door models were hardtops (or convertibles) with vent windows in the front doors and a roll-down rear quarter panel window. Four-door sedans and wagons also had vent windows in the front doors, but one-piece glass in the rear doors. Sedans had no wide windows behind the rear doors, but wagons had a long glass panel running right back to the tailgate.

The GS 350 and GS 400 were marketed as separate series in 1968. The 'muscle-car' market was booming, and the cars were loaded with profitable extras, so the dealers were pushing them. Despite a heavy advertising schedule, the GS never became very popular, and production figures were disappointing. For the 1968 models, all synchromesh transmissions were equipped with column shifts, except for the GS 400, which had Hurst floor shifts for both three-speed and four-speed units. Cool air induction was featured on the 1969 Skylark GS 350 and GS 400. Twin hood scoops were combined with a special air cleaner with compressible muffs connecting to the scoops when the hood was closed. Cooler air, with greater density, gave increased volumetric efficiency compared with an air cleaner drawing in

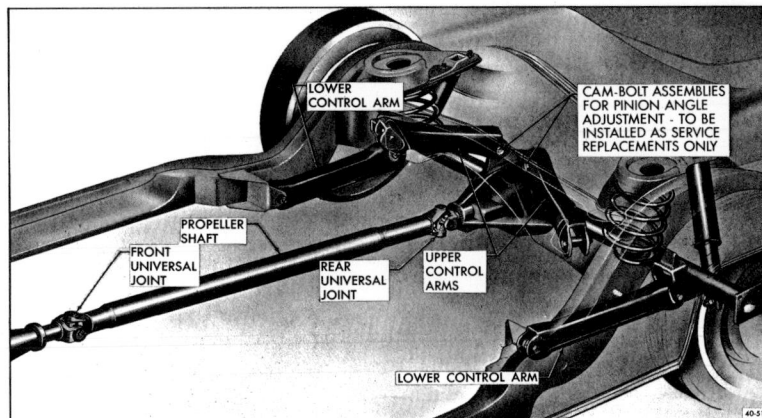

hot air from inside the engine compartment. This cool-air package gave the engine an eight-percent horsepower boost, and also raised peak torque by 6.5 percent. The 1969 Skylark GS models were also available with an optional Stage I package, which included a special camshaft kit, revised fuel pump and carburetor and a modified lubrication system. Stage I modifications also comprised a heavy-duty cooling system, dual exhausts with special mufflers and larger tailpipes, and a Positraction differential with a 3.64:1 final drive ratio. On Gran Sport cars with air conditioning, the final drive ratio was lowered to 3.42:1. For cars with automatic transmissions, the Super Turbine 400 was equipped with a 5200-rpm governor and higher upshift point settings.

Buick's senior series had no significant changes for 1968, as far as anyone could tell by looking at the outside of the car. But there were internal changes. The collapsible steering column had been standardized on all Buicks for 1967. New for 1968 were the installation lap belts for all seats, knee padding and more padding over the instrument panel. One new feature on all 1968 Buicks was the windshield wiper system, which parked the wiper arms in a retracted and concealed position under a lip on the rear edge of the hood, off the windshield base, when not in use. At the same time, subtle engineering development continued. The 1968 LeSabre was equipped with a new, heavy-duty Salisbury-type rear axle, to match the torque of the engine. The pinion and ring gear had twenty-eight percent higher torque capacity and a corresponding increase in fatigue life. The senior-series cars that Buick was building when Lee Mays moved to Flint in April 1969, were almost completely new. Fisher had developed all-new B- and

C-bodies which introduced side impact bars in the doors, eliminated the front door vent window and replaced them with a new system of upper-level ventilation. A new ignition lock that also locked the steering wheel and transmission became standard on the 1969 models. The lock was mounted on the steering column instead of the instrument panel.

Dave Holls had found new varieties of sweepspear design, and the C-body Electra 225 had side sculpturing that differed from the B-body LeSabre and Wildcat. On the Electra 225 the sweepspear grew out of the lip around the front wheel opening and ran in a nearly straight line from the front fender to the rear bumper. On the LeSabre and Wildcat, it ended in the front part of the rear fender, and started afresh from the lip over the rear wheel opening. Belt lines differed, too. On the Electra 225 the rear fender kickup was quite discreet, showing its kinship with the Cadillac (which used the same C-body). The kickup on the B-body Buicks appeared to be taken from the 1968 Skylark rear fender design—another example of upwards mobility in styling details. Before these cars went into production, Dave Holls was transferred from the Buick studio to Chevrolet. Styling Vice President Bill Mitchell made some organizational changes in the styling staff, naming Jack N. Humbert group chief engineer for Buick, Cadillac, Oldsmobile and Pontiac, while Donald Lasky was promoted to chief designer for Buick's exterior studio and A. B. Carr, Jr., to chief designer for Buick interiors.

Chief Engineer Phil Bowser wasted no time in getting his ideas for chassis improvements into production. But he had a lot of new ideas, and all could not happen at once, which is why you'll see important steering and suspension changes each year after he took charge of the technical makeup of Buick cars. The 1969 major series Buicks had new rear suspension systems, each with two long radius arms tying the ends of the axle to brackets mounted on the inside of the frame side-members, plus two short torque arms splayed at an included angle of ninety degrees, tying the top of the differential casing to mounting brackets on the frame cross-member ahead of the axle. This setup was carried over in 1970 and 1971, but in the 1971 models the shock absorbers were moved forward, ahead of the axle, standing on the radius arms, with the top end abutting into a mount on the cross-member. The 1969 major-series Buicks also went to a one-piece propeller shaft, replacing the former design with the split shaft, which needed a center bearing and a special frame cross-member.

During the 1969 model year, the Buick Special and Skylark were assembled at Baltimore, Maryland; Fremont, California; Kansas City, Missouri; Wilmington, Delaware; and Flint. The full-size Buicks were built first and foremost at Flint, but also at Doraville, Georgia; Kansas City, Kansas; Wilmington; and South Gate, California. The Riviera was assembled exclusively

1968 Buick LeSabre features sweepspear-type of accent line, with a three-hole molding on the front fender recalling the ventiports. This was the last year for vent windows in the front doors; wipers had already been concealed.

by the home plant in Flint. In 1969 Buick regained fourth place from Plymouth in the sales race, with 677,319 registrations, but was still a long way behind Pontiac. Buick's market share went up from 6.67 percent in 1968 to 7.17 percent in 1969. We can say that Kessler had prepared the right tools for Mays, and that Mays understood how to use them. Now he began to prepare for the future, and for his own successor, for he was approaching the age of mandatory retirement at GM.

Mays had inherited something of Harlow Curtice's approach to merchandising. He wanted to kill off every fading rose and replace it with a new orchid. The Wildcat had been losing popularity, dropping from 61,000 sales in 1968 to 48,000 in 1969. The base-line Wildcat disappeared at the end of 1969, and for 1970 all Wildcats were Custom Wildcats. At the end of the 1970 year, the Wildcat was replaced by the Centurion, a name first used by Buick for a show car in 1956. The Buick lineup for 1969 included thirty-five models—twenty in the major series and fourteen intermediates, plus the Riviera. The addition of two big wagon models in 1970 was offset by the killing of two Skylarks, so that the total remained the same. The Special name plate was discontinued at the end of the 1969 model year, and for 1970 all intermediate Buicks were Skylarks. The intermediates included the base-line Skylark, Skylark Custom, Gran Sport and Sportwagon. Buick built its ten millionth car in 1960 and the fifteen millionth in 1969. In the late months of 1969 General Motors had a one hundred-day strike, halting all output at the start of the model year, with disastrous results in the market

Left, new type of front-wheel disc brake with floating caliper was adopted for the 1970 Buicks. The caliper had a single cylinder and was automatically self-centering on the disc, working, of course, with friction pads on both sides. Buick Century Regal of 1973, right, shows that an attempt was made to adapt traditional Buick fender lines to a basic body that was shared with three other divisions. Two-door coupe was built on a 112-inch wheelbase, and the list price was $3,412.

The 1969 model was the penultimate Wildcat, for the series was discontinued at the end of the 1970 model year. The wheels are the same as in 1964, and the profile has not changed much, but side sculpturing never ceased to evolve.

place. Still, Buick fared better than some of its sister divisions. Among full-size cars, the big Buick had an outstanding year in 1970, producing better than 100,000 cars more than Oldsmobile, to take its place right behind Chevrolet and Ford. But in the overall sales race, Buick dropped from fourth to sixth during 1970, as registrations fell to 493,207 cars, or 5.88 percent of the market, which had slipped from 9.5 million to 8.4 million cars a year. It was Chrysler that made the biggest gains, so that the ranking list for 1970 ended up this way, from the top: Ford-Chevrolet-Plymouth-Pontiac-Dodge-Buick.

The junior-series Buicks also did remarkably well in view of the lost production. The Skylark ranked fourth among intermediates in 1970, trailing only the Chevelle, Fairlane, and Oldsmobile F-85, and taking a narrow lead over the Tempest. Buick's A-body cars had received new side sheet metal, downplaying the sweepspear, which appeared as an unclearly defined bulge in front and rear fenders. What caught one's attention were horizontal accent lines extending from both front and rear wheel openings, marking a sharp crease in the sheet metal. Buick's senior series had not included a station wagon since 1964, but in 1970 Buick produced an Estate Wagon built on the LeSabre chassis. Buick sold just over 10,000 Sportwagons but nearly 20,000 Estate Wagons, so that the division's share of the station wagon market went up from 3.67 percent in 1969 to 4.07 percent in 1970. Between 1970 and 1971 Buick slashed its model range from thirty-five to twenty-seven models. In the former lineup, there were twenty-two major-line models and twelve intermediates, plus the Riviera. This was cut to sixteen major-line and ten intermediates, with no change for the specialty car.

The big Buicks for 1970 continued the same styling theme but all wheelbases were increased one inch. The LeSabre and Wildcat went to 124 inches, and the Electra 225 to 127 inches.

Engineering improvements abounded. Bowser had become convinced of the merits of variable-ratio power steering—an idea developed by Pontiac and Cadillac together with Saginaw Steering Gear Division, and began pushing for Buick to adopt it. In variable-ratio steering systems, the nut engaged by the worm gear has an hourglass shape, which gives small steering angle changes per degree of steering wheel rotation in the near-straight-ahead position, but rapidly increases front wheel steering angles when the drive continues to turn the steering wheel. Variable-ratio power steering, first introduced as an option on the 1970 Buick, had become standard on the senior series in 1971. The 1970-model power steering system had been improved in the area of oil temperature control.

Under Bowser's direction, Buick also developed a new type of front suspension geometry, known as Accu-Drive. The suspension arms were so arranged that the front wheels would adopt a positive-camber attitude on a full bump, to counteract the harmful effect of bumps on directional stability. Briefly, it reversed the camber curve by widening the distance between the pivot shafts for upper and lower control arms, thus changing the camber thrust from a negative to a positive force, opposing external forces that might try to induce yawing in the car. The engineers who did the test and development work on this were Marlow R. Ladd and R. E. Owen. It was used on some production cars during 1969, and was standardized on all senior-series cars for 1970. The following year, it was further refined and renamed Accu-Drive II. General Motors ordered the other car divisions to adopt it. In return, Buick received for its 1971 LeSabre, Centurion and Electra 225 a new steering linkage, developed by Chevrolet, which had the steering gear located ahead of the front-wheel center line. With the steering linkage aft of the center line, side forces generated in the tires are imposed on the suspension. They cause deflections in the direction of the turn, which is an oversteering effect that tends to make the car feel unstable. With the linkage in front, its rigidity would counteract suspension movements caused by side forces in the tires, and turn the wheels away from the turn, giving an understeering effect. Automatic understeer effects have an important stabilizing influence on the car. Accu-Drive II included camber geometry modified to suit the forward-located steering linkage, so that the front tires kept a wider contact patch on the roadway during severe cornering, with pronounced body roll. Due to the Accu-Drive II system, roll-camber geometry reacted automatically as roll developed to balance the car on its intended course. The 1971 Buicks also received a new independent front suspension system, in which a wide-span pressed-steel lower A-arm replaced a single transverse arm combined with a drag strut.

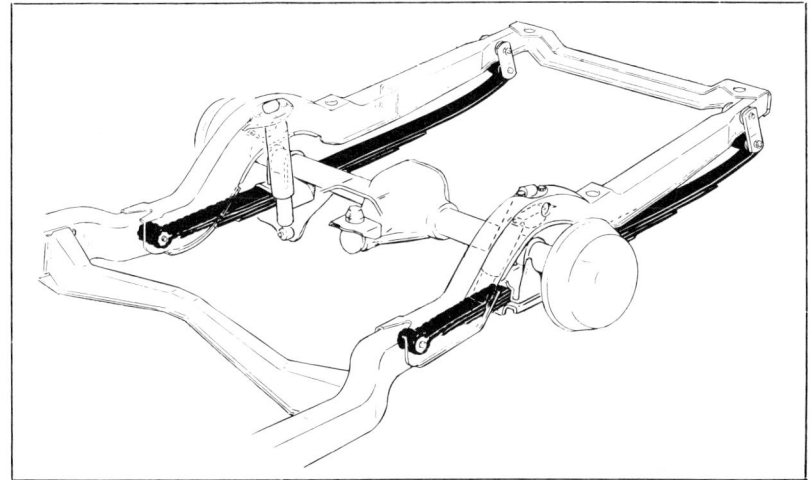

Buick's Estate Wagon from 1971 had its own rear suspension with lead springs instead of coil springs. It was done for space considerations, not for reasons of load capacity, ride or handling. The open propeller shaft was retained.

Justly proud of its finned-aluminum drum brake system, Buick had little immediate need for disc brakes. But GM President Ed Cole wanted to standardize brake systems for all divisions, and he was convinced that disc brakes would, in the long run, turn out to have lower production cost than Buick's very expensive drum brake system. Over in Chevrolet's high-performance vehicle department, Zora Arkus-Duntov wanted four-wheel discs for the 1965 Corvette, and Frank Daley at Delco-Moraine aided in their development and agreed to produce them. Daley spent the next few years developing a simplified front-wheel-only disc brake system, which was offered to all the car divisions. Buick was the slowest in responding. Both Charlie Holton and Phil Bowser recognized, however, that even if their current drum brakes had all the fade resistance they were likely to need, disc brakes offered improved all-weather stability, which is impossible to guarantee in drum brakes. But Buick wanted a fully developed system, with no bugs. Since disc brakes work with small friction areas and very high pressure, there was a much greater risk of leakage than with drum brakes, which have a large surface and low hydraulic pressure. Buick also wanted full satisfaction on service requirements (infrequent pad replacement and

New B- and C-bodies for 1971 were shared by all divisions. Buick revised its side sculpturing and placed less emphasis on the grille. The W-front has been nearly straightened out, and the ventiports are long slots.

quick replacement when needed). Disc brakes became optional on the front wheel of the senior-series Buicks for 1970. The system featured a single-piston floating caliper, with a new tandem power brake booster. A new proportioning valve was inserted in the rear brake line, its task being to restrict line pressure during high g level deceleration in order to prevent premature locking of the rear wheels. The separate front-wheel hub and brake disc of the 1970 design were replaced by an integral hub and disc for 1971. At the same time, Buick adopted a single-piece cast steering knuckle with integral steering arm. This was a Cadillac development.

Buick engineers were taking the lead in engine cooling techniques, having introduced the cross-flow radiator in 1965. The 1970 Buicks had a semi-closed cooling system as standard. The radiator cap was semi-sealed, but the overflow pipe was connected to a separate plastic reservoir, which would collect the coolant when the engine ran hot and automatically return it to the radiator when the engine cooled off. This was another Buick development that was later adopted on a corporation-wide basis. Despite all Buick's pioneer work on automatic drive, a three-speed synchromesh transmission was still standard on the 1970 LeSabre and Wildcat. But the following year, Turbo-HydraMatic was standardized on all senior-series models. The Electra 225 had a 2.56:1 axle in 1970, but with the drop in power resulting from the switch to regular fuel for the 1971-model engines, the final drive ratio was increased to 2.73:1 in order to maintain performance levels.

Only two years after the last change, Buick's 1971 models had all-new Fisher B- and C-bodies with revised styling. Sweepspears provided the styling motif for the body sides, but in a new way. B-bodies had an accent line running from the top of the front fender, through the front door panel, turning into a concave sculpture in the rear door, and ending at the rear bumper. On the C-body, the belt line split in the front door panel, with the high line continuing straight to the rear fender and the lower line running to the rear fender tip, above bumper level.

Front and rear ends contained a number of subtle changes within the overall styling theme which had been so successful since 1967. The 1971 LeSabre and Centurion were built on a 125-inch wheelbase, while the Electra 225 and Estate Wagon wheelbase went to 127 inches. The new Estate Wagon introduced a forward-facing optional third seat, wide enough for two, located in the space between the rear wheel housings. Access was provided by folding one-third of the regular back seat and crawling over the axle kickup in the floorboards. A leaf-spring rear-axle suspension system was adopted for the 1971 Estate Wagon, not because of their greater load-capacity potential, but because the interior arrangement left no room for vertical coil springs. This did not mean a return to the torque tube, however. The open propeller shaft arrangement was kept, and the leaf springs performed all the duties of the four-link suspension system. Simultaneously, the clamshell tailgate was introduced on the Estate Wagon. Patented by GM President Edward N. Cole, it was used on all B-body wagons. The rear glass retracted into the roof, and the tailgate was lowered into a frame under the floor. When fully open, neither glass nor tailgate were visible. It was operated electrically, either by a switch on the instrument panel, or by turning a key in a switch mounted in the body side next to the tailgate.

Buick stayed in sixth place in the 1971 sales race, some 20,000 cars behind Plymouth but 120,000 cars ahead of Dodge. Pontiac was back in third spot, with Oldsmobile fourth. In that 9.7-million car year, Buick's 633,509 registrations gave it a 6.51-percent share of the market. Centurion sales more than doubled from 1970 to 1971, but were still only a small proportion of senior-series cars. In 1970, the LeSabre accounted for forty-eight percent, the Electra 225 for forty-three percent and the Centurion for nine percent of big Buick sales, not counting the Riviera. The Skylark took a smaller proportion of Buick's overall sales, slipping from thirty-five percent in 1970 to thiry-one percent in 1971. Intermediates as a whole were set back that year, from 1.9 to 1.64 million units, and the Skylark did well to hold its fourth place in that class. In 1971 Buick's home plant in Flint produced all Rivieras and a high proportion of Skylarks and senior-series Buicks. The Buick LeSabre, Centurion and Electra 225 were also assembled at Fairfax, Kansas; South Gate, California; and Wilmington, Delaware.

Skylarks were also built at Framingham, Massachusetts; and Fremont, California. In U.S. registrations, Buick ran sixth in both 1971 and 1972, losing fifth place by less than 20,000 cars to Plymouth in 1971, but seeing the gap widen to 45,000 cars the following year. In 1972 Buick was 63,000 cars behind Pontiac and nearly 90,000 behind Oldsmobile, compared with a 40,000-car gap between Buick and Pontiac the year before, when Pontiac was in third place, and there was a 30,000-car separation between Buick and Oldsmobile.

The year 1972 marks a standstill even in product development as far as the LeSabre, Centurion and Electra 225 were concerned. But that was also the year when GM launched a long-overdue group of new A-body cars (intermediates). Lee Mays led Buick into the 1973 model year, but then he retired at year-end 1972. He was succeeded by George R. Elges on January 1, 1973. Elges was a Cadillac man from way back, having gone there to work in 1941 after graduating from Southeastern High School in Detroit. Originally from Erie, Pennsylvania, where he was born in 1923, he had come to Detroit when his family moved there. After World War II, during

which he served in the U.S. Army, he returned to Cadillac and was accepted by the GM Institute. He graduated in 1950 with a degree in industrial engineering. He worked as a maintenance foreman in the Cadillac tank plant in Cleveland, accumulating frequent promotions within the plant maintenance area, and then returned to Cadillac in Detroit in 1953. By 1957 he was Cadillac's superintendent of maintenance. He worked briefly as assistant works manager at Cadillac before being transferred back to Cleveland towards the end of 1961. A year later he was named plant manager there, and in March 1964 he got his first taste of working at Flint,

All-new A-bodies for 1973 were shared by intermediates from Buick, Olds-mobile, Pontiac and Chevrolet. Century grille is anonymous, and front fender lines failed to state Buick identity strongly enough. Still, novelty boosted sales.

Buick revived the Estate Wagon in 1972, placing it right at the top level of the senior series, sharing the Electra grille and other ornamentation. It also had Cole's clamshell tailgate and an optional forward-facing third seat.

when he came to Buick as assistant manufacturing manager (under Kessler). Elges was manufacturing manager of Buick (under Donald F. Taylor, who succeeded Kessler) until February 1966, when he returned to Cadillac as general manufacturing manager. Three years later he was promoted to gen-eral manager of Cadillac and a GM vice presidency.

Not one but two completely new cars were added to Buick's 1973 model range. It was the new A-body car, which revived the Century name, and the X-body car, which had started life as a 1968 Chevrolet Nova, and spread to the other divisions as they felt the demand for a compact car. Buick named its new compact the Apollo. Buick played an important part in the creation of the new intermediates, but the Apollo was basically a 'hand-me-down' that Buick made a few modifications on. Preliminary plan-ning work on the new-generation intermediates began in 1967, with basic design concepts, general specifications, and body types being selected. At first, the intention was to start production in 1971, as 1972 models, but the program was shelved during the one hundred-day strike against GM in the fall of 1969. After the strike, too much time had been lost to get it back on the original schedule. The corporation decided to retain the split-wheelbase concept, without changing the dimensions, for all divisions. What Buick's new intermediate had to share with the Chevelle, Le Mans and Cutlass was the new Fisher A-body, plus a new frame, new front and rear suspension systems and a new steering system. Each division was free to continue its power team lineup, or to develop new versions of existing engines.

The new A-body was the joint responsibility of GM Styling and Fisher Body Division. All the new models from each division had to share the same underbody, which locked them into the same seating positions, and located the entire passenger compartment relative to the wheelbase. But each division had full freedom to design its own outer sheet metal, front end, including grille and head lamp arrangement, and rear end. Three body types were designed: four-door sedan, two-door sedan and station wagon. There were no convertibles, and no hardtops. The main body design fea-tures were a lower belt line, vastly increased glass area, more sloping hood lines and lower-radius curved side glass. Windshields had a gentle, nearly uniform curve throughout, and wiper arms were parked below a lip on the rear edge of the hood. Vent windows were eliminated from the front doors on all models.

New and heavier bumpers were used (required by federal motor vehicle safety standard No. 215), able to withstand a 5 mph frontal impact without damage to vital parts in the body or chassis. Other safety improvements in-cluded a double steel roof and new side guard beams built into the door panels. These items added about 410 pounds to the weight of the four-door sedan. Trunk size increased by one-fifth compared with the 1972 model, and fuel tanks held about one-sixth more.

The new frame originated at GM Research Laboratories and was de-veloped by Chevrolet. Responsibility for the front suspension was also given to Chevrolet, who decided to use the basic geometry from the Camaro in order to build more responsive handling characteristics into the new intermediates. Because of the extra weight, the control arms were beefed up to about the same strength level as the parts for the Impala (full size) chassis. Fisher Body and Pontiac developed a new body mount system, with controlled loading of the body mounts under changing driving conditions. The new mounts had a bell-shaped inner sleeve and a designed-in void to control the loading rate. A soft rate was assured during light-load conditions, and a higher rate for heavier loading. This new system played a major part in improving ride comfort and reducing interior noise levels, in conjunction with frame design, engine mounts, suspension control arm bushings, and exhaust system routing and bracket location.

Buick's task was to develop the brakes, in collaboration with Delco-Moraine Division, which was to manufacture the brakes for all divisions. Buick decided to develop a low-cost system with front disc brakes but without power assist. Even the base-line models, therefore, were to have front discs, and power brakes were made standard for station wagons and high-line models, optional for all others. It was Oldsmobile that developed the new steering gear and linkage, in collaboration with Saginaw Steering Gear Division and Delco. Delco's role was to provide a vibration damper for filtering out road shocks that would lead to kickback and vibration in the steering wheel. This problem had showed up on test cars without power steering fairly early in the game, and the solution was a well-known, well-tried example of Mercedes-Benz engineering, first used on the Model 300 in 1951. It consisted of putting a hydraulic damper, looking very much like a telescopic shock absorber, mounted between the steering linkage and the frame. The Delco steering damper was not used on cars with power steering, since the pump provided the necessary cushioning. In developing the front suspension, Chevrolet adopted the Buick-developed Accu-Drive principles. Rear suspension design and development was entrusted to Pontiac, who chose a four-link system with coil springs, essentially similar to that used for the 1972 models, but including a number of refinements.

Buick's intermediate lineup for 1973 included the base-line Century, the Century Luxus and a high-line two-door coupe named Century Regal. The Century name had been used from 1936 to 1942 and from 1954 to 1958. Now it replaced the Skylark label, which was temporarily displaced from the program.

The Apollo can be traced back to the Chevy II of 1962, a compact car created to compete more effectively against the Falcon, Valiant and Rambler than the Corvair could. Buick had been out of the compact car field since 1963, and it was Lee Mays who got Buick back in. Chevrolet came out with an all-new Nova for 1968, using a maximum of common components with the 1967 Camaro sports car, which used a Fisher F-body. The X-body shared the floor pan with the F-body, but the Nova inherited the

With its 1973½ Apollo, Buick jumped back into the compact car market. But the Apollo was almost indistinguishable from the Chevrolet Nova, and it was given a cool reception in the showrooms, despite its low list price of $2,605.

front and rear suspension systems from the Chevy II. It used a coil-spring independent front suspension, with short and long A-arms, and the rear axle was carried on tapered single-leaf springs. The X-body was a unit-construction from the cowl back, but the front end had a bolted-on stub frame, not unlike Chrysler's bodies. Two body styles were made, a four-door sedan and two-door coupe.

Buick's Apollo used the Chevrolet six-cylinder engine as standard, with the Buick 350 V-8 as an option. It was launched as a 1973½ model, in February 1973. No sheet metal was changed from Chevrolet's design. The only change was that all Chevrolet identification was replaced by Buick labels. Buick did not even assemble the car. It was built in GM Assembly Division plants in Willow Run, Michigan; and Van Nuys, California.

Convertibles disappeared from the A-body Buicks at the end of the 1972 model year. For 1973 the LeSabre and Electra convertibles were discontinued. The only 1973 Buick convertible was the Centurion, and it was downgraded to LeSabre rank when the Centurion name plate was discontinued at the end of the 1973 model year. It lived on through 1976. Only a few years earlier, Buick had offered no less than five different convertibles. In 1963 there were convertibles in both the Special and Skylark series, plus LeSabre, Invicta, Wildcat and Electra 225 convertibles. What killed the convertible? Above all, it was air conditioning. The interstate highway system

1975 Buick Apollo shows elegant new roofline and a belt line that seems lower but wasn't. Sales were disappointing, as the car was too clearly the same as the Chevy Nova, but listed at a higher price. Technical specification is quite modern.

repeating the grille theme. Heavier-gauge face plate material was used, with additional steel reinforcement to back it up. The 1972 Centurion had a frontal aspect that differed from the LeSabre only in having vertical bars in the grille and the inside sections of the opening in the bumper face. The bumper face was equipped with a full-width rubber strip. The 1972 Electra 225 had the same front and rear bumpers as the lower-priced senior series. Front end sheet metal was also the same, but the Electra had a different grille with a mouth-organ pattern appearing in the main grille between the head lamps as well as in the lower open sections in the bumper face. The same basic designs were retained in 1973 and 1974. The Centurion was merged into the LeSabre series for 1974. At the same time, the LeSabre Custom was renamed LeSabre Luxus.

Buick shared in the general prosperity of 1972-73 and maintained its market share at just over six percent, in a car market that expanded from 10.5 to 11.35 million units. It's the model-by-model breakdown that tells the real story, however. The big Buick was tops in its market segment in 1973, leading Oldsmobile by a small margin and Pontiac by a considerable margin. With a model-year output of 298,467 cars, Buick's Century ran fourth among intermediates in 1973, topped only by the Cutlass (405,000 units), Ford Torino (332,000 units) and the Chevelle (328,000 units). The following year, the Century sank to fifth place and an output of 190,607 cars, and the Chevrolet Monte Carlo moved up. But the Apollo was a failure at the start. In the 1973 model year, when Chevrolet made nearly 370,000 Novas and Oldsmobile over 60,000 Omegas, Buick held its compact-car production down to just under 33,000 units. The 1974-model Apollo did better, with nearly 57,000 compact cars produced. That compares well with 50,000 for the Omega, but the public shunned both because people felt they could get the same car at a much lower price from a Chevrolet dealer. They sold 390,000 Novas that year.

During 1973 Buick held 3.54 percent of the station wagon market, with the full-size Estate Wagon leading the Century by 2.29 over 1.25 percent. The following year, the Century wagon slipped to 1.19 percent, and the Estate fell to 1.55 percent, for a Buick total of only 2.74 percent. What Elges ran into was the fuel shortage during the 1973-74 winter. Buick had to stockpile both intermediates and full size cars, while the public wanted nothing but 'small' cars. Buick's total domestic sales during 1974 stopped at 428,000 after having been within reach of the 700,000-mark the year before. Buick's market share dropped below five percent and its rank fell to seventh place. Again, there is a story in how the different series performed in the market that year. Electra 225 sales plunged from 150,000 a year to 92,000 units. The Century took a similar beating, dropping from the

helped cut the demand for convertibles, too; at 70 mph the wind buffeting made driving disagreeable for men and almost impossible for women. And if those two had not done it, the federal safety standards would eventually have put it under.

Styling changes in the senior series were soft-pedaled in both 1972 and 1973. Some new front end touches may be worth mentioning. The 1972 LeSabre had a low, wide grille, with a small number of horizontal bars. Side-by-side dual head lamps in square bezels flanked the grille. The bumper had a level upper surface, with curved ends and a recessed understructure. There was provision for a license plate between simulated overriders in the center section. Openings in the bumper face on both sides accommodated the turn signals and parking lights, with their inner sections

244,000-unit level to 142,000 units. Station wagon sales were down to sixty-two percent of the previous year's volume for the Century and forty-five percent for the Estate Wagon. The Apollo, as we have seen, was not the tool Buick needed to compete in the compact car market. All of GM was hard hit. Car sales for all divisions fell to 3.6 million from 5.05 million units, as the total car market shrank to 8.7 million. GM's market share dropped from 44.3 to 41.9 percent. GM President Elliott M. 'Pete' Estes and Chairman Thomas A. Murphy instigated major programs to move the corporation's center of gravity away from the heavy end of the car market, and participate at all price levels with new, more intelligently designed, space-efficient and fuel-efficient products. This meant additional proliferation for Buick, entering the subcompact market with its 1975-model Skyhawk.

General Motors seems to have had more than a fair share of safety problems during the years Elges was head man at Buick. The car companies had always coped with production defects by calling them back for fixing, usually at the dealer level. Some secrecy tended to surround these campaigns, because each car company wanted to protect its image. But after the National Highway Traffic Safety Agency (NHTSA) was formed in 1966, consumer activists and consumer protection groups, aided by an anti-industry daily press, received notice of all callback programs and gave them wide publicity. The Insurance Institute for Highway Safety even published reports of investigations of suspected defects, most of which resulted in nothing. It's against this background that we must look at Buick's safety-callback cases.

One lawsuit was still pending hearings in 1975 and concerned a number of 1966 Buicks that might be subject to a fire hazard from faulty carburetor plugs. The cars in question were equipped with Rochester Quadrajet carburetors that, according to the NHTSA, created "a high probability of fire and unreasonable risk of accidents, deaths, and injuries." The problem was a press-fit aluminum plug on the fuel-intake side of the carburetor, that could work loose because of vibration and fuel pressure. If it dropped out of place, it would leave a half-inch opening from which raw gasoline might be spilled onto the hot manifold. The opening was not needed for operational reasons, but was strictly a hole for materials handling and location during assembly. The manufacturer was blamed for not having made any fail-safe means for keeping the metal plug in place. The NHTSA said that engine fires had occurred in a majority of all such carburetor failures reported to it. In July 1974, General Motors offered a rebuttal to federal charges that the carburetors might have defective fuel inlet plugs. Cliff Studaker pointed out that the cars (approximately 336,000 Chevrolets and Buicks) equipped with these carburetors had been operated over more than twenty-five billion miles with only 947 cases of fuel-plug dropout. Accord-

The 1975 Buick LeSabre managed to show a semblance of a sweepspear in the body side sculpturing, but the only thing that identifies the grille as a Buick is the triple-shield emblem, prominently displayed. LeSabre prices that year started at $4,771.

ing to Studaker, the GM data showed that the failure rate up to July 1974 had amounted to only one in each twenty-five million miles, and affected only three cars in 1,000 over an eight-year period. Despite this evidence, General Motors was fined $400,000 for the Rochester Quadrajet defects by a court order issued at the end of July 1976. GM had refused to issue a defect notice, though the corporation did not contest the existence of the defect itself.

In August 1972, the National Highway Traffic Safety Administration issued a consumer protection bulletin to warn owners of 1971 and 1972 General Motors automobiles that certain models ran a risk of steering lock-up. The Buicks involved were the LeSabre, Wildcat, Electra 225 and Riviera. What could happen was that cars being used on bad roads could suffer from gravel or rocks becoming lodged between front lower frames and the steering coupling at the base of the steering column. This would cause an interference problem on left turns. After a certain point, any further turn to the left would be blocked. When the steering wheel was turned to the right, the stone would be dislodged. First, General Motors issued a service bulletin for its dealers to provide, under regular warranty coverage, an expensive 'gravel shield' (Part Number 231 480) to owners who had this problem or anticipated it. The bulletin also advised frequent inspection in order to keep lower frame members free of stones and gravel. Before long, twenty-three accidents due to this problem were reported—mostly Chevrolets, not Buicks. The corporation was forced to call back the entire 1971-72 output of standard-size Buicks, Chevrolets, Pontiacs and Oldsmobiles, at an estimated cost of $16 million.

Another suit was concerned with the Cruise Control automatic speed control feature. It involved 441,000 Buicks (1965-68 Wildcat and Electra 225, plus some early-production 1970 Cadillacs). The NHTSA said these cars were subject to failure of their engine mounts, resulting in possible sudden jamming of the throttle and loss of control. General Motors settled the suit by agreeing to call in 1965-model Wildcats and Electra 225's, and 1967-model Wildcats and Electra 225's equipped with Cruise Control. For owners who were to respond to the defect notice, GM would correct the condition on a no-charge basis. The corporation was also ordered to pay the government a civil penalty of $95,000. Originally, General Motors had considered a voluntary callback for these cars in 1972, but rejected it. Eventually, it happened in February of 1973. About 3.7 million cars were involved.

As late as May 1975, the National Highway Traffic Safety Administration announced that a safety defect existed in the power-brake vacuum check valves installed on the 1968 Buick Special and Skylark, 1967-68 LeSabre, Wildcat, Electra and Riviera. The NHTSA said that its investigation identified two vacuum check valve designs which showed significantly greater failure rates than those of other GM vehicles and those used by other domestic automobile manufacturers. The vacuum check valve showed unforewarned separation of the cap from the body, resulting in the loss of the power assist. By that time the designs in question were no longer in production. They were originally supplied by Delco-Moraine Division, and production was terminated at the end of the 1970 model year in favor of another check valve design. In a prepared statement, General Motors disputed the existence of a safety problem. "There is no unreasonable risk of injury accidents since a check valve failure only results in a loss of power-brake assist," said the GM document. "The hydraulic brakes, which remain

effective, allow the driver to stop the vehicle." Attorneys acting for General Motors also argued that the cars had been driven "billions of miles" and that the actual experience could not justify calling them all back for fixing because the government had "reported only thirteen cases of personal injury and no fatalities allegedly due to a failed check valve." That ended it for the time being.

Without testing the issue in court, General Motors recalled 843,000 cars in December 1973 for possible loose nuts in the front suspension. The Buick models involved were the LeSabre, Wildcat, Electra 225 and Riviera. The cars were built from August to October 1973 and were all 1974 models. The nuts were part of the front suspension system, and if they worked loose, it could lead to breakage of a shaft in the steering linkage that was part of an assembly holding the front wheels in proper alignment. If the shaft broke, one of the wheels could go sharply out of line, causing the steering wheel to pull to one side. General Motors maintained there was no risk of a front wheel becoming detached, and claimed there was no risk of the car becoming uncontrollable. But Ralph Nader, in a letter to the National Highway Traffic Safety Administration, contended that the car could become unsteerable and might also suffer partial loss of braking due to the same nuts coming loose. General Motors agreed to replace the nuts that might work loose with special locking-type nuts, already ordered, and to be in the dealerships by mid-January 1974. On the assembly line the problem was corrected by either welding the old-type nuts in place or fitting locking-type nuts. As a voluntary action in August 1974, Buick Motor Division said it was calling back 7,300 Estate Wagons of 1974-model year production to repair a defect that could cause rear brakes to fail. The company said that the rear brake pipe might be improperly installed, causing the pipe assembly to bend or break under heavy loads or on bumpy roads. Buick reported fifteen cases of failure, but without accidents or injuries. The defect could be repaired by putting a clamp on defective rear brake pipes to keep them from bending.

On the whole, Buick maintained good quality in its cars during the Kessler and Elges periods, and the publicity around the alleged safety defects served mainly to illuminate some interesting differences between what happens to cars tested by professional drivers on the proving grounds and what can go wrong with them after they come into the hands of consumers. Failures that had not been detected during, say, three million miles of proving-ground driving, would suddenly show up under some combination of circumstances that the programmed tests could not possibly include. While we certainly do not want to whitewash GM for its attitude, which was not one of bending over backwards to inspect all cars that could possibly have the same defect as each one suddenly reported from the field, neither do we believe that the government always understood or presented its case in its actual dimensions or implications. Perhaps due to the newness of the subject matter (and their authority) there was an overreaction among the legislators who wrote the Highway Safety Act and their staffs; among those at all levels of the Department of Transportation; and in the daily press. After ten years, safety defect reports and investigations are now treated routinely, objectively, and without all the histrionics that accompanied the initial actions of the NHTSA. We have recounted a few instances to show what Buick was up against at a critical time in its history.

Buick Century Special for 1976 had a slight backwards tilt on the grille to improve airflow characteristics. Rectangular head lamps are well integrated with front end styling. List price was $4,838 for this V-8-powered model.

CHAPTER

13

Today and Tomorrow

ON THE EVE of its seventy-fifth year of operation, Buick was poised to set new production records, and to carve out a bigger slice of the domestic car market. For 1976, Buick was planning to build 900,000 cars and aimed for a 7.5-percent market share. Actual production reached 818,000 cars and the market penetration came within 0.3 percent of the ambitious target. On May 31, the twenty-millionth Buick rolled off the Flint assembly line. It was a four-door LeSabre sedan. In the future, Buick will not be satisfied with less than 7.5 percent of the market, and production will be expanded to keep pace with the growth in the market.

How Buick won its new strength is no mystery. The credit must be shared among management, product planning, product engineering, manufacturing and distribution. Some important personnel changes were made in October 1975. First, George R. Elges was named group vice president in charge of GM car and truck divisions, and David C. Collier took over as general manager of Buick. A Canadian by birth, Collier was president of GM of Canada before moving to Buick. Before that, he worked as a top finance man in GM's New York office, having formerly been on the comptroller's staff in Detroit. Born in Hardisty, Alberta, in 1929, he first became a teacher but went back to school and graduated in 1956 with a degree in business administration from the University of Montana. The following year he joined General Motors as a summer trainee on the financial staff.

Though highly deserving of promotion, Chief Engineer Phil Bowser was passed over for promotion to general manager of Buick twice, but in October 1975 was named general manager of Delco-Moraine. However, he belonged more in engineering than in management, and in July 1976 he was appointed technical assistant to George R. Elges, his former boss at Buick. To fill Bowser's place at Buick, Lloyd Reuss was transferred from Chevrolet. This was a most fortunate choice for Buick, for there was a great risk that the technical directions in the engineering center in Flint would fall into a void after the departure of a strong-willed, hard-driving man like Bowser, who came as close to being indispensable as anyone since Charlie Chayne.

Reuss (pronounced Royce) is one of those few engineers who really understands the whole car and sees the car as an entity, instead of as a composite of various mechanical units. That must not lead anyone to think he doesn't have a full grasp of all the details. He is a stickler for precision, as he proved while working as a project engineer on automatic transmissions at Chevrolet in 1965, for instance. But most engineers tend to be accurate and meticulous. What's so rare about Reuss is his ability to grasp at once the effect on the whole car of making a change in any part of it. He is also outstanding for his vision of where car design and engineering are going—not futuristic dreams for the twenty-first century, but for cars that

ENGINE

TRANSMISSION

SPRING & FORGE

FOUNDRY

GEAR & AXLE

PERSONNEL
RELIABILITY & QUALITY CONTROL
PROCESS ENGINEERING
WORKS STANDARDS & PLANT LAYOUT
CHEMICAL & METALLURGICAL LABS
MAINTENANCE & TOOLING

SHEET METAL FABRICATION

PRODUCT ENGINEERING

FINAL ASSEMBLY

ACCOUNTING
SALES
PURCHASING
DATA PROCESSING

The home of Buick in Flint, Michigan, is a small city in itself. Modernization and reconstruction projects succeed each other ceaselessly, to improve employee job satisfaction as well as productivity.

143

Left, David C. Collier is a Canadian businessman who has been general manager of Buick since October 1975. He is a financial man who has been with General Motors since 1956, but the Buick appointment was his first in an executive office. Right, Lloyd Reuss (pronounced Royce) has been chief engineer of Buick since October 1975. He was formerly with Chevrolet and has a thorough background in transmission work, prototype development and forward planning. He shepherded the 1977 LeSabre into production.

Basic C-body for 1977 is this sedan, shared by Buick, Oldsmobile and Cadillac, each different mainly in grilles and minor decor. The Electra 225 takes over Mercedes-type grille from intermediate series, has small-block V-8 as standard.

must be planned in the next few years. Reuss is very forward-looking, but at the same time an extremely practical engineer with both feet on the ground. Reuss hails from Belleville, Illinois, where he was born on September 22, 1936. He graduated from the University of Missouri at Rolla with a degree in mechanical engineering in 1957 and joined GM Engineering Staff in 1959 after two years in the U.S. Army Corps of Engineers. He was transferred to Chevrolet in 1960 and worked for five years at the proving grounds as a development engineer. He moved to Chevrolet's engineering center in 1965, and a year later was named assistant staff engineer for axles and transmissions. In 1968 he became staff engineer of administration, but

soon got back into more creative work as chief design engineer for the Nova and Camaro. Suddenly, Lloyd Reuss had to take over the half-born Vega after the former project manager, James Musser, had left Chevrolet. The basic design was frozen and only small changes could be made after the day he was appointed chief engineer for the Vega in January 1970, less than eight months before production was due to start. By 1973 he had sorted out the Vega's worst problems, and worked 2½ years as manager of forward product planning for Chevrolet, laying some of the groundwork for the project that was to become the 1977 B- and C-body cars for all divisions.

On arriving at Buick, Reuss began to make some changes in his department. Earlier, C. R. Davis had replaced Hagler as assistant chief engineer, and then Reuss replaced Davis with H. J. Presser. Cliff Studaker and George W. Drew completed the top-level team. Product planning and engineering at Buick was, of course, subordinate to corporate directions. And the new top management—which had taken office in October 1974, with Elliot M. 'Pete' Estes, an engineer, as president; and Thomas A. Murphy, a financial man, as chairman—had decided to spend $15 billion to revamp the car programs for all divisions over the coming six-year period. One of the reasons for the immensely costly budget was that the government had responded to the energy problem by passing laws which specified gasoline mileage for future cars: 18.5 miles per gallon in 1978, twenty in 1980, and 27.5 in 1985. These figures are to be understood on a sales-weighted basis, so that the car makers will still be free to make heavy luxury cars, as long as their higher fuel consumption is balanced by building larger numbers of small cars with better-than-average fuel economy. In order to try and meet these goals, General Motors began an immediate and wholesale program to get smaller cars into production, and replace the biggest models with smaller models. Buick had got its first subcompact Skyhawk at the start of the 1975 model year. Both it and the compact Apollo stemmed from Chevrolet.

The relationship between the Buick Apollo and the Chevrolet Nova was explained in the preceding chapter. The Apollo was cleverly redesigned for 1975, acquiring a completely new look despite only minor retooling and low cost. Only two basic versions of the X-body were built, a four-door sedan and a two-door coupe, but the coupe was available either as a hatchback or with a normal trunk. A station wagon was contemplated, but Fisher Body presented some estimates of the tooling costs that were so high the corporation vetoed the wagon. Both sedan and coupe had new, flatter roofs, and the windows were extended upwards into the roof to give the car a modern look and improve the driver's visibility. It had the effect of making it look as if the belt line had been lowered. No underbody changes were made. The cowl structure and front sub-frame remained the same, and the rear window base stayed in the same position. But new hoods and front ends gave the impression of more modern proportions. The cars were much quieter than before, due to a new body mounting system, with larger, softer mounts for improved insulation. At the same time, the compact Buick (along with its sister cars in the other divisions) adopted the front suspension and steering from the Camaro, which gave higher directional stability and faster steering response. A torsion spring was built into the steering gear to provide more positive returnability (self-centering action). Steel-belted radial-ply tires were standardized, and the suspension system adapted for the radials.

Calendar-year sales figures show that the Apollo was tenth among compacts in 1974, behind the Valiant, Nova, Dart, Maverick, Camaro, Hornet, Comet, Firebird, and Ventura, and had only a narrow lead over the last-placed Omega.

The Skylark name was revived for two 1975-model coupes in the Apollo line: the basic Skylark and Skylark S/R. (The following year the Apollo name was dropped altogether.) Built on the same 111-inch Apollo wheelbase the new compact Skylark had a wider track: 61.3 inches in front and fifty-nine inches in the rear. Overall length was 200.3 inches, and curb weight was 3,499 pounds. This was hardly a compact car by 1961 definitions, but a large model having interior space comparable with the senior series of 1955! Yet, because Buick built two larger sizes of cars in 1975, the public perceived the Skylark as a small car. Buick's compact had climbed from 47,500 sales in 1974 to nearly 64,000 the following year, and hit 104,000 in 1976. The Skylark (including Apollo) accounted for thirteen per-

The four-door 1977 LeSabre carries wheels using the Wildcat design from 1964, but otherwise is outwardly difficult to pin down as a Buick. All GM's 1977 B-body cars were developed as part of the Chevrolet Caprice program, and the other divisions were not given time and opportunity to avoid the look of sameness.

cent of Buick's total domestic sales in 1975 and increased that to just short of fifteen percent in 1976. In 1975, it jumped ahead of the Ventura, Comet and Firebird, but still ranked only ninth in its class, because of Ford's new entries (Granada and Monarch) which jumped to prominence. Skylark beat out the Hornet in 1976, and the ranking list now had the Granada on top, followed by the Nova, Volare, Camaro, Aspen, Monarch and Maverick, putting the Buick compact in eighth place.

A small number of 1975-model Buick Apollo and Skylark cars were called back for inspection of two possible problems. One was concerned with the carburetor throttle cable on the 260-cubic-inch V-8 engine, which Buick purchased from Oldsmobile. The cable housing might break and cause a sharp bend in the cable. Should this occur, the throttle would not return to idle position when the driver removed his foot from the accelerator pedal. In all, some 16,000 cars were involved (X-body cars from Buick, Oldsmobile, Pontiac and Chevrolet). The second problem was concerned with the same cars having been assembled with insufficient torque on the steering shaft clamp bolt-nut, which implied a threat of steering shaft separation and a loss of steering control. Only 3,100 cars in all were estimated to be affected.

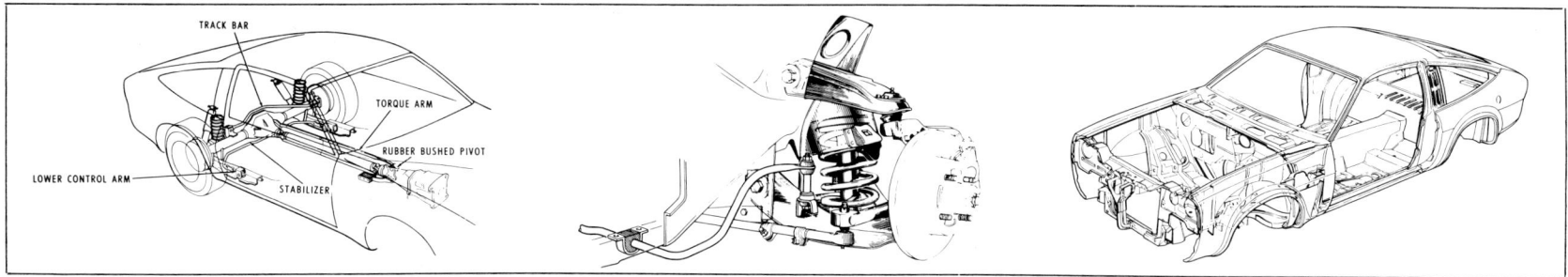

Left, with low-powered four-cylinder engines, the basic suspension was adequate to handle rear-axle torque and thrust loads. With Buick's V-6, a torque arm running alongside the propeller shaft protected the universal joints from axial overloads. Middle, Skyhawk front suspension shows basic simplicity, with few parts involved. Both steering linkage and stabilizer bar were located ahead of the front wheel axis for improved stability. Right, the HS-body shell used floor pan from basic H-body and retained same 97-inch wheelbase, but was first built as a fastback with a rear hatch which needed structural reinforcements in the rear floor and B-post areas.

The 1977 compact Skylark was available in three levels: Skylark 'S,' Skylark, and Skylark S/R. The 'S' was built as a coupe only, while the others were available in sedan, coupe and hatchback versions. Skylarks for 1977 had no sheet metal changes. And the car will remain essentially the same in 1978. After eleven years in production (counting from the 1968 Nova) it will then be overdue for replacement. It is scheduled to be replaced by a totally new car, smaller and lighter, built on a 102-inch wheelbase, with front-wheel drive, for the 1980 model year. Engines will be Buick's own V-6 and a four-cylinder Pontiac.

Buick's subcompact Skyhawk was not successful in its original form. Although it made its debut as recently as a 1975 model, it is an old design and an obsolete concept. It is one of a corporate family of HS-body cars, derived from the basic H-body of the 1971-model Chevrolet Vega. The Vega project started in 1966. It was then code-named XP-887. Its four-cylinder aluminum engine had actually been under development since 1961, and in its early stages of in-car road-testing, it was installed in a Fiat 124 sedan. Later test cars were Opel Kadetts. Due to the small size of the car, it was decided to use unit body construction as in the Fiat and Opel. The shape of the new H-body, created by the Chevrolet styling studio and Fisher Body Division, was based on the Fiat 124 Sport Coupe, with a certain amount of Camaro influence. When the seating package was finished the wheelbase was set at ninety-seven inches. When the chassis elements were off the drawing board, a new prototype was made, using an Opel

body split in two down the center and welded up again with pieces inserted in the middle to give it the extra width. Only minor chassis modifications were made during the further development period. By September 1969 the final H-body was ready, and prototypes began to appear at the GM proving grounds.

The H-body is significant because it introduced some new design techniques, such as that which GM engineers call 'modular construction design.' It is a method that utilizes as many large body panels as possible put together with highly automated equipment, thereby eliminating a number of small parts used in conventional body construction processes. The basis for the H-body was a single platform weldment with front wheel housings and underbody, suspension mounting brackets, cowl and dash panels. The roof panel included the outer top cowl sheet metal, windshield and rear window frames. Left- and right-hand body sides included the door posts, rocker panels, door sills and rear quarter panels. The body shell was then made up as a box by combining these four pieces.

XP-887 was an economy car project, and the only radical thing about it was the engine. The chassis was as conventional as the average production car of the time. It was no Corvair, with rear-mounted engine and all-independent suspension. It was just a plain, conventional American car built to a smaller scale. As the XP-887 was too small to use any components from the Camaro or Nova, its chassis was designed from scratch. The front suspension was sort of a scaled-down version of the Camaro geometry, with transverse A-arms and coil springs. The rear axle was located by a four-link suspension system, also using coil springs (in contrast with the leaf-spring suspension of the Camaro and Nova). The main reason for choosing the four-link type of rear suspension was to prevent vibrations from the four-cylinder engine from being transmitted via the propeller shaft to the rear axle, and through the rear suspension into the body structure. That would have been a problem with leaf springs, but a four-link system

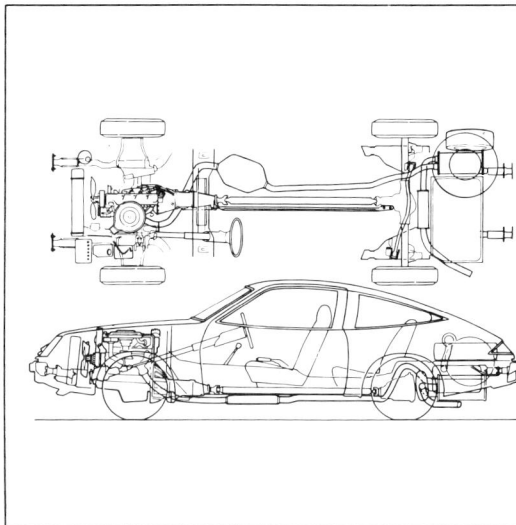

Buick's Skyhawk began life as a V-6-powered version of the Chevrolet Monza (shown left with four-cylinder engine), which in turn was derived from the Vega. High price ($4,216 in 1976) was a deterrent to reaching the economy car market with this subcompact. The 1976 Buick Skyhawk, right, is Flint's version of the super-Vega, developed by Chevrolet. The Skyhawk has Buick power, however, in the form of its V-6 engine. Transmission options included a Borg-Warner five-speed synchromesh gearbox.

with amply-sized rubber insulation could eliminate it. It made sense to use coil springs, once the decision to go with the four-link design was taken, to avoid the universal-joint disturbances and excessive axle movements that come with a softening of leaf springs. The suspension system was tuned to a new A78-13 tire that was developed concurrently with the vehicle. The steering gear with its parallelogram linkage was located ahead of the front suspension, in the pattern that Chevrolet engineers set for the whole corporation. Front disc brakes were part of the basic design, with drums on the rear wheels. Static brake force distribution put seventy percent of the effort into the front discs, which were solid rotors of ten-inch diameter, integral with the wheel hubs, and fitted with single-piston floating calipers.

Three types of H-body were made: two-door sedan, two-door hatchback coupe and two-door wagon. The HS-body was to be a fastback sports coupe with its own skin and more distinctive styling. It started in 1972 as a Chevrolet project, to be the corporation's first production model powered by the GM rotary engine then under development. When the RC engine program was shelved in September 1974, Chevrolet hurriedly developed a small V-8. Buick and Oldsmobile decided to use the Buick V-6 for their versions of the HS-body car. Buick called it Skyhawk. There were some important engineering differences. A heavy radius arm was added to the rear suspension, running straight forward from the axle, just left of the differential, to an anchorage point on the transmission casing where it was held in

a rubber-bushed pivot bearing. This arm assisted the lower control arms in taking up the driving thrust and controlling torque reactions and rear axle wind-up forces. A rear stabilizer bar was added as standard equipment. The Skyhawk, then, should have been a fully developed car, able to meet Buick standards for quality and reliability. It's part of the story that the Vega had the worst call-back record of any American-made passenger car. In April 1972, GM called back 130,000 Vegas to fix a possible fire hazard in the fuel and exhaust system. In May 1972, Chevrolet had to call back 350,000 cars to strengthen the solenoid bracket on the carburetor to guard against throttle sticking. In July 1972, 500,000 Vegas were called back for inspection of the rear axle shafts and replacement of those that had been ground too thin by faulty machining (a bad batch had found its way to the assembly line despite having been spotted early). And some problems still remained after the HS-body cars went into production.

All Buick Skyhawks built in 1975 were called back in February 1976 because the front disc brake calipers might be displaced from their proper position after repeated hard braking. This could cause a loss of front wheel braking action, the corporation admitted. But there had been no reports of accidents or injuries related to this problem in the field. Buick sold 2,976 Skyhawks from the day it went on sale to the end of the 1974 calendar year. Throughout all of 1975, however, only 28,642 Skyhawks were registered, and the following year was not much better, with 30,326 sales. Skyhawk sales accounted for only 5.8 percent of Buick's trading volume during 1975, and fell to 4.3 percent in 1976. Both years it was vying with the Oldsmobile Starfire for rock bottom position among its group of subcompact sports cars, which was led by the Ford Mustang II and Chevrolet Monza.

All Skyhawks were assembled at Sainte-Therese, Ontario, Canada, alongside the other HS-body cars (Chevrolet Monza and Oldsmobile Starfire), adding capacity at South Gate, California, in 1976. Apollo/Skylark assembly points in 1975 were Van Nuys, California; and Leeds, Missouri. In 1976, the Tarrytown, New York, plant also began building Skylarks. The Century was assembled in 1975 at Framingham, Massachusetts; Fremont, California; and in the home plant at Flint; but the following year Baltimore replaced the Framingham plant in that role.

Buick's intermediate cars, despite their weight and bulk, which threatened sales during the fuel shortage, proved to be a definite asset to the division. The Century ranked fourth among all intermediates in 1974 with a sales volume of 152,000 cars, behind the Ford Torino, Chevelle and Oldsmobile Cutlass. It was Buick's leading car line, accounting for 35.5 percent of the division's sales. The Special name was brought back for a 1975 model, a V-6 coupe in the Century series.

Positions were reshuffled in 1975, as GM had the intermediate field practically all to itself, with the Cutlass first, Chevelle second and Century third. Buick's intermediate reinforced its position within the division, accounting for 37.5 percent of all its sales, with a volume of 183,666 units. In February 1975, General Motors decided to call back about 220,000 of its 1975-model intermediates, including the Buick Century, for inspection. The reason was a possible defect in the rear wheel bearings. GM said it learned of the defect from field reports indicating that up to 4,500 side thrust plates might have been improperly manufactured. The side thrust plate is part of the rear wheel bearing. Failure of the rear wheel bearing can cause the rear wheel to fall off. At the time, GM said there had been only one minor accident, and no injuries, due to rear wheel bearing failure. In 1976 Century sales topped 283,000 units, and over forty percent of all Buicks sold that year were intermediates. It came within 45,000 units of catching the Chevelle, and had an unassailable lead over the LeMans as well as the Ford Motor Company and Chrysler Corporation intermediates.

From 1973 through the 1975 model year, there were few styling changes on the Century, and no sheet metal changes. But the 1976 models had new skin, eliminating the sloping front fender line and going to a slab-sided look. New grilles broke completely with the style of recent Buick front ends. The Special grille slanted backwards and contained three broad horizontal wire-mesh air intakes. The Regal grille looked as if it belonged on a Cadillac. These designs continued practically without alteration for 1977, as the A-body was being restyled and reengineered for 1978. The 1978 Century has a 108-inch wheelbase and is shorter overall by eighteen inches. It is also nearly seven inches narrower and about 650 pounds lighter. Inside, however, dimensions are substantially increased. Because of the weight reductions, power steering and power brakes were made optional instead of standard equipment. That will help hold the price level down. Buick's V-6 will continue as the basic power unit in the intermediates.

"We think the V-6 is the engine of the future," Chief Engineer Lloyd Reuss stated firmly. "The weight and packaging features are its top features." The in-line Chevrolet six is too long to fit under the hood of the 1978-model A-body Buicks, and is expected to be phased out of production entirely. Three body styles are a four-door sedan, a notchback coupe and a fastback coupe. The style is sober, with short, sloping hoods and front ends presenting a blunter face to the wind for aerodynamic reasons. Glass areas are no more generous than on previous models, and belt lines remain high.

Until the new front-wheel-drive compacts get into production, Buick will thus find itself in the situation of selling intermediates that are smaller and lighter than its compact cars! This is just one of the many anomalies that result from the phasing program the corporation chose for the wholesale renovation of its car lines. The full-size 1977 models were, in many cases, smaller and lighter than their intermediate counterparts. For instance, the base-model LeSabre weighed 3,615 pounds, or one pound less than the base-model Century. The Estate Wagon, at 4,135 pounds, was 290 pounds lighter than the V-8-powered Century wagon. Wheelbases and lengths were closely similar. The redesign of Buick's senior series for 1977 took place over a three-year period during which only the necessary minimum of changes were made to these cars. They were the biggest problem in the market place, and consequently it was most urgent to develop new and smaller models to replace them. That's why they were renewed a year before the intermediates and two or maybe three years before the compacts.

Buick's senior series as a whole could not defend their position after the setback of big-car sales in the wake of the fuel crisis of 1973/74. Their share of Buick's total domestic sales shrank from 53.4 percent in 1973 to 48.4 percent in 1974 and 40.7 in 1975, and slumped to 37.7 percent in 1976. The major-line models were built at Flint; Fairfax, Kansas; and Wilmington,

LeSabre Custom coupe for 1977 served as spear-carrier for Buick's senior series in the new reduced size. V-6 engine is standard. Vestigial ventiports are among small touches that identify the car as a Buick.

Intermediate Buick series for 1977 included this Regal coupe on a 112-inch wheelbase, with a grille that's more Mercedes than Buick, and a profile devoid of Buick identification.

Delaware in 1975. For 1976 the Wilmington plant switched to Chevette assembly, and East Coast Buick assembly operations moved to Linden, New Jersey. The LeSabre Luxus was renamed LeSabre Custom for 1975. Radial-ply tires were made standard, and in a curious reversal of the horsepower race, the V-6 (231 cubic inches) replaced the small-block V-8 (350 cubic inches) as the base power unit for LeSabre. LeSabre sales were really in the doldrums in 1974, with a volume of 102,500 cars. The following year failed to bring the expected recovery as sales fell further to 94,000 cars in 1975. Even 1976 was disappointing, as LeSabre did not get far beyond 128,000 units.

On the other hand, the Electra 225 had fared better throughout the fuel shortage and was quicker to recover. Its sales volume, including the Estate Wagon, bottomed out at 105,000 units in 1974, stayed level in 1975, and climbed to 135,600 in 1976. Apparently unsure of the market trends, Buick introduced a new Limited as part of the Electra 225 series for the 1975 model year. The Limited had not been built since 1942, when it was known internally as the Series 90. The Electra Limited was a top-of-the-line prestige limousine, and there were only two levels of Electra 225, the Custom and the Limited, but no base model. The Electra 225 became involved in the call-back campaign of some 1,800 GM cars equipped with air bags in 1975. Three divisions had sold cars built with air-cushion passive restraint systems (Buick, Oldsmobile and Cadillac). The corporation said there was a possibility that on some of these vehicles the driver's air bag (carried in the steering wheel hub) might have an insufficient amount of gas propellant needed to inflate it. As a result, the driver's air cushion might not deploy normally in case of the car's becoming involved in a frontal impact severe enough to activate the system. GM said replacements were to be made free

of charge. Buick's sales volume soared by fifty-six percent from 489,000 cars in 1975 to 701,000 in 1976, but the division lost its fourth place behind Chevrolet, Ford and Oldsmobile to Pontiac, which made even more spectacular gains, and got ahead of Buick by less than 6,000 cars. In terms of market shares, Buick advanced from 5.9 percent in 1975 to 7.2 percent in 1976.

Compared with its predecessor, the 1977 LeSabre sedan was ten inches shorter, 2.7 inches narrower and 665 pounds lighter. At the same time, the interior was made larger, with greater headroom and rear legroom, and trunk space was increased from 19.7 to 21.2 cubic feet. Five LeSabre models included coupe and sedan styles at two levels, plain and Custom, plus the exclusive LeSabre Sport Coupe. In the Electra family, there were the Electra 225 and Limited coupes and sedans, plus the base-line and Limited Estate Wagons. At the very top of the line was a Park Avenue sedan.

"In 1977 we changed emphasis in marketing Buicks," said Lloyd Reuss, "instead of building the biggest cars on the road, we placed first priority on building an efficient car. That means it is lighter, smaller, and easier to drive, but no less elegant than before. We have to build a high-quality car in each series we produce. The 1977 model line is part of a major redesign that will extend to the entire Buick product range." With reduction in size, General Motors had to weigh the decision of whether to use unit body con-

In the intermediate line, this 1978 Century sedan has gracefully sloping lines for a new aerodynamic design. It is some seven inches narrower, eighteen inches shorter and 600 pounds lighter than its 1977 counterpart. Standard in all Buick intermediates, except wagons and the Regal Sport coupe, is a 3.2-litre (196 cid) V-6 engine.

struction or separate frames. After considering all the pros and cons of each, GM opted for separate frames. The frame for the 1977 LeSabre, Electra and Riviera is a perimeter design without torque boxes. Instead the side members curve gently in to make room for the wheels, but run right out to door-sill width inside the wheelbase. "We made fuller use of the computer in designing the 1977 models than at any time in the past," explained Lloyd Reuss. "We started with computer design of the body. After we had that, we knew that we could build-in the chassis with little fear of making big mistakes."

Computers also played an important role in cutting the lead time involved in getting the car off the drawing board and onto the assembly line. Computers were used not only in design but also in testing. As Lloyd Reuss expressed it: "The result is that through the prototype testing stage we had fewer iterations—less of the old routine of building a prototype, road-testing it, finding a flaw, sending it back for redesign, incorporating the new design, taking it back out for road test, and so on. The computer can divide the body, frame and suspension into finite elements," Lloyd Reuss went on. "We can separate out any part of the car we want, and then apply the strain it would receive in actual driving. If it shows up weak, we test a

stronger design on the computer. When we get the problems fixed, we start to build the car." He added: "The smaller size and the computer design allowed us to cut weight by building strength into the basic body and not depend on reinforcement rods and cross members to strengthen a weak area that showed up during testing."

Greater efficiency means less waste, and that refers above all to fuel waste. Buick wanted to waste less energy on overcoming air drag at highway speeds, and that meant streamlining the bodies more. This was done in the wind tunnel. The designs from GM Styling were, of course, made to look streamlined, but what it looks like the airflow will do and what it actually does can be two very different things. That's where wind tunnel testing comes in. There are several visualization techniques that enable you to see and photograph air flow, and analyze it, while the effect of changes can be measured by keeping track of the forces acting on the platform that holds the car or model. Buick worked with quarter-scale models first, and later with full-scale clay mockups. As a result of the wind tunnel tests, leading edges were softened, and windshield pillars smoothed over. On some models, air deflectors were added below the front bumper to divert air flow from the drag-inducing areas under the car. "With the body design completed," Reuss explained, "the frame and suspension posed no problems. Actually, the frame and suspension were designed with the aid of a computer, too. So, we had tested a mathematical model of the body design on a mathematical model of the proposed frame and chassis even before we drove the prototype on the road. If we found a design problem in the computer test results, we did the iteration right there on the computer. We didn't have to wait until the design was out on the road before a mistake showed up. The result was that the car was designed better right from the start, and testing went more smoothly throughout the prototype stage." Computers are not creative, of course. The ideas and the choices must come from human brains. In this case, the guiding word was 'efficiency.' "Just look at the cars and you can see the emphasis on efficiency," said Lloyd Reuss. "Even the sheet metal styling reflects this. We want to have the high-luxury car in each line. This year's LeSabre Sport Coupe embodies all that we're trying to accomplish. It's better-handling than the regular models, it's fuel-efficient and at the same time has good performance."

The LeSabre Sport Coupe was made different from the other models by using the same sort of improvements that made the GS cars different from other Skylarks ten years earlier. The 1977 LeSabre Sport Coupe has stiffer front and rear springs, a reinforced front stabilizer bar, a rear stabilizer that isn't part of the base-model specification, specific shock absorber valving, and faster-geared steering for better response. It also had an exterior appearance that set it apart. A triple-shield stand-up hood ornament gave the

The 1978 Regal Sport coupe, a personalized luxury car in the intermediate line, is one of the two American production cars with a turbocharged engine. Both the Regal Sport coupe and the LeSabre Sport coupe offer the turbocharged V-6 with either a two-barrel or four-barrel carburetor. The Regal Sport coupe is distinguished by a bubble at the rear of the hood with the inscription 'Turbo 3.8 Litre' on the sides.

keynote address, assisted by black vertical bars in the grille, black anodized windshield frame moldings and black louvered rocker panel moldings. Chrome wheels and white-striped tires were also included in the styling touches. For the 1977 model year, Buick discontinued its big-block V-8's, and began buying a 301-cubic-inch Pontiac V-8 engine and a 403-cubic-inch Oldsmobile engine. Normally, the 1977 LeSabre Sport Coupe was powered by the 301-cubic-inch V-8, using the 350 as standard for cars going to California and high altitude areas. The 403 became the top power option. The 301-cubic-inch V-8 weighs 567 pounds, and is now America's lightest V-8 passenger car engine. Oldsmobile's 260-cubic-inch V-8 from 1976, which Buick also used in some models, was the former lightweight champion, at 574 pounds.

Buick's product development is now planned in outline at least as far as 1985. What we hope for in the immediate future, as well as in the long term, is that the corporation will leave more room for individuality in the cars of each division. Buick cars, we firmly believe, will be better cars if greater design and engineering antonomy are restored to Flint. This belief is based on what we hear from the people at Buick. For instance, we asked the chief engineer about the differences between working at Chevrolet and working at Buick. Lloyd Reuss gave his answer: "One of the big benefits of the Buick setup is that I can see virtually all the facilities right here from my office. From the foundry to the machining plants—you get the whole picture. We have the entire engine built here in Flint. We have the Fisher Body plant next door for our bodies, and assemble them right here, too. We even have finance and purchasing, all on the same premises. That means we can keep track of any phase of the business in this one central plant."

151

Nearly two feet shorter than last year, the 1978 Century Station Wagon has a two-piece tailgate with a flip-up glass, making loading and unloading more convenient.

New in the Electra series for 1978 is the Park Avenue coupe, featuring a new grille with a horizontal band in the center.

Buick's manufacturing complex in Flint is often referred to as 'Buick's Busy Acres.' It is General Motors' largest single-site manufacturing installation in the United States and second largest in the world, exceeded only by the Opel plant in West Germany. Buick, in relation to Flint, is a city within a city. The Buick plant has a population of about 20,000, with its own power station, communications, hospital, police, water treatment, fire department and many other operations vital to its basic functions. In 1968 Buick's central office operations moved into a new three-level building containing more than 284,000 square feet of office space. The former Buick office building was erected in 1917 and was in use for fifty-one years. Buick's facilities in Flint take up an area more than two miles long, containing more than 300 acres. It contains a foundry, engine machining and assembly plants, transmission plant, axle plant, stamping and body assembly plants. The Buick assembly plant in Flint turns out new Buicks at the rate of about one every minute. Buick's engine plant, which was completed in 1952, now has more than one million square feet of floor space and comprises three separate engine lines.

To this day, Buick has coordination responsibility for transmissions for all GM cars. That does not necessarily include manufacturing, but Buick does build a quantity of Turbo-HydraMatic 350 units (as does Chevrolet).

Smaller and larger transmissions (the THM 200 and THM 400) are manufactured exclusively by HydraMatic Division at Willow Run. Buick's task is to match transmissions with engines on a corporation-wide basis, with maximum standardization of parts and pre-settings. We believe Buick should play a greater role in this scheme of coordination. Channeling technical evolution through one single path may save money, but it does not necessarily provide the best results. We suggest that General Motors will need Buick to supply alternative solutions for future engine programs, suspension and steering developments, and brake systems. From Buick's viewpoint, it is potentially harmful that its cars should be produced as a montage of mechanical units created by other scources, just because the corporation thinks it cannot afford multiple programs, when Buick itself has the capability to engineer, design and manufacture cars that are different, possibly superior, and above all, Buicks.

Appendix I
Technical Evolution of Buick Models

Year	Wheelbase (inches)	Overall length	Overall width	Overall height	Curb weight (pounds)	ENGINE Cu. in.	HP	Axle ratio	Turn diameter (feet)	Tire size
ROADMASTER										
1946	129	217.1	78.6	65.1	4,125	320	144	4.10	40.2	7.00-15
1947	129	217.1	78.6	65.1	4,125	320	144	4.10	40.2	7.00-15
1948	129	217.125	78.6	65.15	4,125	320	150	4.08	40.2	8.20-15
1949	126	214.125	78.6	65.1	4,117	320	150	4.10	40.2	8.20-15
1950	126.25	208.75	78.6	65.1	4,055	320	152	3.91	40.2	8.00-15
1951	126.25	208.75	80	63.3	4,060	320	152	3.91	40.9	8.00-15
1952	126.25	215	80	63.2	4,090	320	170	3.60	41.8	8.00-15
1953	125.5	215.6	79.9	63.4	4,100	322	188	3.60	39.5	8.00-15
1954	127	216.8	79.8	62.6	4,250	322	200	3.40	43	8.00-15
1955	127	216	80	62.7	4,278	322	236	3.40	43	8.00-15
1956	127	213.6	80	62.7	4,280	322	255	3.36	43	8.00-15
1957	127.5	215.3	77.6	59.1	4,377	364	300	3.07	44.5	8.00-15
1958	127.5	219.1	79.8	59.6	4,544	364	300	3.23	44.5	8.00-15
SPECIAL										
1946	121	207.5	77.8	66.7	3,822	248	110	4.454	40.1	6.50-16
1947	121	207.5	77.8	66.7	3,820	248	110	4.454	40.1	6.50-16
1948	121	207.5	77.8	66.7	3,820	248	110	4.454	40.1	6.50-16
1949	Special production suspended									
1950	121.5	204	79.4	63.9	3,695	248	115	4.10	39.8	7.60-15
1951	121.5	204.8	76.7	63.4	3,711	263	120	3.90	39.7	7.60-15
1952	121.5	204.8	76.7	63.4	3,730	263	120	4.10	39.5	7.60-15
1953	121.5	205.9	76	63.4	3,710	263	125	3.90	39.5	7.60-15
1954	122	206.3	76.6	60.5	3,735	264	143	3.90	41.6	7.60-15
1955	122	206.7	76.2	60.4	3,742	264	188	3.60	41.6	7.10-15
1956	122	206.7	75.5	60.4	3,790	322	220	3.90	41.6	7.10-15
1957	122	208.4	74.8	58.4	3,845	364	250	3.58	41.6	7.10-15
1958	122	211.8	78.1	57.6	3,889	364	250	3.58	41.6	7.10-15
SUPER										
1946	124	212.5	78.6	64.9	3,962	248	110	4.454	40.2	6.50-16
1947	124	212.5	78.6	64.9	3,965	248	110	4.454	40.2	6.50-16
1948	124	212.375	78.6	64.9	4,018	248	115	4.454	40.2	7.60-15
1949	121	209.5	78.6	64.9	4,000	248	115	4.454	40.2	7.60-15
1950	121.5	204	80	63.9	3,835	263	124	4.10	39.8	7.60-15
1951	121.5	206.2	80	62.8	3,848	263	124	4.10	39.8	7.60-15
1952	125.5	210.2	80	62.8	3,887	263	124	3.90	41.5	7.60-15
1953	125.5	211.6	79.9	62.8	3,905	322	164	3.90	39.5	7.60-15
1954	127	216.8	79.8	62.4	4,105	322	182	3.40	43	7.60-15
1955	127	216	80	62.5	4,141	322	236	3.40	43	7.60-15
1956	127	213.6	80	62.5	4,200	322	255	3.36	43	7.60-15
1957	127.5	215.3	77.6	59.4	4,354	364	300	3.07	44.5	7.60-15
1958	127.5	219.1	79.8	59.4	4,500	364	300	3.23	44.5	7.60-15
CENTURY										
1954	122	206.3	76.6	60.5	3,805	322	195	3.90	41.6	7.60-15
1955	122	206.7	76.2	60.6	3,807	322	236	3.40	41.6	7.60-15

Appendix II
Buick Literature 1946-1953
Compiled by Jeffrey I. Godshall and Autoenthusiasts International

1946:
Folder, 8½ x 11, full-line, color, 5-46
Folder, 8½ x 11, full-line, color
Folder, 8½ x 11, Super/Roadmaster, color, 10-45
Catalog, 12 x 9, full-line, color, 20p., 3-46
Folder, 8½ x 3½, Venti-Heater, b&red

1947:
Catalog, 12 x 9, full-line, color, 24p., 1-47
Folder, 8½ x 10½, full-line, color, 1-47

1948:
Folder, 11 x 8, full-line, color, 2-48
Catalog, 9 x 6½, Roadmaster Custom Interior, color, 4p., 4-48
Catalog, 9 x 7, Dynaflow, color, 16p., X-495, 4-48
Folder, 11 x 8, full-line, color, 4-48
Catalog, 8½ x 7, "Vibra-Shielded Ride," color, 12p., 4-48
Catalog, 9 x 7, Dynaflow, color, 16p., X495, 5-48

1949:
Folder, 10½ x 8½, Super/Roadmaster, color, 5-49
Booklet, 4 x 5, Dynaflow, 2-color, 12p.

1950:
Folder, 8 x 5½, heater, color, X961, 11-49
Catalog, 11 x 8, full-line, color, 8p., 11-49
Catalog, 11 x 8, full-line, color, 8p., 1-50
Catalog, 11 x 8, full-line, color, 8p., 4-50
Folder, 8½ x 10½, Special, color, 7-49
Folder, 8½ x 10½, Special, color, 9-49
Catalog, 7 x 5, "Always on Level," b&w&yellow, 12p., 11-49

Year	Wheelbase (inches)	Overall length	Overall width	Overall height	Curb weight (pounds)	ENGINE Cu. in.	HP	Axle ratio	Turn diameter (feet)	Tire size
1956	122	205.1	75.5	59.8	4,000	322	255	3.36	41.6	7.60-15
1957	122	208.4	74.8	58.7	4,156	364	300	3.07	43.2	7.60-15
1958	122	211.8	78.1	57.9	4,267	364	300	3.23	43.2	7.60-15

LE SABRE

Year	Wheelbase (inches)	Overall length	Overall width	Overall height	Curb weight (pounds)	ENGINE Cu. in.	HP	Axle ratio	Turn diameter (feet)	Tire size
1959	123	217.4	80.7	57.1	4,266	364	250	3.58	44	7.60-15
1960	123	217.9	80	57.2	4,269	364	250	3.91	44	7.60-15
1961	123	213.2	78	56.3	4,129	364	250	3.07	44	7.60-15
1962	123	214.1	78	56.3	4,156	401	280	2.78	45.9	7.60-15
1963	123	215.7	78	55.9	4,233	401	280	2.78	45.9	7.60-15
1964	123	218.9	78.1	56.4	4,072	300	210	3.42	43.9	7.10-15
1965	123	216.8	80	55.2	4,080	300	210	3.55	39.7	8.15-15
1966	123	216.9	80	57.1	4,061	340	220	3.36	39.7	8.15-15
1967	123	217.5	80	55.6	4,067	340	220	3.36	42.2	8.45-15
1968	123	217.5	80	55.5	4,158	350	230	3.23	46.4	8.45-15
1969	123.2	218.2	80	55.3	4,176	350	230	3.23	45.6	8.55-15
1970	124	220.2	80	55.4	4,252	350	260	3.23	47.1	H78-15
1971	124	220.7	79.7	54.4	4,321	350	230	3.42	46.8	H78-15
1972	124	220.9	79.7	54.4	4,436	350	150	3.08	44.1	H78-15
1973	124	224.2	79.6	53.8	4,487	350	150	3.08	45.3	H78-15
1974	124	225.9	79.9	54	4,516	350	150	3.08	42.9	H78-15
1975	124	226.9	79.9	54	4,568	350	165	3.08	41.7	HR78-15
1976	124	226.9	79.9	54	4,455	231	105	3.23	48.8	HR78-15
1977	115.9	218.2	77.2	55.3	3,615	231	105	2.73	43.0	FR78-15

ELECTRA

Year	Wheelbase (inches)	Overall length	Overall width	Overall height	Curb weight (pounds)	ENGINE Cu. in.	HP	Axle ratio	Turn diameter (feet)	Tire size
1959	126.3	220.6	80.7	57.3	4,641	401	325	3.23	45.7	8.00-15
1960	126.3	225.9	80	57.5	4,653	401	325	3.23	45.7	8.00-15
1961	126	219.2	78	57	4,417	401	325	3.23	45.7	8.00-15
1962	126	220.1	78	57	4,390	401	325	3.23	47.6	8.00-15
1963	126	221.7	78	57.5	4,260	401	325	3.23	47.6	8.00-15
1964	126	222.8	78.1	57.2	4,256	401	325	3.07	45.6	8.00-15
1965	126	224.1	80	56	4,250	401	325	3.07	43.3	8.85-15
1966	126	223.4	80	57.5	4,255	401	325	3.23	43.3	8.85-15
1967	126	223.9	80	56.2	4,260	430	360	2.78	44	8.85-15
1968	126	224.9	80	56.3	4,372	430	360	2.78	49.4	8.85-15
1969	126.2	224.8	80	55.8	4,390	430	360	2.78	49.0	8.55-15
1970	127	225.8	80	55.9	4,422	455	370	2.56	47.1	H78-15
1971	127	226.1	79.7	54.9	4,480	455	315	2.73	46.8	J78-15
1972	127	226.9	79.7	54.9	4,560	455	225	2.93	46.8	J78-15
1973	127	229.8	79.3	54.9	4,625	455	225	2.73	46.8	J78-15
1974	127	231.5	79.9	55	4,740	455	210	2.73	43.5	J78-15
1975	127	233.4	79.9	55.1	4,750	455	205	2.73	44.3	JR78-15
1976	127	233.4	79.9	54.5	4,700	455	205	2.56	47.9	JR78-15
1977	118.9	222.1	77.2	55.7	3,870	350	155	2.41	44.1	HR78-15

INVICTA

Year	Wheelbase (inches)	Overall length	Overall width	Overall height	Curb weight (pounds)	ENGINE Cu. in.	HP	Axle ratio	Turn diameter (feet)	Tire size
1959	123	217.4	80.7	57.1	4,373	401	325	3.23	44	7.60-15
1960	123	217.9	80	57.2	4,365	401	325	3.23	44	7.60-15
1961	123	213.2	78	56.3	4,179	401	325	3.07	44	7.60-15
1962	123	214.1	78	56.3	4,159	401	325	3.23	45.9	7.60-15
1963	123	215.7	78	57.9	4,225	401	325	3.23	45.9	7.60-15

Folder, 9 x 4, mailer, Conv.-Wagon-Riviera, color
Booklet, 5 x 6½, "Buick...Features," b&w&red, X-967, 12-49
Folder, 5 x 8, "Weather in Special," 1-color, 8-49
Catalog, 11 x 8, full-line, color, 8p., 12-49
Folder, 8½ x 10½, Special, color, 8-49
Booklet, 6 x 4, "Beauty on Duty," b&w&blue, 12p., X960, 11-49
Folder, 8½ x 5½, "All Seasons...Spring," color, X961, 11-49, (venti-heater)
Booklet, 4 x 5½, Dynaflow, b&w&brown, 16p., X962, 11-49
Folder, 8½ x 4, "It's Beautiful...," red&green&b&w, 100MN 504, 3-50
Mailer, 8 x 4, Dynaflow (pop-out type folder), color
Booklet, 4 x 5, "Easy Going...Dynaflow...," b&w&mustard, 16p., X1248-S, 7-50
Card, 9 x 6, Special tourback sedan, b&w, N505, 5-50
Card, 8½ x 6, Super Riviera, b&w, N506, 5-50
Catalog, 8 x 5½, Body by Fisher, 2-color, 20p.

1951:
Catalog, 11 x 8, full-line, color, 8p., 1-51, (with Custom Special)
Catalog, 11 x 8, full-line, color, 8p., 2-51
Folder, 8½ x 5½, Heating & Ventilation, color
Catalog, 4 x 5, Dynaflow Driving, b&w&green, X1352, 12-50 S
Mailer, 4 x 3, flip-type, full-line, color
Mailer, 11 x 5, full-line, brown&white, X1368

1953:
Folder, 4 x 7, access., blue&red&w, X-2012, 1-53

Year	Wheelbase (inches)	Overall length	Overall width	Overall height	Curb weight (pounds)	ENGINE Cu. in.	HP	Axle ratio	Turn diameter (feet)	Tire size
CENTURION										
1971	124	220.7	79.7	53.8	4,515	455	315	3.42	44.1	H78-15
1972	124	220.9	79.7	53.8	4,615	455	225	2.93	44.1	H78-15
1973	124	224.2	79.6	53.8	4,525	350	175	3.08	44.1	H78-15
WILDCAT										
1962	123	214.1	78	56.3	4,159	401	325	3.23	45.9	7.60-15
1963	123	215.7	78	57.9	4,242	401	325	3.23	45.9	7.60-15
1964	123	218.9	78.1	56.4	4,225	401	325	3.42	43.9	7.60-15
1965	126	219.8	80	55.2	4,266	401	325	3.42	43.3	8.45-15
1966	126	219.9	80	57	4,212	401	325	3.23	43.3	8.45-15
1967	126	220.5	80	55.6	4,240	430	360	3.07	44	8.45-15
1968	126	220.5	80	55.3	4,360	430	360	3.07	49.4	8.45-15
1969	123.2	218.2	80	55.3	4,345	430	360	3.07	45.6	8.55-15
1970	124	220.2	80	54.4	4,456	455	370	2.78	47.1	H78-15
RIVIERA										
1963	117	208.0	76.6	53.2	4,136	401	325	3.23	43.6	7.10-15
1964	117	208.0	76.6	53.0	4,085	425	340	2.78	43.6	7.10-15
1965	117	209.0	76.6	53.0	4,141	401	325	3.23	43.6	8.45-15
1966	119	211.2	79.3	54.4	4,316	425	340	3.07	44.0	8.45-15
1967	119	211.3	79.4	53.2	4,342	430	360	3.07	42.3	8.45-15
1968	119	215.2	78.1	53.2	4'360	430	360	3.07	46.9	8.45-15
1969	119	215.2	79.2	53.2	4,327	430	360	3.07	46.0	8.55-15
1970	119	215.5	79.3	53.6	4,342	455	370	2.78	46.0	H78-15
1971	122	217.4	79.9	54.0	4,502	455	315	2.93	46.5	H78-15
1972	122	217.3	79.9	54.0	4,497	455	250	2.93	46.5	H78-15
1973	122	223.4	79.9	54.0	4,647	455	250	2.93	46.5	H78-15
1974	122	226.4	80.0	53.7	4,732	455	230	2.93	41.7	J78-15
1975	122	223.0	79.9	53.7	4,680	455	205	2.93	41.7	JR78-15
1976	122	223.0	79.9	53.0	4,676	455	205	2.56	41.7	JR78-15
1977	115.9	218.2	77.2	54.6	3,944	350	170	2.41	42.9	GR78-15
TWO-DOOR A-BODY INTERMEDIATES										
Special/Skylark										
1964	115	203.5	73.4	54.4	2,992	225	155	3.23	40.6	6.50-14
1965	115	203.4	73.6	54.0	3,035	225	155	3.23	40.6	6.95-14
1966	115	204	75.5	55.9	3,046	225	160	3.23	40.6	6.95-14
1967	115	205	75.4	54.0	3,050	225	160	3.23	40.6	7.75-14
1968	112	200.7	75.6	53.5	3,369	250	155	3.23	42.2	7.75-14
1969	112	200.7	75.6	53.4	3,357	250	155	3.23	42.9	7.75-14
1970	112	202.2	77.3	53.1	3,381	250	155	3.23	44.0	G78-14
1971	112	203.2	77.3	53.8	3,396	250	145	3.08	44.5	F78-14
1972	112	202.8	76.5	53.8	3,426	350	190	3.08	45.3	G78-14
Century										
1973	112	210.7	78	53.5	3,692	350	150	3.08	41.5	G78-14
1974	112	212	79	53.3	3,748	350	150	2.73	41.4	G78-14
1975	112	209.5	79	53.3	3,750	231	110	2.73	41.4	GR78-15
1976	112	209.7	77	52.8	3,680	231	105	3.08	42.5	GR78-15
1977	112	209.8	76.5	52.7	3,485	231	105	3.08	42.5	FR78-15

Year	Wheelbase (inches)	Overall length	Overall width	Overall height	Curb weight (pounds)	ENGINE Cu. in.	ENGINE H.P.	Axle ratio	Turn diameter (feet)	Tire size
FOUR-DOOR A-BODY INTERMEDIATES										
Special/Skylark										
1964	115	203.5	73.4	54.4	3,078	225	155	3.23	40.6	6.50-14
1965	115	203.4	73.6	54	3,105	225	155	3.23	40.6	6.95-14
1966	115	204	75.5	55.9	3,146	225	160	3.23	40.6	6.95-14
1967	115	205	75.4	54	3,165	225	160	3.23	40.6	7.75-14
1968	116	204.7	75.6	54.2	3,448	250	155	3.23	42.2	7.75-14
1969	116	204.7	75.6	54.1	3,412	250	155	3.23	42.2	7.75-14
1970	116	206.2	77.3	54	3,476	250	155	3.23	44.8	G78-14
1971	116	207.2	77.3	54	3,515	250	145	3.08	45.3	F78-14
1972	116	206.8	76.5	54.3	3,510	350	190	3.08	45.3	G78-14
Century										
1973	116	212.4	78	54.4	3,725	350	150	3.08	45.3	G78-14
1974	116	213.5	79	54.1	3,747	350	150	2.73	45.3	G78-14
1975	116	213.5	79	54.1	3,889	350	145	2.56	41.7	GR78-15
1976	116	213.5	79	53.6	3,820	350	140	2.56	43.6	FR78-15
1977	116	213.6	79	53.6	3,790	231	105	2.41	43.6	FR78-15
COMPACTS										
Special										
1961	112	188.4	71.3	52.5	2,615	215	155	3.36	38.1	6.50-13
1962	112	188.4	71.3	52.5	2,620	215	155	3.23	38.1	6.50-13
1963	112	192	70.2	52.8	2,696	198	135	3.23	38.1	6.50-13
Apollo										
1973	111	197.9	72.4	53.9	3,140	250	100	3.08	43.8	E78-14
1974	111	200.3	72.7	52.8	3,250	250	100	3.08	41.2	E78-14
1975	111	200.3	72.4	54.2	3,300	250	100	2.73	38.1	FR78-14
Skylark										
1976	111	200.3	72.7	53.1	3,260	231	105	3.08	41.7	ER78-14
1977	111	200.2	72.7	53.1	3,240	231	105	3.08	41.7	E78-14

Appendix III
Switching From SAE Gross to SAE Net Horsepower

ENGINE Cyl.	Carb.	Cu.in.	Type	1971 Hp @ rpm	1971 Torque @ rpm	1972 Hp @ rpm	1972 Torque @ rpm
Six	1-bbl	250	All	145 @ 4000	230 @ 1600	110 @ 3800	185 @ 1600
V-8	2-bbl	350	All	230 @ 4400	350 @ 2400	150 @ 3800	265 @ 2400
V-8	4-bbl	350	All	260 @ 4600	360 @ 3000	190 @ 4000	285 @ 2800
V-8	4-bbl	455	Std	315 @ 4400	450 @ 2800	225 @ 4000	360 @ 2600
V-8	4-bbl	455	Riv	330 @ 4600	455 @ 2800	260 @ 4400	380 @ 2800
V-8	4-bbl	455	GS	340 @ 5000	460 @ 3000	270 @ 4400	390 @ 3000

Appendix IV
Buick Production Statistics

MODEL YEAR	SPECIAL	SUPER	CENTURY	ROADMASTER	LIMITED	TOTAL
1946	4,502	122,135		32,091		158,728
1947	34,270	163,410		79,454		277,134
1948	36,187	112,441		81,090		229,718
1949	92,444	229,032		87,662		409,138
1950	256,514	253,352		78,573		588,439
1951	165,554	172,235		66,868		404,657
1952	120,898	136,404		46,443		303,745
1953	217,624	191,894		79,237		488,755
1954	191,484	119,375	81,983	51,767		444,609
1955	381,946	133,208	158,796	64,864		738,814
1956	313,915	81,500	122,985	53,700		572,024
1957	220,700	70,600	66,000	47,786		405,086
1958	133,500	42,500	33,000	23,767	9,125	241,892

Senior Series

MODEL YEAR	LE SABRE	INVICTA	ELECTRA ELECTRA 225	ESTATE WAGON	WILDCAT	CENTURION	TOTAL
1959	157,300	46,700	66,600	14,400			285,089
1960	144,700	40,300	56,300	12,100			253,999
1961	105,300	28,700	20,900	8,000			189,982
1962	127,200		62,500	13,700	43,300		245,683
1963	161,700		58,700	13,000	35,700		269,068
1964	135,163		68,912		84,245		288,320
1965	144,996		86,810		98,787		330,593
1966	147,399		88,225		68,584		304,208
1967	155,190		100,304		70,881		326,375
1968	179,748		125,362		69,969		375,079
1969	197,866		159,618		67,453		423,937
1970	200,622		150,201	28,306	23,615		402,744
1971	153,835		126,036	24,034		29,398	333,303
1972	183,322		172,122	28,968		36,435	420,847
1973	197,281		177,772	35,795		44,976	455,824
1974	113,792		99,414	14,412			227,618
1975	109,201		94,930	13,740			217,871
1976	137,107		124,559	20,374			282,040

MODEL YEAR	COMPACTS	INTERMEDIATES	SKYHAWK	RIVIERA	SENIOR SERIES	TOTAL
1961	87,444				189,982	277,426
1962	154,467				245,683	400,150
1963	149,538			40,000	269,068	458,606
1964		185,688		37,658	288,320	511,666
1965		234,969		34,568	330,593	600,148
1966		209,314		45,348	304,208	558,870
1967		193,333		42,799	326,375	562,507

MODEL YEAR	COMPACTS	INTERMEDIATES	SKYHAWK	RIVIERA	SENIOR SERIES	TOTAL
1968		227,460		49,284	375,079	651,823
1969		188,613		52,872	423,937	665,422
1970		226,421		37,336	402,744	666,501
1971		184,075		33,810	333,303	551,188
1972		225,346		33,728	420,847	679,921
1973	32,793	298,467		34,080	455,824	821,164
1974	56,709	190,607		20,129	227,618	495,063
1975	63,133	183,458	4,000	17,306	217,871	481,768
1976	117,900	316,300	10,000	20,000	282,040	746,240

Appendix V
Buick Models

Year	Compact	Skyhawk	Intermediate	Riviera	Senior series	Total
1946					9	9
1947					10	10
1948					10	10
1949					11	11
1950					19	19
1951					19	19
1952					15	15
1953					15	15
1954					16	16
1955					18	18
1956					18	18
1957					22	22
1958					20	20
1959					19	19
1960					19	19
1961	6				17	23

Year	Compact	Skyhawk	Intermediate	Riviera	Senior series	Total
1962	7				14	21
1963	8			1	18	27
1964			10	2	17	29
1965			10	2	24	36
1966			15	2	21	38
1967			14	2	21	37
1968			11	2	20	33
1969			12	2	20	34
1970			10	2	17	29
1971			9	1	15	25
1972			9	1	15	25
1973	3		7	1	14	25
1974	3		8	1	14	26
1975	6	1	9	1	12	29
1976	7	2	9	1	12	31
1977	7	3	8	1	11	30

Appendix VI
Buick Straight-Eight Engine Data

Years	Cu.in.	Bore x stroke	Hp @ rpm	Application	Remarks
1931	220	2.875 x 4.25	77 @ 3000	Series 50	1-bbl updraft carburetor
1931-32	272	3.067 x 5.00	90 @ 3000	Series 60	
1931-33	344	3.625 x 5.00	104 @ 3000	Series 80 and 90	Vacuum spark advance
1932	230	2.932 x 4.25	80 @ 3000	Series 50	1-bbl updraft carburetor
1933	230	2.932 x 4.25	86 @ 3200	Series 50	
1933	272	3.067 x 5.00	97 @ 3200	Series 60	
1934	233	2.95 x 4.25	88 @ 3200	Series 50	1-bbl updraft carburetor
1934-35	278	3.09 x 4.625	100 @ 3200	Series 60	New block
1934-35	344	3.625 x 5.00	116 @ 3200	Series 90	
1936	233	2.95 x 4.25	93 @ 3200	Special	1-bbl downdraft carburetor
1936	320	3.437 x 4.312	120 @ 3200	Century and Roadmaster	Aluminum pistons
1937	248	3.09 x 4.125	100 @ 3200	Special	New camshaft
1937	320	3.437 x 4.312	130 @ 3400	Century, Roadmaster, Limited	
1938-39	248	3.09 x 4.125	107 @ 3400	Special	
1938-40	320	3.437 x 4.312	141 @ 3600	Century, Roadmaster, Limited	
1940	248	3.09 x 4.125	107 @ 3400	Special and Super	
1941	248	3.09 x 4.125	115 @ 3500	Special	
1941	248	3.09 x 4.125	125 @ 3800	Super, optional on Special	Compound carburetion
1941	320	3.437 x 4.312	165 @ 3800	Century, Roadmaster, Limited	
1942	248	3.09 x 4.125	110 @ 3400	Special	Cast iron pistons
1942	248	3.09 x 4.125	118 @ 3600	Super, optional on Special	Compound carburetion
1946-47	248	3.09 x 4.125	110 @ 3600	Special and Super	
1946-49	320	3.437 x 4.312	144 @ 3600	Roadmaster	
1948-49	248	3.09 x 4.125	115 @ 3600	Special and Super	With synchromesh gearbox
1948-49	248	3.09 x 4.125	120 @ 3600	Special and Super	With Dynaflow
1950-51	320	3.437 x 4.312	152 @ 3600	Roadmaster	
1950-52	263	3.1875 x 4.125	124 @ 3600	Super	With synchromesh gearbox
1950-52	263	3.1875 x 4.125	128 @ 3600	Super	With Dynaflow
1950-53	248	3.09 x 4.125	115 @ 3600	Special	With synchromesh gearbox
1950-53	248	3.09 x 4.125	120 @ 3600	Special	with Dynaflow
1952	320	3.437 x 4.312	170 @ 3800	Roadmaster	4-bbl carburetor

Appendix VII
Buick Model Lineups

Year	4-door sedan	4-door hardtop	2-door sedan	2-door hardtop	2-door coupe	Conv.	Wagon	Total
SPECIAL								
1946	1		1					2
1947	1		1					2
1948	1		1					2
1949	1		1					2
1950	4		2		1			7
1951	4		2		1			7
1952	1		2	1	2	1		7
1953	2		2	1		1		6
1954	1		1	1		1	1	5
1955	1	1	1	1		1	1	6
1956	1	1	1	1		1	1	6
1957	1	1	1	1		1	2	7
1958	1	1	1	1		1	2	7
SUPER								
1946	1		1			1	1	4
1947	1		1			1	1	4
1948	1		1			1	1	4
1949	1		1			1	1	4
1950	2		1	1		1	1	6
1951	2		1	1		1	1	6
1952	1			1		1	1	4
1953		1		1		1	1	4
1954		1		1		1		3
1955	1		1	1		1		4
1956	1	1		1		1		4
1957		1		1		1		3
1958		1		1				2
CENTURY								
1954	1			1		1	1	4
1955	1			1		1	1	4
1956		1		1		1	1	4
1957	1	1		1		1	1	5
1958	1	1		1		1	1	5
ROADMASTER								
1946	1		1			1		3
1947	1		1			1	1	4
1948	1		1			1	1	4
1949	1		1	1		1	1	5
1950	2			2		1	1	6
1951	2			2		1	1	6
1952		1		1		1	1	4
1953		1		1		2	1	5
1954		1		1		2		4
1955	1	1		1		1		4
1956	1	1		1		1		4
1957		3		3		1		7
1958		1		1		1		3
LIMITED								
1958		1		1		1		3
ELECTRA								
1959	2	3		2		1		8
1960	2	3		2		1		8
1961	1	3		2		1		7
1962	1	2		1		1		5
1963	1	1		1		1		4
1964	1	1		1		1		4
1965	2	2		2		1		7
1966	2	2		2		1		7
1967	2	2		2		1		7
1968	2	2		2		1		7
1969	2	2		2		1		7
1970	2	2		2		1		7
1971		2		2			1	5
1972		2		2			1	5
1973		2		2			1	5
1974		3		3			1	7
1975		2		2			1	5
1976		2		2			1	5
1977	2			2			2	6
LE SABRE								
1959	1	1	1	1		1	1	6
1960	1	1	1	1		1	1	6
1961	1	1	1	1		1	1	6
1962	1	1	1	1				4
1963	1	1	1			1	1	6
1964	1	1		1		1	1	5
1965	2	2		2		1		7
1966	2	2		2		1		7
1967	2	2		2		1		7
1968	2	2		2		1		7
1969	2	2		2		1		7
1970	2	2		2		1		7
1971	2	2		2		1		7
1972	2	2		2		1		7
1973	2	2		2				6
1974	2	2		2		1		7
1975	2	2		2		1		7
1976	2	2		2		1		7
1977	2			3				5

Year	4-door sedan	4-door hardtop	2-door sedan	2-door hardtop	2-door coupe	Conv.	Wagon	Total
INVICTA								
1959	1	1		1		1	1	5
1960	1	1		1		1	1	5
1961		1		1		1	1	4
1962		1		1		1	1	4
1963		1		1		1	1	4
WILDCAT								
1962				1				1
1963		1		1		1	1	4
1964	1	1		1		1		4
1965	2	3		3	2			10
1966	1	2		2	2			7
1967	1	2		2	2			7
1968	1	2		2	1			6
1969	1	2		2	1			6
1970		1		1	1			3
CENTURION								
1971		1		1		1		3
1972		1		1		1		3
1973		1		1		1		3
SPECIAL								
1964	2		2			1	2	7
1965	2	1				1	2	6
1966	2		2	1		1	2	8
1967	2	1	1				2	6
1968	1	1					2	4
1969	1		1				2	4

Year	4-door sedan	4-door hardtop	2-door sedan	2-door hardtop	2-door coupe	Conv.	Wagon	Tot.
SKYLARK								
1964	1			1		1		
1965	1		1	1		1		
1966		1	2	2		2		
1967	1	1	2	2		2		
1968	2	1		2		2		
1969	2	1		3		2		
1970	3	1	1	3		1	1	1
1971	2	1		3		2	1	
1972	2	1		3		2	1	
CENTURY								
1973	2				3		2	
1974	3				3		2	
1975	3				4		2	
1976	3				4		2	
1977	3				4		1	
SPECIAL								
1961	2			1			3	
1962	2		1	1			3	
1963	2		1	1		2	2	
APOLLO								
1973	1				2			
1974	1				2			
1975	2				4			
SKYLARK								
1976	2				5			
1977	2				5			

Index